Public Administration's Final Exam

Public Administration's Final Exam

A Pragmatist Restructuring of the Profession and the Discipline

MICHAEL M. HARMON

The University of Alabama Press
Tuscaloosa

The University of Alabama Press
Tuscaloosa, Alabama 35487-0380
uapress.ua.edu

Copyright © 2006 by the University of Alabama Press
All rights reserved.

Hardcover edition published 2006.
Paperback edition published 2016.
eBook edition published 2011.

Inquiries about reproducing material from this work should be addressed to the University of Alabama Press.

Typeface: Palatino

Manufactured in the United States of America
Cover design: Paul Moxon

∞
The paper on which this book is printed meets the minimum requirements of American National Standard for Information Science–Permanence of Paper for Printed Library Materials, ANSI Z39.48-1984.

Paperback ISBN: 978-0-8173-5870-9
eBook ISBN: 978-0-8173-8135-6

A previous edition of this book has been catalogued by the Library of Congress as follows:
Library of Congress Cataloging-in-Publication Data
Harmon, Michael M., 1941–
Public administration's final exam : a pragmatist restructuring of the profession and the discipline / Michael M. Harmon.
p. cm.
Includes bibliographical references and index.
ISBN-13: 978-0-8173-1539-9 (cloth : alk. paper)
ISBN-10: 0-8173-1539-X (alk. paper)
1. Public administration—United States. 2. Civil service—United States. I. Title.
JK421.H295 2006
351.73—dc22
2006008284

To Frank P. Sherwood,
mentor and fellow pragmatist

Contents

Tables

Preface

Public Administration's Final Exam began as a one-page handout that I prepared, if memory serves, nearly twenty years ago for my Introduction to Public Administration course at The George Washington University. The handout listed four conceptual distinctions presupposed by, and thus tacitly legitimating, Woodrow Wilson's hoary, much-reviled "dichotomy" between politics and administration. For more than half a century no credible scholar of public administration has taken the dichotomy seriously as a valid descriptor of real-world governance practices, but only a very few have seriously challenged the coherence of the dichotomy's supporting conceptual distinctions. The persistence of that implicit disconnect between public administration "practice" and "theory" has sown much confusion among the field's academics, especially those concerned with the purportedly theoretical problem of reconciling the factual reality of administrative discretion and involvement in policy formation with the normative imperative of democratic accountability. That confusion can only be dissipated, or so I argue here, by acknowledging that the politics/administration dichotomy has not, despite claims to the contrary, been substantively discredited or discarded by what I term public administration's standard narrative. Rather, Wilson's ghost continues to haunt, tricking the field into posing unsolvable theoretical problems, thereby diverting attention from the important practical problems of governance to which there can be no theoretical solutions.

In this book I hope to make clear that the principal division of opinion within the contemporary discourse of public administration lies not between the "rationalist" and "normativist" wings of its standard narrative—between, for example, Herbert Simon's modern disciples, rational choice theorists, or advocates of the New Public Management, on the one hand, and the administrative ethicists, institutionalists, or "rule of law" traditionalists, on the other. The contributors to the standard narrative uniformly embrace most, if not all, of the conceptual distinctions (which I will term "dualisms") on which Wilson's dichotomy is predicated, and they differ from one another only on which of the two opposing elements (or "moments") to accord greater normative validity or temporal priority. Instead, the great divide within the discipline as a whole is between those who, if only in the breach, honor those conceptual dualisms—namely, *both* branches of the standard narrative—and those who don't. Most conspicuous among those who don't, at least in the United States, are the pragmatists. My purpose in "restructuring" the discourse on public administration is to banish Wilson's (not to mention Descartes's) ghost in order, as I conclude in my epilogue, to "clear away the theoretical and ideological debris that has obscured an already present, though only partially articulated, conception of governance, which from pragmatism's alternative vantage has long been visible and compelling."

Acknowledgments

During the three years since this book's inception I have profited greatly from the advice, criticism, and support of colleagues and friends. As usual, Orion White and Cynthia McSwain were indispensable to my completion of the project; each read an early draft of the manuscript, offering unfailingly wise suggestions about how to fill in important gaps in the book's argument and reassuring me, when I needed reassuring, that the project was worth doing. More broadly, the book can be seen as an extended footnote to our ongoing conversation of more than twenty-five years.

Professor Thomas Catlaw of Arizona State University commented extensively on a draft of chapter 6, which focuses directly on his own important and original critique of the concept of the popular sovereignty. His expression of satisfaction that I truly understood his argument was, in turn, a source of satisfaction to me.

Carolyn Harmon edited the first draft of the manuscript, finding numerous lapses in syntax, clarity of exposition, and cogency of argument. If good friends are those who on timely occasions save us from embarrassment, she surely qualifies as one.

Professor Robert Kramer of the American University read a major portion of chapter 3's critique of empiricist methodology and offered several helpful suggestions for tightening my argument. I was relieved to learn that he shared my opinions concerning the limitations of empiricist social science, especially in view of his own extensive experience in teaching and using its methods.

I credit Marcus Raskin, my colleague at George Washington's School of Public Policy and Public Administration, for prompting me to write the book's "Postscript on the Personal/Political Nature of Epistemological Choice" and for his supportive criticisms of chapter 3. Our too infrequent conversations during the past two years have served to remind me of the presence of at least a few local allies on the pragmatist side of the great divide.

Professor Peter Bogason of Roskilde University in Copenhagen read a late version of the manuscript in its entirety and provided several helpful references to buttress my argument. His keen editorial eye also spotted several lapses and inconsistencies in my argument, most of which (I hope) I have been able to remedy.

Annette Beresford read the manuscript's early portions, detecting many instances in which I had failed to be as clear as I had supposed. Still, she said that, overall, she liked what she read a great deal, and I'm especially grateful for that.

My graduate assistants, Pei Liu (for the first two years of the project) and Rachel Krefetz and Nathaniel Taylor (for the third), provided invaluable help in tracking down references, toting books and journals to and from George Washington's Gelman Library, providing editorial assistance, and preparing the index.

My colleagues at the School of Public Policy and Public Administration have cheerfully (or so I have assumed) indulged my frequent lamentations about the slow pace of the book's progress and have otherwise been supportive of what many of them no doubt regard as a somewhat eccentric project. I would especially like to thank Bill Adams, Lori Brainard, Jennifer Brinkerhoff, Dylan Conger, Joe Cordes, Dwight Cropp, Donna Infeld, Phil Joyce, Jed Kee, Kathy Newcomer, and Mike Worth.

I owe perhaps my greatest debt, however, to the two anonymous reviewers invited by the University of Alabama Press to critique the manuscript. Both, though generally supportive of my project, pointedly criticized major aspects of its execution. Their criticisms, even if I did not always agree with them, were always accompanied by constructive recommendations about how I might improve the manuscript. The final product is, as a result, substantially longer than I had first anticipated; but, more importantly, it is a much better book.

Public Administration's Final Exam

A Prologue on Adolescence

> Intellectual progress usually occurs through sheer abandonment of questions. . . . We do not solve them; we get over them.
>
> —John Dewey

> Youth is fleeting. Immaturity, however, can last forever! Happy Birthday
>
> —greeting card by Avanti Press, Inc.

The standard version of American public administration's historical narrative typically marks the field's birth with Woodrow Wilson's (1887) and Frank Goodnow's (1900) pronouncement of a dichotomy between politics and administration. The field's coming-of-age—its loss of innocence and consequent maturity—then follows, or so the narrative assumes, with the dichotomy's subsequent rejection. While innocence lost may satisfy a precondition for maturity, however, it is insufficient for maturity's fuller attainment. A more accurate interpretation of the field's historical development, therefore, holds that public administration's rejection of the dichotomy as a practical possibility—beginning with Luther Gulick in 1933—merely ushered in a period of sustained adolescence from which it has yet to emerge.[1]

Adolescence involves profound conflict and ambivalence born of wanting to be taken seriously by one's elders while at the same time seeking independence from them. The metaphor of adolescence thus seems apt for depicting public administration's struggle to achieve legitimacy as a politically accountable—but at the same time professionally independent—voice in defining and responding to the public interest. These twin "problems," however, cannot be solved within the terms that the adolescent assumes. In their ordinary connotations, accountability and independence are irreconcilable goals inasmuch as each can be achieved, if at all, only at the expense of the other. Moreover, striking a balance between them or subordinating one to the other, which the standard narrative often confuses with reconciling them, simply makes matters worse. Maturity involves, instead, comprehending the futility of that reconciliation through a revised account of what is at stake.

Public administration's distinctive claim to maturity has traditionally been both asserted and contested within what is now commonly called its "legitimacy project": the field's more-than-seventy-year struggle to justify its unique entitlement to speak truth to power from a posture of political subordination. That claim, however, has entailed a disguised presumption of moral innocence by virtue of the field's continued acceptance of four conceptual distinctions (or dualisms) on which the politics/administration dichotomy—the original source of its claim to innocence—is itself grounded: value and fact, thinking and doing, ends and means, and theory and practice. This book's critique of these dualisms, and of dualistic thinking more generally, exposes the costs to public administration of its paradoxical presumptions of innocence and worldliness, of accountability and independence.

My principal purpose, however, is not critique for its own sake. Rather, by dissolving the dualisms that still underwrite the legitimacy project of public administration's standard narrative, I hope to remove the conceptual impediments to imagining an alternative—and more authentically mature—approach to governance. The chief impediment, I will argue, is the legitimacy question itself, which, like the philosophical questions alluded to in Dewey's epigraph, we need to "get over" rather than "solve." The alternative "unitary" conception of governance that I will propose, long extant though partially concealed behind a veil of dualisms, has its main roots in the century-old tradition, and now the revival, of American pragmatist philosophy. As I suggest in the epilogue, pragmatism, including its implied notion of "practical maturity," is an idea whose time has finally come—now rendered persuasive and even compelling by the transition from the failed promises of the modern era to the uncertainties and interdependencies of the global age.

1
The Question

Louis Menand has likened pragmatism's message to formalist philosophers to an admonition that, if taken to heart, would lift from their shoulders "a pressing but vaguely understood obligation—[as if notifying them] . . . that some final examination for which they could never possibly have felt prepared has just been cancelled" (1997, xi–xii). The examination metaphor blends nicely with the metaphor of public administration's adolescence for the obvious reason that most adolescents know what it means to study for final exams, and with rare exceptions they have also fantasized on occasion about their being canceled. Extending the metaphor a step further, the adolescent might eventually rue the exam's cancellation for its hastening the moment when he or she has to face the prospect of doing something useful, such as getting a job. This observation, too, bears on a cardinal theme of pragmatism—William James (1898) called it the "cash value" of ideas—that will be revisited later.

Despite the appealing prospect of a respite from grading exams, professors are nevertheless reluctant, as a common practice, to cancel them. Not only do examinations provide the chief means by which they certify students, but through that certification professors also validate the content and standards of their disciplines. Public administration's overarching final examination, "written" soon after Luther Gulick first announced the demise of the politics/administration dichotomy, has consisted of a single four-part question. Unbeknownst to its authors, it is a trick question inasmuch as the terms and assumptions that underlie its formulation preclude the possibility of a coherent answer. Detailed instructions precede the question itself:

(*circa* 1933)
This is a take-home examination, so be sure to use a typewriter and remember to double-space. Take as much time as you need to write your response; in fact, you are allowed up to seventy years to complete it. Also, there is no space limitation; indeed, you may have to produce many volumes before you are ready to turn in your final answer. Although the faculty expects you to demonstrate a comprehensive knowledge of the relevant literature, including thorough documentation and meticulous footnotes, we will otherwise be quite generous in our grading standards. This is because we can't agree upon what constitutes a correct or even a satisfactory answer to the examination's question. We ask that you keep this confidential inasmuch as public knowledge of that disagreement might damage our credibility and alarm prospective students. Moreover, for reasons we don't fully understand, some dissident colleagues, including the pragmatists over in Philosophy (as if it were any of their business), don't like the question. Please keep this quiet, too. Good luck!

The Question:
Mr. Gulick has recently observed, and we soon anticipate almost unanimous agreement with him from the public administration academy, that politics and administration are fundamentally inseparable, therefore making inevitable discretionary judgments by administrators in initiating and interpreting policy decisions. Presuming that you, too, agree with him, write an essay that both defines and circumscribes the legitimate exercise of administrative discretion, which is to say, policy (as opposed to purely technical) judgments, decisions, and actions that professional public administrators independently make, initiate, or recommend. In addition to whatever else you might wish to write on this topic, make sure that your case for administrative discretion satisfies all four of the following requirements:

1. The core values that inform the exercise of administrative discretion must be shown to be consistent with and subordinate to the values and purposes of legally enacted public policies and other constitutionally legitimate decisions made by political authorities. You will receive extra credit if you can show that these values are, in addition, "universal," "transcendental," or modified by some other adjective signifying that they

are *not* merely matters of personal, local, or historical opinion. At the very least, discretionary acts informed by the public administrator's core values must be shown not to violate the letter, intent, or spirit of such policies and decisions. (Satisfying this requirement will solve, or at least avoid, the vexing problem of moral relativism.)

2. Public administrators must be shown to be capable of exercising discretion effectively and responsibly, owing to their unique possession of relevant knowledge, skills, techniques, or other kinds of expertise. That is, administrators must be able to show that they possess vital expertise that others don't. (After all, if non-experts such as ordinary citizens or political hacks could do the job just as well, why invest time and money to produce trained professionals?)
3. Not only must public administrators possess a common (and unique) body of expertise and a defensible set of core values, but they must also be able to show that their application across cases of a similar class will produce uniform and consistent decisions, recommendations, or outcomes, and that the application of such expertise and core values by various administrators to the *same* case would result, within tolerable limits, in the same decision, recommendation, or outcome. (Why train experts, in other words, if they can't agree with one another?)
4. After showing how the first three requirements can be satisfied, answer either a or b.
   a. What kinds of "objective" legal, institutional, and/or managerial controls—either already in place or readily imaginable—provide, or could provide, realistic assurance that administrators will apply their unique expertise responsibly, effectively, and in the public interest?
   b. What "subjective" factors—for example, professional socialization, appeals to democratic values, satisfying public administrators' "higher" psychological needs—obviate, or substantially diminish, the need for the kinds of controls called for in 4.a? (Even if public administrators know what they ought to do and how to do it, how can the public be confident that they will actually do it?)

The Structure of the Argument

My purpose in this book is to explain why, owing to some dubious assumptions that it takes for granted, public administration's final exam question cannot be answered, and therefore that the so-called legitimacy project that the field's standard narrative has pursued for nearly three quarters of a century ought to be abandoned. I hope to show, in other words, that the problem the question asserts cannot be solved by starting from the assumptions on which it is framed, but only *dis*solved by exposing those assumptions as specious. Chief among those assumptions is the acceptance of four analytical distinctions, or dualisms, that underlie the standard narrative's taken-for-granted distinction between politics (and policy) and administration. The four dualisms—value and fact, thinking and doing, ends and means, and theory and practice—provide the philosophical backdrop against which the field of public administration has traditionally tried to justify its legitimate relation to politics. These dualisms not only separate the two terms in each pair from one another but also specify a temporal and normative priority between the two terms in order to justify administration's subordination to politics.

When practical problems of governing arise regarding the maintenance of that subordination, factions of the standard narrative resort to either of two strategies for dealing with them. One faction uses what I will call "splitting" strategies, which are intended to reaffirm the separation of administration from politics; a second, more dominant faction pursues "reconciling" strategies for managing the tensions caused by their inevitable overlap. Both factions of the standard narrative, however, leave unchallenged the four underlying dualisms on which the coherence of the politics/administration distinction depends.

The pragmatists' principal challenge to the standard narrative entails a demonstration of why both splitting and reconciling strategies necessarily fail. The theoretical reasons for their failure help to explain why practical problems of administrative discretion and accountability, the role of technical expertise, the resolution of disagreement, and so forth, persist despite the best efforts of the standard narrative to either eliminate or effectively manage them. Pragmatism, one of several "critical" discourses outside public administration's standard narrative, attributes the failure of these efforts to public administration's unexamined acceptance of the four dualisms on which the politics/administration distinction is parasitic. Pragmatists use either "inverting" strategies, which reverse the temporal and normative priority of the two terms in each dualism (e.g., doing precedes thinking, rather than the other way about), or more radical "dissolving" strategies, which reveal those dualisms as contrived and misleading to begin with. That is, each dualism masks a "unitary" or "fused" activity. The analytical distinction between thinking and doing, for example, misrepresents the unitary quality of action at both an individual and a collective level.

Dissolving these dualisms, then, enables a parallel dissolving of the analytical distinction between politics and administration. The result is a unitary conception of governance, one that does not depend, at least conceptually, on any distinction between politics and administration. The U.S. government's constitutional legacy of separation of powers and the emergence of an "administrative state" roughly a century after the republic's founding, however, have produced institutions of government and a concomitant set of public beliefs about "the way things are" that are distinctly inhospitable to this unitary view of governance. It would be grandly naive, therefore, to presume that history might be erased and current institutions dismantled in order to construct, de novo, new institutions of governance from whole theoretical cloth. No matter how persuasive my critique of public administration's standard narrative, which is itself a product of that history and those beliefs, some nominal distinction between "politicians" (policy *makers*) and "administrators" will persist for the foreseeable future, including continuing concerns about their proper spheres of influence and relation to one another.

My concluding proposal for a unitary conception of governance (appearing near the end of this book) is thus, at least mainly, a proposal for rethinking the relation between politics and administration (and citizens, as well) implied by inverting and dissolving the dualisms that have led the standard narrative astray. All of those suggestions, however, presume that the relation between policy makers and administrators is not, and should not be regarded as, a normative (or "legitimacy") problem, as the standard narrative assumes. That is, the proper relation between them is more productively viewed as a strictly practical problem.

The plausibility of a unitary conception of governance, however, requires the introduction of two additional dualisms depicting the analytical distinctions implicit in two quite different, though often conflated, historical variants of the "P/A" dichotomy: *policy* and administration, and *politics* and administration. The first, the policy variant, connotes the distinction between the *general* and the *particular,* in which (and like all of the other dualisms) the first element is assumed to be temporally and normatively prior to the second element. The dichotomy's *politics* variant presupposes the distinction between *expression* (of, e.g., the popular will or public sentiment) and *execution,* Woodrow Wilson's original synonym for *administration.* In chapter 6 I will argue not only that each dualism is problematic when analyzed separately but that their errors are compounded when the two dualisms are conflated. Dissolving both dualisms while insisting upon an analytical distinction between policy and politics enables a radical reframing of the notion of governance that renders moot public administration's long-standing and misplaced preoccupation with the question of its legitimacy. Rid of that unneeded burden, the field's final examination question might then be rewritten in a manner that realistically clarifies the possibilities for its transition from adolescence to maturity.

To ease the difficulty readers might experience in following the book's complex line of argument, I have organized each of the remaining chapters according to a common architecture depicted in Table 1.1. Chapters 2 through 5 each explicate one core dualism (listed in the table's first column), while chapter 6 covers two dualisms. The table's second column identifies the "problematic virtue" that an acceptance of each dualism implies, while the third column identifies the generic "pseudo-problem" similarly implied by that acceptance. The fourth column labels the concealed "unitary" idea or activity exposed by means of dissolving each dualism. The fifth (right-hand) column identifies the "real" problem—the heretofore repressed ideological issue—made evident by dissolving each dualism and in reference to which, therefore, the field's examination question ought to be rewritten.

Public Administration's Grand Dualism: The Politics/Administration Dichotomy

Had Woodrow Wilson not later been elected president of the United States, it is safe to assume, his now-revered and frequently reinterpreted essay, written when he was a young political science professor at Princeton, would forever have languished in obscurity. During the more than sixty years following its initial publication in 1887, "The Study of Ad-

Table 1.1: Dualisms, Problematic Virtues, and Pseudoproblems

Dualism	Problematic virtue implied by the dualism	Pseudoproblem produced by the dualism	Unitary activity/ idea concealed by the dualism	Problem revealed by dissolving the dualism
1. Politics (Policy)/ Administration	Accountability	Legitimacy	Governance	(See items 6 & 7)
2. Value/Fact	Moral justification	Relativism	Belief	Moralism
3. Thinking/Doing	Instrumental rationality	Irrationality	Action	Rationalism
4. Ends/Means	Effectiveness/ Efficiency	Ineffectiveness/ Inefficiency	Organizing	Managerialism
5. Theory/Practice	Expertise	Uncertainty	Praxis	Technicism
6. General (*Policy*)/ Particular (Administration)	Social equity (Fairness)	Inequality	Universal equality as "infinite difference"	Presupposition of sameness (Homogeneity)
7. Expression (*Politics*)/Execution (Administration)	Representation	Threats to the popular sovereignty	Administration as "a politics of the subject"	The *myth* of representation

ministration" was rarely discussed or even cited in public administration's academic literature. It finally received prominent consideration with the publication, in 1948, of Dwight Waldo's *The Administrative State.*[1] Waldo's influential volume, subtitled *A Study of the Political Theory of American Public Administration,* was among the first to credit Wilson's essay as an important early statement of what subsequently became, during the first third of the twentieth century, an "orthodox" distinction between politics and administration.[2] Wilson, however, was not the first to make that distinction; Dorman B. Eaton had remarked upon it in 1879 in a report on governmental reform produced at the request of President Rutherford B. Hayes. Moreover, the frequency with which Wilson's essay has been commented upon *since* 1948 very likely owes as much to its ambiguity and internal contradictions as to its cogency and depth of insight (Van Riper 1984).

"Wilson's dichotomy" clearly qualifies as a dualism in the sense described earlier: its two "moments" are temporally separated and hierarchically ordered, with politics (and therefore policy) both preceding and commanding authoritative priority over administration. Wilson's essay was published just four years after the creation of the U.S. Civil Service by the passage, in 1883, of the Pendleton Act, the signal event of the governmental reform movement begun in the late nineteenth century and extending into the early twentieth. Although the essay caught a rising tide of public reaction against the corrupting influences of Jacksonian democracy, Wilson's critique more explicitly targeted the constitutional framers' guiding doctrine of separation of powers. Like his contemporary Frank Goodnow (1900), Wilson believed that although the separation of governmental functions (politics from administration) was a good thing, separation of political powers was decidedly bad, the twin consequences of which were governmental inefficiency and the irresponsible exercise of political power induced by its fragmentation. As Rohr (1984) has noted in this regard, "Wilson shared with the framers the fear of . . . [the] excesses [of popular democracy], but he found wanting their reliance on separation of powers. He would amend their means, but not their ends. Wilson hoped enlightened administration would replace separation of powers in the noble task of saving democracy from its own excesses" (45)—brought upon, for example, by the spoils system and the influx of immigrant groups of heretofore unfamiliar ethnicity, customs, and speech.

Wilson's (and soon thereafter Goodnow's) distinction between politics and administration implied two somewhat different, and quite possibly contradictory, qualities to be desired of the latter: first, its subordination to legitimate political authority; and second, its independence from illegitimate political pressures, including the vagaries of public opinion about which Wilson, as a political conservative, was deeply suspect (Rohr 1984). Wilson's failure to explain how to distinguish the former from the latter, however, generated disagreement among his later interpreters as to which of those two qualities he valued more highly. Whether Wilson was chiefly concerned with subordinating administration or with protecting it, however, is perhaps less important than his urging its functional separation from politics. His advocacy of that separation constituted a direct assault upon the Federalist principle of separation of powers, augmented by the promise of administrative efficiency produced by the application of modern business principles. As Waldo (1948) has noted, "Generally speaking, students of administration have been hostile to the tripartite separation of powers. . . . This lack of sympathy . . . was nourished by admiration for British practice [of unified cabinet government] and American business organization; and it found expression typically in proposals to deflate the judiciary, to aggrandize the executive, to distinguish more sharply 'decision' and 'execution'" (104–5). Only to the extent that deciding and executing were separated in practice could the criterion of administrative efficiency in principle be satisfied. And Wilson's vision of two separate functional spheres has, in retrospect, been at most only partially affirmed by later U.S. Supreme Court decisions. The Court, as Rosenbloom (1984) explains, has consistently upheld prohibitions against political patronage in awarding administrative appointments, while typically leaving intact government policy practices that co-mingle, rather than separate, the political and administrative spheres: "[The Supreme Court] has strongly supported far-reaching limitation of those rights where partisan-patronage politics is at issue, such as in regulations for political neutrality. Rather, the Court's actions reflect its support for the constitutional values of political competition and political diversity as opposed to Wilsonian administrative values seeking to promote effectiveness, efficiency, and economy through the depoliticization of public employees" (105). Measured, then, against his ambitious hope of ridding administration of policy politics, Wilson's vision of efficient governance would have to settle for the fractionally more modest victory of civil service reform.

Although the Wilsonian dichotomy could not supplant the founders' earlier and still dominant aim of separating political power in order to prevent its arbitrary exercise, it did set, or at least anticipate, the terms on which the meaning of administrative responsibility would later be debated. Wilson's, along with Goodnow's, essentially "organic" conception of the state (Waldo 1948; Rohr 1984) as embodying a unitary, homogeneous "will" predisposed both men toward a view of administrative responsibility as strict accountability to political authority. The strictness of that view was modulated, however, by their recognition of the countervailing need for administrative independence in making technical judgments and saying "no" to political interference in administrative questions. Goodnow, perhaps more than Wilson, seemed to appreciate, even if he could offer no clear formula for resolving, the practical question of how to distinguish between politically legitimate oversight and politically *il*legitimate "meddling."

Nearly half a century after the publication of Wilson's essay, new voices began to express more radical notions of what administrative independence might properly mean. With Gulick in 1933, followed soon afterward by Friedrich in 1940, administrative independence began to assume a connotation of administrative discretion no longer restricted to purely technical judgments. As I noted in the prologue, for Gulick "the seamless web of [administrative] discretion and action" (1933, 61) implied the obsolescence of the politics/administration dichotomy, an opinion echoed by Friedrich's declaring that the dichotomy had "become a fetish, a stereotype in the minds of theorists and practitioners alike" (1940, 6). In the years following World War II, opinion among scholars representing public administration's standard narrative has been divided, not chiefly over the dichotomy's empirical accuracy, but on normative questions of administrative conduct revealed by the now widespread recognition of its demise. As I will argue in the following section, the two contending factions of the standard narrative, notwithstanding their real and substantive disagreements, are nevertheless implicitly united by their common acceptance of not only the analytical distinction between politics (and policy) and administration but also of the underlying conceptual dualisms that support the illusion of its plausibility.[3]

The Standard Narrative

At the beginning of this chapter I referred, perhaps too cryptically, to public administration's standard narrative, the standpoint from which the field's final exam was originally written. As with any grand narrative, its contributors disagree on many things—the narrative, that is, should not be mistaken for orthodoxy—but they do share a number of beliefs, usually tacit, that provide a common basis for clarifying their disagreements. The persistence for more than half a century of what appear to be divisive issues within that narrative suggests, however, that those issues' perpetuation rather than their resolution is the chief consequence, even the implicit purpose, of the arguments waged by the narrative's contributors (McSwite 1997). That is, they seem to know that resolving their differences, whatever might be the benefits of doing so, could also produce a new orthodoxy that would obviate the very point of the narrative itself. If the contributors to the standard narrative settled all their arguments, they might have nothing left to do. Thus, continuing the arguments for their own sake provides energy and even a sense of urgency to those who engage in them. Moreover, in public administration's standard narrative, the continuation of its arguments according to long-established terms of disagreement is virtually guaranteed by an underlying agreement on beliefs that render its final exam question unanswerable.

Contributors to the standard narrative appear to share at least three key beliefs about the relation between politics and administration. First, they generally accept as unproblematic the core functional meanings of the two words. *Politics,* at least insofar as its relation to administration is concerned, refers to activities bearing upon the formulation of public policy, while *administration* refers to activities pertaining to its implementation, or, formerly, its "execution." Accordingly (and obviously), "politicians"—that is, elected officials and their appointees chosen mainly for their political loyalty—are the chief makers of policy, while "administrators"—selected for their professional expertise or experience—are chiefly involved with its implementation. Virtually all contributors to the standard narrative now agree, however, that in practice considerable overlap occurs: politicians often make "administrative" decisions, and, more significantly for the standard narrative, administrators often make policy or otherwise influence its formulation.

At this point there is little factual dispute within the standard narrative regarding the extent of administrators' actual involvement in policy making. And, the disagreements that *can* be detected result from confusing and conflating the use of *administrative* as, on the one hand, the adjectival form of *administration* as a functional category of practices with, on the other hand, its use as a qualifier to describe both "administrative" *and* "nonadministrative" (policy-*making*) activities that public administrat*ors* often perform.[4] In the standard narrative, then, what sometimes passes for substantive disagreement is merely evidence of terminological confusion. Nevertheless, everyone now agrees that there is not, and probably has never been, a strict dichotomy between politics and administration, and that an astute reading of the field's two chief founders of a century ago, Wilson and Goodnow, reveals that they, too, were to some degree aware of this, thus giving the lie to caricatures of them as naive perpetrators of a pernicious myth that has distorted public administration's self-understanding (Lynn 2001; Svara 2001).

Second, notwithstanding its nearly universal rejection on empirical grounds of a dichotomy between politics and administration, the standard narrative is firmly agreed on the normative priority of politics (and therefore of policy) over administration. Given that priority, the standard narrative typically concedes that tensions may and often do arise when, on the basis of discretionary judgments informed by their expertise and experience, administrators act in ways that contradict or otherwise collide with the wishes of their political masters. What unifies the narrative on this issue is the belief that such tensions can—at least in principle—be effectively reduced either by splitting politics and administration *from* one another or by reconciling them *with* one another.[5]

Splitting strategies stem from the belief, now largely but not entirely in disfavor, that any observed tension between administrative discretion and political accountability necessarily results from the failure of administrators to confine their judgments to those informed by technical or professional expertise, which, by virtue of its politically "neutral" nature, could be deployed in the effective and efficient attainment of any political end. This normative depiction of the public administrator as neutral expert finds some echo in both Wilson and Goodnow, but its origins are most often traced to Frederick Taylor's (1947) scientific management movement, and it later received a more nuanced and sophisticated formulation by Herbert Simon in his classic work, *Administrative Behavior* (1947).

At least two limitations of splitting strategies, however, are immediately apparent. First, if successful, they would have the effect of instituting a strict dichotomy between politics and administration, which most public administration scholars, beginning with Gulick in 1933, have already claimed to be neither practically possible nor normatively desirable. That is, splitting strategies would entail a claim to the recovery of lost innocence in which public administrators would stand wholly apart from and wholly subservient to politics and the policy-making process, thus forfeiting any normative claim as active and "mature" participants in the larger process of democratic governance.

And second, if successful, such strategies would make public administration even more vulnerable than it now is to the many radical critiques, issuing from outside the field's standard narrative, of "technical rationality" and its associated managerialist (note the pejorative connotation of the *ist* suffix) values of effectiveness and efficiency. Beginning with Weber (1968) and as recently as Adams and Balfour (2004), those critiques have disputed the comforting belief that technical expertise *can*, even in theory, be morally and politically neutral. Although representing varied intellectual and ideological viewpoints, most authors of these critiques would probably regard MacIntyre as aptly summarizing their sentiments: "[T]he whole concept of effectiveness is . . . inseparable from a mode of human existence in which the contrivance of means is in central part the manipulation of human beings into compliant patterns of behavior; and it is by appeal to his own effectiveness in this respect that the manager claims authority within the manipulative mode" (1984, 74). The opposing stances of the standard narrative and its critics on this point might thus be summarized as follows: The dominant faction of the standard narrative regards as naive the belief that administration is, can, or should be characterized by the dominance of politically neutral expertise; that is to say, administrators both do and should participate in policy making, and therefore do and should contend with political and value questions as well as technical ones. The radical critics, by contrast, regard as naive the belief that expertise itself *can* be politically neutral owing to its manipulative character, but believe that the collective mind-set of public administrators is nevertheless (unconsciously) suffused to a far greater degree by the myth of political neutrality—which itself constitutes a source of hidden political power—than the standard narrative cares to admit or can even comprehend.

Perhaps aware of these pitfalls of splitting strategies, the standard narrative's more typical strategy for dealing with the tensions between administrative discretion and political accountability is to try to show how they might be reconciled with one another by asserting that both in theory and in much observed practice they are essentially complementary to, rather than antagonistic toward, one another. The frequent tensions between them that do arise, therefore, must result from an absence of enlightened leadership by and mutual respect between politicians and administrators. The job of the standard narrative is to show a conceptual way out of their temporary and essentially needless conflict. A recent example of such a reconciling strategy is provided by Svara (2001), whose proposal for managing the tensions between administrative expertise and political accountability is based explicitly on the assumption of their underlying complementarity. (I confess that I was prompted, at least in small part, to quote liberally from and then comment upon Svara's article because in it he appears, if only in passing, to have enlisted me as a likely opponent of his position.) Svara writes:

> The complementarity of politics and administration is based on the premise that elected officials and administrators join together in the common pursuit of sound governance. Complementarity entails separate parts, but parts that come together in a mutually supportive way. One fills out the other to create a whole. Complementarity stresses interdependence along with distinct roles; compliance along with independence; respect for political control along with a commitment to shape and implement policy in ways that promote the public interest; deference to elected incumbents along with adherence to the law and support for fair electoral competition; and appreciation of politics along with support for professional standards. The issue is not whether public administrators are "instrumental or usurpative" . . . but how they are both instruments and contributors to the political process, that is, instrumental and constitutive. . . .
>
> Complementarity reconciles what have *seemed* [emphasis added] to be contradictory—even paradoxical (Harmon 1995)—aspects of public administration. How can politicians maintain control and,

> at the same time, allow administrators to maintain their independence to adhere to professional values and standards and to be responsible to the public? The reconciliation comes from recognizing the reciprocating values that underlie complementarity. Elected officials, could, in theory, dominate administrative practice, but they are constrained by a respect for administrative competence and commitment. Administrators could use their considerable resources to become self-directed, but they are restrained by a commitment to accountability in the complementary relationship. (2001, 179)

Knowing that the unconscious abhors coincidence, I felt moved, while reading Svara's argument for complementarity, to ponder why I had begun to hum the tune to "The Farmer and the Cowman Should Be Friends" from Rodgers and Hammerstein's *Oklahoma.* Readers might recall that this song is Auntie Eller's plea for mutual understanding and friendship between farmers and ranchers locked in a bitter dispute over the settlement of and grazing access to land in the newly opened territory. She tries to convince the two sides that, despite their differences, they have more in common than they realize and that a little goodwill and common sense would surely reveal the folly of their present acrimony. At one level the song could be heard as simply a sincere plea for reconciliation, a sentiment that Rodgers and Hammerstein indulged, sometimes to cloying excess, in several of the songs in their later musicals. In the present instance, however, that is hardly their intent. Instead, the song is meant to be amusing, even hilarious, owing to the naïveté and futility of Auntie Eller's admonition. The audience, that is, intuitively knows (or is supposed to know) that the farmers and ranchers won't heed a word of her advice, a suspicion confirmed at the song's conclusion when a brawl ensues.

One might imagine, somewhat fancifully, this situation as the object of analysis by a group of overly serious social scientists (or, alternatively, some very droll ones with lots of spare time). To begin, the group's anthropologist casts her analysis in terms of the opposing myths that constitute the "structural" conditions determining (1) how farmers and ranchers variously define the situation, (2) the possibilities each side is therefore able to conceive for acting toward the other, and (3) the "readings" of the motives that the two sides attribute to one another. The Marxist, predictably, stresses the "contradictions" among the underlying economic conditions that make intractable the present conflict between the two sides, both of which are, in turn, simply pawns in a larger play of material forces during the period of early capitalism. The group's rational choice economist is especially sensitive to the opposing logics—for example, individual versus collective rationality, long-term versus short-term considerations of rational self-interest, "the tragedy of the commons," and the "free-rider" problem—that make predictable the farmers' and ranchers' turning a deaf ear to Auntie Eller's plea. The Jungian analyst in the group cites the reciprocal unconscious projection of both sides' unresolved psychological conflicts as a chief barrier to their reconciliation. Finally, the (nondirective) Rogerian psychotherapist reminds the group that farmers and ranchers, like people generally, almost always reject advice, especially moralistic advice, whenever and by whomever it is given.

By now, only the least alert readers will have failed to spot the parallel between "politicians and administrators" and "the farmer and the cowman," or failed to suspect, therefore, that advising the former pair to reconcile their differences in a spirit of mutual respect is as likely to succeed as Auntie Eller's exhorting the latter to be friends. In proffering their advice, then, Svara and other "reconcilers" ignore the structural and other largely hidden forces—cultural, economic, organizational, linguistic, psychological—that make tension and conflict between politicians and administrators predictable and pervasive. This is not to deny the practical possibility of sometimes effectively managing these conflicts on a case-by-case basis, but it does suggest that a fuller account is needed of the conditions that make their reconciliation in any larger sense both unlikely and difficult. More importantly, structural analysis of this kind suggests vastly different definitions of the problem than the one proposed by Svara, who assumes that conflicts must, on their face, result from an absence of mutual respect, reasonableness, and appropriate deference by each side to the other. By construing problems of conflict in such moralistic terms, Svara unsurprisingly dismisses contradiction and paradox as mere appearances rather than regarding them as subjects that merit serious attention. Instead, he defines these problems away by starting from a wishful premise—"elected officials and administrators join together in the common pursuit of sound governance"—followed by substituting in place of argument an extended truism: complementarity enables interdependence and mutual respect, which in turn reconcile values and interests that are really reciprocal owing to their complementarity.

The third core belief of public administration's standard narrative rejects on factual grounds a strict dichotomy between politics and administration while nevertheless retaining both a functional and therefore a normative distinction between them. By definition, that is, politics involves policy making, while administration is construed as policy implementation. In accepting that distinction, however, the standard narrative undermines its own efforts to "solve" the normative problem of public administration's legitimacy by putting itself between a conceptual rock and a hard place. By conceding that the dividing line between politics and administration is (and, as a practical matter, has to be) blurred in actual practice, asserting the normative priority of politics over administration becomes increasingly unrealistic as a guiding normative principle. The more the practical distinction is blurred—the more forcefully, that is, the dichotomy is "rejected" as a valid descriptor of the real-world practice of governance—the less realistic it is to assert the normative priority of politics over administration in order to resolve the tensions between these two domains. The appearance of worldliness that administrators claim by means of their active participation in policy making is thus immediately contradicted by the claim to innocence inhering in their morally and politically subservient status. *Reconciliation,* a favored word in the standard narrative, is merely a euphemism for *subordination.* Despite appearances, in the standard narrative the hoped-for reconciliation is not *between* politics and administration as equal partners in governance, but the reconciling *of* administration *to* politics.

I can anticipate the reply that I have merely stated the obvious, namely, that when tensions between politics and administration occur (as they often do), politics should trump administration whenever reasonableness and goodwill on the part of either side fail to resolve them. In view of their structural origins, however, such tensions may very often be hidden from the awareness and scrutiny even of those who are parties to them, and are therefore immune to the kind of resolution that either reasonableness or authoritative political command promises. More basic, however, are the standard narrative's underlying assumptions regarding the functional distinction between politics and administration. That distinction presupposes at least four other, largely hidden and implicit, dualisms required for making public administration's legitimacy project theoretically coherent.

The remainder of this book is devoted chiefly to destabilizing and then dissolving those dualisms in order to reveal the legitimacy project as a theoretical dead end. If the analytical distinctions that have historically underwritten the politics/administration distinction are themselves based on dubious beliefs and assumptions, then the simultaneously moral and practical problem of how we—politicians, administrators, and citizens alike—govern ourselves needs to be fundamentally recast. In order to begin work on that problem, however, we first need to rethink how we think about some rather basic issues, including thought itself, action, and judgment.

Dualisms, Justification, and Innocence

The discussion of public administration's final examination begins by highlighting what may seem both obvious and uncontroversial, namely, that the question is a demand for justification. That is, to establish their collective legitimacy as an independent discretionary voice in policy making, public administrators must justify that voice to their political superiors and to the public at large. As I hope to show, however, demands for justification in any strong sense of the word cannot be satisfied. And if this conclusion is correct then the very point of the question is itself called into question as a coherent strategy for establishing the legitimacy of administrative discretion or anything else.

To justify means to establish a claim for one proposition, principle, or action by logically deducing it from, or showing its indisputable empirical connection to, some prior and already accepted proposition, principle, or action. In the sense of the word that the question assumes, justification implies a relation of an "if-then," "in terms of," or "in order to" sort. These three phrases share a common connotation that any successful claim for a proposition is extrinsic rather than inhering within the proposition as a unitary entity. Dichotomies, especially Wilson's and Goodnow's asserted dichotomy between politics (or policy) and administration, initially seem well suited as devices for justifications of this kind. *Dichotomy* not only connotes an analytical distinction between one element and another but also packs the added punch of suggesting that the distinction between the two elements is especially clear cut, or "radical," and even that their relation is contradictory or antagonistic. Further, one might choose to reject the existence of a dichotomy between politics and administration on the ground that, as a factual matter, the activities that each of the two domains comprise inevitably intrude into those of the other. In order to make any sense, however, the statement requires a prior analytical (functional) distinction in the absence of which we could not know what is intruding into what.

The standard narrative's dualisms also stipulate which of their two elements precedes the other. Politics (or policy) precedes administration, thinking precedes doing, ends precede means, and theory precedes practice. The lone possible exception is the dualism between values and facts, in which the two elements might appear to have coequal status. As the value/fact dualism is used in the public administration literature (Simon 1947), however, the relevance of facts depends upon the prior identification of values in whose service they are employed. So, as a practical matter, values also precede facts in a manner paralleling the other dualisms.

The priority of the first over the second element in each of these dualisms is not, however, merely temporal, nor is it analytical in a neutral sense; it is also normative by virtue of implicitly prescribing a proper and legitimate priority between the two elements. That is, none of these dualisms consists of separate-but-equal parts, being arranged instead in a simple normative hierarchy. When Wilson and Goodnow, for example, sought to separate politics from administration, they did so not in order to distinguish between them for purely analytical purposes, and not, at least mainly, to urge the independence of each from the other in practice, but rather to make clear administration's normative subordination to politics. (This last sentence requires some qualification inasmuch as Wilson, especially, wanted public administration to be protected from, and therefore in a sense independent of, the corrupting influence of politics, but most assuredly *not* from the mandates of legitimate political authority to which he regarded administration as properly subordinate.)

The point of this rather technical discussion is to show why, owing to their undeniably normative character, the dualisms of the standard narrative seem convenient and even compelling as rhetorical devices for justifying public administration's existence as both a discipline and a profession. Much of the reason has to do with the sheer simplicity of the apparent connection between the first and second element of each dualism: owing to the hierarchical relation between the two elements of each dualism, administration derives its justification from politics; facts are deemed relevant from the standpoint of previously validated public values; "doing" is rendered sensible and therefore justified in terms of decisions arrived at through "rational" thought; and means have no justification—indeed, they could not be conceived *as* means—independently of previously established ends.

Assuming (but only for the moment) that these dualisms are conceptually valid, they should thereby be capable of grounding the in-terms-of or if-then kind of justification for administrative discretion that the standard narrative asserts. Such a justification is paradoxical, however, because the implicit syllogism with which it begins leads to a self-contradictory conclusion. To see why, we should notice that *discretion* connotes a degree of latitude in choice and action that, in the administrator's judgment, cannot in the final analysis be adjudicated by recourse to authoritative rules or commands. At least two reasons account for this: first, rules are very often, and perhaps always, ambiguous, therefore requiring interpretation of their relevance to the situation at hand; and second, in deliberately making exceptions to seemingly *un*ambiguous rules, administrators deem such judgments to be warranted within the context of the situation, not "in terms of" their match with external (and authoritative) standards of correctness that rules and commands are supposed to provide. *Discretion* thus refers to actions that are deemed appropriate or fitting (internally) but not, at least necessarily, justified (externally). A "justifiable act of discretion," by implication, is a contradiction in terms. If a particular act were to be justified through reference to either an unambiguous rule or an authoritative (external) interpretation of a rule—as most contributors to public administration's standard narrative recommend—the act would by definition not be discretionary.

Exercising discretion thus means that administrators end up, in Sartre's (1989) famous phrase, with "dirty hands" insofar as they deny the moral and practical possibility of safe and final recourse to authoritative rules. "Dirty hands" is Sartre's metaphor for lost innocence, which, in the present context, could be interpreted as acknowledging the futility of trying to justify what, by definition, cannot be justified. The standard narrative's depiction of public administration's "mature" (rather than simply technical and/or obedient) participation in democratic governance is revealed to be paradoxical inasmuch as its justification of administrative discretion entails a disguised effort to reclaim the profession's moral innocence. *Justification, however, is itself a claim to innocence;* and this holds true both with respect to arguments for or against administrative discretion in general and with respect to arguments that justify or condemn particular discretionary acts.

To say that justification entails a disguised claim to moral innocence is, in effect, to restate Sartre's better-known assertion as to the personal nature of responsibility, which he defines as the individual's "consciousness of being the incontestable author of an event or an object" (1956, 553). Because they are irreducibly personal, responsible actions are necessarily those that are self-aware and freely chosen rather than dictated or determined externally. The reciprocal relation of responsibility to freedom, however, is at best a mixed blessing for Sartre, for he dolefully remarks that we are all "condemned to be free" (553), and therefore condemned to get our hands dirty in the responsible—which is to say, discretionary—exercise of that freedom. Thus, if discretion in the sense that I have described it excludes the possibility of final justification in terms of impersonal standards of correctness, then "responsible discretion," including actions that might range from submission to defiance, takes on a far different meaning from that envisioned by either faction of public administration's standard narrative. Administrators get their hands dirty in messy situations in which the contrived distinction between the personal and the institutional is always blurred; and any attempt, therefore, to justify their actions from the standpoint of dualistic logic produces instead paradoxical moral choices from which they can find no safe or authentic escape.

Four Strategies for Dealing with Dualisms

Earlier I noted that public administration's standard narrative characteristically employs either of two strategies for handling the relation between politics and administration. Both strategies—splitting and reconciling—accept as given a commonsense distinction not only between politics and administration but also, though often only implicitly, between the two elements of the various "supporting" dualisms upon which the politics/administration distinction is based. Advocates of what I have termed splitting strategies not only accept the analytical distinction between politics and administration but also urge as a practical matter the institutional separation of these activities to the fullest extent possible. Advocates of reconciling strategies also leave these vari-

Table 1.2: Strategies for Dealing with Dualisms

Standard Narrative	*Strategies*
Rationalism	Splitting
Normativism	Reconciling
Critical Discourses	*Strategies*
"Eccentric" Organization Theory	Inverting
Pragmatism	Dissolving

ous distinctions conceptually intact, but in the case of politics and administration they are concerned with practical questions of how effectively to manage problems associated with their inevitable overlap.

Two other strategies—inverting (or eccentric) and dissolving—offer substantial promise for diagnosing problems and paradoxes generated, or at least left unresolved, by the former two strategies. Both of these latter strategies take more seriously than the first two the problematic character of the supporting dualisms that ground the standard narrative's analytical distinction between politics and administration. Inverting strategies are more conventional than dissolving strategies because they accept, up to a point, these supporting dualisms as valid. However, inverting strategies can be thought of as eccentric inasmuch as they reverse the commonsense normative and temporal priority of the elements in each pair, namely, administration precedes politics (Thayer 1980, 1981); facts precede, and are thus more problematic than, values (Garfinkel 1967); doing precedes thinking (Weick 1979); means precede ends (March 1976; Cohen, March, and Olsen 1972); and practice precedes theory (Argyris and Schön 1974).

Dissolving strategies are more radical than inverting strategies because they contest the very coherence of these dualisms. According to those who pursue dissolving strategies, such dualisms misleadingly depict what are more sensibly seen as the "unitary" activities of belief, action, organizing, and praxis. Various enduring practical problems of governing—itself more properly construed as a unitary activity that for more than a century has been misleadingly bifurcated by the analytical separation of politics and administration—are symptoms of, and explicable chiefly in terms of, an acceptance of those supporting dualisms.

Unless and until they are effectively dissolved, public administration's—or, more accurately, government's—final exam question will not only remain unanswered but (and worse) will still be asked in its current, unanswerable form. The particular relevance of pragmatism to transforming the theory and practice of governing lies precisely in its potential for showing how they might be dissolved.

Pragmatism as an Antiformalist Movement

In this book I will not presume to consider all or even most of the core ideas that have influenced pragmatist thinking, nor will I comment, except very briefly, on pragmatism's rich intellectual tradition—started by William James (1898, 1907), Charles Sanders Peirce (1878, 1991), Oliver Wendell Holmes (1870, 1920), and John Dewey (1896, 1976–83)—that has since evolved in the United States for more than a century. A similar disclaimer is also in order regarding my coverage of pragmatist public administration and management scholars, beginning with Mary Parker Follett (1918, 1924, 1940) and succeeded, with a gap in between of almost fifty years, by a now-expanding cadre of her intellectual heirs. I draw from their ideas selectively, though liberally, rather than with a view toward synthesizing the "essential messages" that, from their own varied perspectives, pragmatism offers. The pragmatist character of *Public Administration's Final Exam* is instead restricted, if that is the right word, to an analysis of governance from the standpoint of one central theme of pragmatist thought: the fundamental epistemological error of dualistic thinking and the unfortunate practical consequences produced by its commission. In defense of that apparent restriction, however, I should note that the pragmatist critique of dualisms is protean enough to subsume insights related to other core themes of the pragmatist literature.

In order to orient readers unfamiliar with that literature and to provide some hint as to the style of argument developed here, I will include both a short comment on what seems most distinctive about pragmatism as a philosophical movement, from its origins up to the present, and a recommendation of where to begin reading more about it. Two books by Louis Menand, one authored and the other edited, suit these two purposes well. In telling the life stories of pragmatism's progenitors and examining the historical context in which their ideas were forged, Menand's prize-winning *The Metaphysical Club: A Story of Ideas in America* (2001) provides an indispensable and engrossing portrait of pragmatism's first half century.[6] Blending biography with political and social history, *The Metaphysical Club* explains the movement's emergence as a product of America's disenchantment, in the wake of the devastation wrought by its recently concluded Civil War, with its essentially European intellectual and philosophical roots. The book's title is ironic in that it is the name given by its members—prominent among them James, Peirce, and Holmes—to an informal association of young Massachusetts intellectuals (several, veterans of the war) united mainly by their *scorn* for metaphysics and other, characteristically European, modes of abstract philosophizing. In rejecting metaphysics, the Metaphysical Club initiated, not a coherent and clearly identifiable philosophy, but a loosely shared agreement about how to *do* philosophy—and how to think about practical problems—unencumbered by foundational beliefs about truth and other traditionally "philosophical" questions.

In his introduction to an earlier edited volume of essays, Menand (1997) summarizes four original strands of pragmatist thought, each later explicated more fully in *The Metaphysical Club,* that energized its resurgence beginning in the late twentieth century.[7] The first is an acceptance, indeed the celebration, of individual and group differences—"of cultural pluralism in response to the xenophobia induced by the turn-of-the-century waves of immigration and exacerbated by America's entry into the First World War" (xxvii). James, for example, preferred "multi-verse" rather than "universe" for describing a social world that is never synthesized, unified, or completed and in which differences are never fully transcended but instead are permitted to retain a mutually respectful separation from one another. The second strand, reflecting the influence mainly of Holmes and Dewey, was a commitment to experimentation and social reform in which government plays a vital role in conducting experiments and the law provides the instrument for protecting its right to do so. Holmes and Dewey were thus intellectual allies of the early-twentieth-century Progressive movement, although Holmes himself was often pessimistic about the likelihood of success for its proposed reforms. The third pragmatist strand is evident principally in Dewey's educational philosophy of "learning by doing," which held that knowledge should not be valued for its own sake but rather for its practical value. Dewey's conception of practical knowledge, however, was by no means synonymous with instrumental or technical knowledge, nor could it be neatly divided into the separate academic disciplines that increasingly (and, for Dewey, disconcertingly) typified the structures of schools and universities during the time he wrote. For Dewey, practical knowledge instead meant knowledge required for responsible citizenship in a culturally diverse world.

Finally, because pragmatism is antiformalist, it is ever suspicious of attempts to erect from contingent knowledge (philosophy included) an edifice on which truths might be confidently and permanently arrayed. Instead, Menand says, pragmatism acts "the role of termite—undermining foundations, collapsing distinctions, deflating abstractions, suggesting that the real work of the world is being done somewhere other than in philosophy departments" (1997, xxxi). Perhaps more than the other three strands, this one proved to be the main source of pragmatism's temporary, though extended, decline. Even in the United States, most philosophy departments of Dewey's time steadily aligned themselves with formalist Continental movements—in particular, analytic philosophy, along with its several variants that dominated academic philosophy on both sides of the Atlantic for most of the twentieth century.

If pragmatism's antiformalism had earlier provoked Continental philosophers' strongest objections, that same antiformalism has also figured prominently in pragmatism's resurgence and transformation since the 1970s. During the past three decades pragmatism's termite-like activity has taken the form of intellectual guerrilla warfare against the idea of philosophically secure foundations of knowledge. To the consternation of some and the delight of others, antifoundationalism signals the "end of philosophy" (Bernstein 1991), including the end of metaphysics, as an authoritative arbiter of claims to truth. To the extent that pragmatists have achieved some success (or at least notoriety) in conducting that war, however, they have done so with the aid of allies—notably, Jacques Derrida (1982), Michel Foucault (1997; Rabinow 1984), and Hans-Georg Gadamer (1975)—from the continent that had once spurned them.

Although my own argument, paradoxically, may itself appear somewhat "formal" in its architecture, its principal focus is an outgrowth of this antiformalist strand of pragmatist thought. A signature tactic used in pragmatism's war against philosophical formalism consists of what Menand earlier called "collapsing distinctions," or what I term here "dissolving dualisms." Dissolving dualisms, as I hope to make clear, offers a fruitful angle for challenging—for subjecting to constructive ridicule—theoretical assumptions that serve only to generate questions that cannot be answered and demands that cannot be met. The other three strands, however, also weave throughout the book: chapter 6, for example, proposes a "politics of difference" as a cardinal principle of pragmatic governance; collaborative experimentation, discussed most extensively in chapters 3 and 4, describes its essential social dynamic; and chapters 2 and 5 identify practical knowledge as the only kind worth having, and practical problems as the only real ones. To dissolve dualisms, then, is to dissolve (rather than solve) "theoretical" problems—and thus rid ourselves of unnecessary burdens such as final exams.

2
Values, Facts, and the Problem of Moralism

Within public administration's standard narrative, the apparent division between normativists (who characteristically employ reconciling strategies) and rationalists (those who use splitting strategies) is less contentious than might be supposed, resembling, rather, an amicable division of labor born of indifference toward one another's interests.[1] I identify as normativists those scholars who write chiefly about "value," or "philosophical," concerns such as administrative ethics and responsibility, the public interest, democracy, and social equity; in contrast, rationalists, following Simon's (1947) lead, focus on "factual," or "scientific," issues pertaining to problems of efficiency and effectiveness.[2] To a normativist the ideal administrator is one who is morally, ethically, and legally accountable either to political authority or to one or another conception of the public good, while the rationalist's exemplary administrator is the value-neutral efficiency expert. Insofar as the administrator as neutral expert typically uses his or her expertise in a politically accountable manner, however, no conflict between normativists and empiricists need be assumed.[3]

With varying degrees of explicitness, representatives of both factions of the standard narrative accept as unproblematic the analytical distinction between values and facts, which in turn grounds their common epistemological distinction between politics and administration. Although it may have been implicit in the mainstream public administration literature much earlier, the analytical distinction between values and facts as it bears upon the politics/administration distinction was first made explicit half a century ago. Within a period of six years, David Easton (1953) influentially defined politics as the "authoritative allocation of *values* for a society" (129, emphasis added),[4] while Simon, with the publication of *Administrative Behavior* in 1947, located his own project of a rational science of administration squarely in the domain of observable *facts,* radically separated from the metaphysical—and therefore, to Simon, irrational—realm of values. Both writers were early and major figures in the behavioral methodology movement then sweeping virtually all of American social science. Simon, more directly than Easton, acknowledged his—and by implication behavioralism's—debt to the analytical separation of values and facts posited nearly thirty years earlier by the logical positivists of the Vienna Circle. To Simon the very idea of rationality was conceivable only in terms of that distinction. Rational administration, to him, entailed the marshaling of facts relevant to the development of means for the efficient achievement of ends derived from previously "validated" political values. (Although Simon [1952] does in fact use the term *validated* in this context, he used it ironically owing to his disdain for philosophical discourse about values.)

Whether used disparagingly or approvingly, the word *rationalist,* employed as either a noun or an adjective, connotes precisely the separation between value and fact that Simon and the logical positivists insisted upon. Although the more ambiguous term *rational,* on the other hand, may (for authors such as Simon) also connote that separation, it is more generically used as merely a rough synonym for *sane, sensible, reasonable,* or *justifiable* and thus necessarily implies no particular stance on the relation between facts and values. Normativists are also ration*alists* insofar as they take for granted the fact/value distinction, but they characteristically differ from the Simon faction on whether values may be rationally derived and justified. Followers of the Simon tradition, insofar as they embrace the legacy of logical positivism, resoundingly answer "no," while most normativists, especially those having Kantian or communitarian leanings (Geuras and Garofalo 1996; Hart and Wright 1998), reply with an equally emphatic "yes."

As we will see shortly, pragmatists are ardently *anti*-rationalist by virtue of rejecting the analytical distinction between values and facts in the first place. For this reason they also reject the notion of "rationally derived values," which they regard as meaningless abstractions owing to their radical disconnect from particular substantive, "factual" contexts. For pragmatists, the words *value* and *fact* typically require scare quotes to signal that the ideas they ostensibly connote cannot as either a practical *or* an analytical matter be separated from one another.

A Preliminary Comment on the Fact/Value Controversy in Philosophy

Although the two opposing factions—the rationalists and the normativists—of public administration's standard narrative by and large accept the fact/value distinction at a commonsense level, they differ with respect to the relative priority of its two terms in guiding the field's scholarly agenda. Recent argument among philosophers, however, has centered on the coherence of the fact/value distinction itself rather than on the relative priority of its two elements. Whether that distinction ought to be honored, moreover, is implicated in a larger controversy about the nature and purpose of philosophy as an intellectual enterprise.

In *Philosophy and the Mirror of Nature* (1979), Richard Rorty divides the opposing camps on the fact/value question into the foundationalists, who practice "systematic" philosophy, and (appropriating a term earlier explicated by Gadamer [1975]) the hermeneuticists, who write what Rorty calls "edifying" philosophy. Foundationalists, in furthering the otherwise diverse traditions begun by Plato, Descartes, Kant, and various strains of twentieth-century positivism, regard philosophy's chief task as "mirror[ing] accurately, in our own Glassy Essence, the universe around us . . . [on the belief that it] is made up of very simple, clearly and distinctly knowable things, knowledge of whose essences provides the master-vocabulary which permits commensuration of all discourses" (Rorty 1979, 357). More simply, foundationalists are concerned with the identification of truth, and in particular with the role of language in accurately representing ahistorical essences or justifying particular claims regarding them. Like the opposing factions of public administration's standard narrative, the foundationalists in philosophy are also divided internally, however, on whether truth, as they variously conceive of it, can intelligibly refer only to "factual" knowledge claims (as with the positivists) or can also include claims concerning "moral" truths (as with some Kantians).

Of the two foundationalist factions, the positivists have held the upper hand for nearly a century and thus provide the chief target of the hermeneutic critique, led, in *Philosophy and the Mirror of Nature,* by Rorty himself. (Rorty's pragmatist self-identification occurred shortly after *The Mirror of Nature*'s publication with the appearance, in 1982, of *Consequences of Pragmatism.*) His project in the final chapter of *The Mirror of Nature* is to challenge the foundationalist assumption that language can mirror—that is, represent—the essence of anything, and indeed to question the coherence of the idea of "essence" itself.[5]

I will defer until chapter 5's discussion of the "ocular metaphor" and chapter 6's discussion of Catlaw's epistemological critique of political representation a fuller account of Rorty's reasoning on this matter, and proceed directly to his chief recommendation to his fellow philosophers: "We must get the visual, and in particular the mirroring, metaphors out of our speech altogether. To do that we have to understand speech not only as not the externalizing of inner representations, but as not a representation at all. We have to drop the notion of correspondence for sentences as well as for thoughts, and see sentences as connected with other sentences rather than with the world" (1979, 371–72). If Rorty is right in asserting that language cannot "represent" (mirror) nonlinguistic essences or "express" (externalize) prior nonlinguistic thoughts, then the foundationalist hope of systematic philosophy—that of developing a super-vocabulary of "universal commensuration" in terms of which competing claims to objective truth may ultimately be adjudicated—would appear futile. From the standpoint of hermeneutical philosophy, all that "objectivity" can reasonably mean is conformity to the historically contingent norms of justification that people happen to believe in at present. In the absence of any firmer, more foundational ground for objectivity than this, the possibilities for redescribing, and thus of remaking, the (our) world(s) are revealed as radically open-ended. The "edifying" project of hermeneutical philosophy is thus to explore just those possibilities, and to do so rid of any pretense to superior knowledge or intellectual authority.

What bearing does this have on the fact/value dichotomy? In answering this question I should note, first, that asserting, as the foundationalists do, the possibility of objective truth is simply another way of asserting the possibility of a value-free vocabulary of empirical description separate and distinct from a parallel (though sometimes subordinate) vocabulary of moral appraisal and judgment. That is, the fact/value dichotomy presupposes the possibility of objective empirical truth uncontaminated by value considerations, even if the dichotomy's foundationalist adherents disagree with one another about the possibility of a similarly "objective," or universal, vocabulary of values. But, if what now passes for objective description is historically and locally contingent —that is, merely subjective description in authoritative disguise—then the radically open-ended possibilities for inventing alternative descriptions necessarily incorporate, as an integral feature of those activities, what are commonly thought of as value judgments. These latter kinds of judgments, however, are not separate cognitive activities from "factual judgments" inasmuch as redescribing ourselves simultaneously entails remaking ourselves through self-constituting projects that embody our moral aspirations, even if we are sometimes only dimly conscious of them. "The trouble with the fact-value distinction," Rorty says, "is that it is contrived precisely to blur the fact that alternative descriptions are possible in addition to those offered by the result of normal inquiries" (1979, 363). For hermeneutical (edifying) philosophy, by contrast, value and fact are fused in practical/moral acts of redescribing/remaking, in which human beings exist and act "both *pour-soi* and *en-soi,* as both described objects and describing subjects" (378).

Beginning with chapter 3, most of the remainder of this book's attention to the fact/value issue focuses on why empiricist social science's long-standing goal of developing an objective, value-free brand of inquiry is fundamentally misguided; and, in the light of that critique, it explains how empiricist notions of rationality conceal a latent ideological bias that impedes the practice of truly democratic governance. From chapter 3 onward, that is, the chief target of criticism includes strands of thought identified mainly with the rationalist faction of public administration's standard narrative, whose writings chiefly emphasize the *fact* side of the fact/value dichotomy. The rest of this chapter, by contrast, approaches the dichotomy from the opposite direction by examining how the standard narrative's normativist (or moralist) faction, by virtue of its emphasis on the *value* side of the dichotomy, misconceives, at least from a pragmatist point of view, "normative" questions about governance. At the end of the chapter, however, I will argue that rationalism and moralism are guilty of parallel errors. Despite the seemingly different kinds of issues with which the two factions are chiefly concerned, the critique of rationalist empiricism of the sort made by Rorty applies with equal force to the way in which public administration's normativist/moralist faction deals with the issue of values.

Moralism and Relativism

Except when provoked, as Simon was by Dwight Waldo in the early 1950s (Waldo 1952; Simon 1952; Harmon 1989b), rationalists have by and large absented themselves from the broadly philosophical debates within the discourse of public administration for nearly half a century.[6] During the past twenty years especially, the most prominent collision of philosophical viewpoints in the discipline have involved the normativists, representing the standard narrative, and various (and often-overlapping) critical discourses from outside that narrative, such as the Frankfurt school, phenomenology and interpretivism, post-Marxism, structuralism and poststructuralism, Lacanian psychoanalytic theory, and pragmatism. All of these critical discourses in one way or another dispute, or simply dismiss as naive and irrelevant, the fact/value distinction as well as the normativist claims that values are rationally defensible and that agreement about them is a precondition for a stable and just society. Of these critical discourses I will focus here chiefly on pragmatism, for which the dissolving of the fact/value distinction, along with other parallel analytical distinctions, has long been a core intellectual objective.

A brief but revealing way to tell the difference between normativists of public administration's standard narrative and pragmatists is to highlight the pejorative labels with which each group describes the other. To the normativists, pragmatists are "relativists," who, by insisting that it is not possible to transcend their own cultural and political history in order to identify universal, transcultural values, *must* therefore be claiming that any value is just as good as any other. Normativists believe that this is a sure recipe for social disintegration, nihilism, the war of all against all, and other forms of disarray that erode the moral foundations upon which people, cultures, and nations can hold each other accountable. Values, decided upon and justified through reasoned discussion and then enforced through authoritative means, provide the bulwark against the evils that relativism inevitably spawns (Hart 1994; Denhardt 1988).

Pragmatists, for their part, often refer to normativists as "moralists," a seemingly innocuous, even laudatory, label were it not for the pejorative connotation that the *ist* (or *ism* or *istic*) suffix has steadily attained in recent decades. In everyday language, for example, being called a *racist* or a *sexist* is quite obviously anything but a compliment; while, in the more esoteric vocabularies of academe, *managerialism* and *scientism*, to mention only two of many recently coined "isms," are always subjects of criticism rather than approval. Similarly, to be a moral*ist* in the pejorative sense that pragmatists intend is equivalent to being called "moralistic" (or to be said to "moralize"), that is, to be preachy, dogmatic, and unwilling to reconsider one's own values and feelings on the basis of encounters with others. Moralism thus violates the attitude of tentativeness and an appreciation of context that pragmatists claim to hold dear.

In order to dampen my own inclination to vituperate against the normativists, I offer here a less inflammatory definition of moralism implied by the prior discussion of the fact/value distinction: *Moralism is a posture toward discourse and action in which moral, or value, questions precede, and are radically distinct from, practical questions.*[7] Moralism presumes, therefore, that particular actions must be justified in terms of previously agreed-upon or authoritatively enforced values and moral principles, in the absence of which those actions would necessarily be "arbitrary" (a partner epithet of "relativist"). A corollary assumption of moralism holds that, in order to qualify for "objective" status, the facts that constitute particular contexts of action should ideally be free of the contaminating influence of values. The blurring or blending of facts and values with one another thus poses a threat to that objectivity, producing so to speak an epistemological fall from grace (Harmon 1989a). Students of philosophy might therefore detect some irony in the debt that moralism, at least in the discipline's standard narrative, evidently owes to logical positivism on this score. Like the contemporary normativists in public administration, the logical positivists did insist upon the analytical separation of values and facts; but, and unlike the normativists, they did so in order to further their "scientific" aspiration of ridding philosophy of its traditional metaphysical baggage of values, morals, and ethics, which they regarded as hopelessly subjective and thus immune to rational justification.

The connection between public administration's normativists and the Vienna Circle is in any case loose and tangential. Because the normativists' moralism derives mainly from their intuitive conviction that values must have a rationally defensible basis, little purpose would be served here in rehearsing the many arguments later lodged against the logical positivists' radical epistemological distinction between values and facts. A more fruitful avenue for assessing the controversy about the relation of values to facts in public administration is to consider whether the normativists' worry about pragmatism's purported moral relativism is warranted. In order to do so, however, we need to examine various meanings that *relativism* has acquired to see which, if any, best depicts the pragmatists' position with respect to values. Rorty is especially helpful in this regard, listing "[t]hree different views . . . commonly referred to by this name. The first is the view that every belief is as good as every other. The second is the view that 'true' is an equivocal term, having as many meanings as there are procedures of justification. The third is the view that there is nothing to be said about either truth or rationality apart from descriptions of the familiar procedures of justification which a given society—*ours*—uses in one or another area of inquiry. The pragmatist holds the ethnocentric third view" (1991, 23, emphasis in source).

Although he prefers the third view, Rorty nevertheless doubts that *relativism* is really an appropriate word to describe it. Pragmatists, he says, do not have a conception of truth that would allow them to make the positive claim "that something is relative to something else" (23), which is what the first view asserts. In addition to being self-contradictory, it does not even qualify as relativist in a strict sense: to say that any belief (or value) is just as good as any other itself presumes a positive theory of truth—a *non*ethnocentric and therefore *non*relativist standpoint—from which to declare their moral equivalence. But this is not what pragmatists are saying. They are making, Rorty says, "the purely *negative* point that we should drop the traditional distinction between knowledge and opinion, construed as the distinction between truth as correspondence to reality and truth as a commendatory term for well-justified beliefs" (23–24, emphasis in source). The first and third meanings, therefore, are quite distinct from one another. Owing to their failure to grasp that distinction, normativists (whom Rorty calls "realists") can only conclude that pragmatists must either (1) have no moral convictions whatsoever, thus prompting the charge of nihilism; (2) possess moral convictions that, while possibly heartfelt, have no justifiable basis; or (3) be disingenuous, or at best naive, about the actual reasons for their moral commitments, in which case they must be closeted moralists. Sometimes normativists conflate all three of these possibilities.

The pragmatists respond that they, too, can and do have moral convictions just like the normativists and virtually everyone else, that their convictions are fully as heartfelt as those of the normativists, and that having these heartfelt convictions in no way makes them closeted moralists. Pragmatists would add, moreover, that they form those convictions in precisely the same way that normativists do, namely, on the basis of their necessarily ethnocentric experience in dealing with actual rather than purely hypothetical situations. Moral convictions are neither, as a factual matter, deduced from a priori abstract principles nor, honestly at any rate, justified (or justifiable) post hoc in terms of them.

At this point in the conversation, normativists may resort to what they regard as their trump card, namely, their assertion that, even if the pragmatists were right in claiming that people's moral convictions, values, and principles are ethnocentric in the way that Rorty asserts, we would then be left with no plausible basis from which to adjudicate opposing moral claims of radically differing cultures and political systems. We could have no possible "answer to Hitler" (nor he to us); collectively we could have no shared—in particular, no rational—basis on which to reason together in trying to settle our differences.

This shift in the normativists' debating tactics brings to mind the excellent story, set in the early 1900s, of a dinner party hosted by an aristocratic English dowager. She sat herself next to a young scientist, who spent most of the meal enthusiastically telling her of Darwin's theory of natural selection, including in particular the part about the evolution of our own species. The dowager was skeptical about, even appalled by, what the scientist told her; but mindful of the courtesy that her role as hostess required, she replied, "Yes, young man, but if you and Mr. Darwin are indeed correct in saying that we are all descended from apes, I certainly hope that that fact does not become widely known." Like the dowager, the normativists are deeply troubled about what they see as the practical consequences of taking the pragmatists' position seriously, even conceding to them the best of intentions and most cogent of arguments.

To show how the argument between the normativists (the moralists) and the pragmatists (the ethnocentrists) plays out with respect to a vital contemporary issue, consider the question "Can Relativists Condemn Terrorism?"[8]—the title of a symposium published in *The Responsive Community* (Etzioni 2002). By "relativists" the journal's editor, Amitai Etzioni, would probably include most pragmatists, but more broadly he seems to mean anyone with postmodernist sympathies.

A pragmatist's short answer to the question might be: "Most certainly! Not only *can* I condemn terrorism, I in fact *do*." When pressed by the moralist to explain why, the pragmatist replies: "I condemn it for the same reasons, presumably, that *you* do, namely, because I'm horrified, angered, and saddened by the killing and suffering that terrorism causes." Still not satisfied, the moralist clarifies his last question, saying that by "explain" he really meant "justify," to which the pragmatist asks in return:

> Justify to whom? Do you really believe that terrorists either want or are able to engage in "reasoned" discussion about why they do what they do? I'm trying to imagine what you, as a moralist, might say to a terrorist: "My good man, perhaps you've merely forgotten this trenchant passage from Kant. . . . " Your question, even if you got the answers that you wanted, serves no useful purpose. The trouble with you moralists, with all of your talk about values, principles, and reason, is that the only people you could possibly convince by your philosophical justifications are those who already agree with you. Meanwhile, we are left with the tough and scary problems of, in the near term, protecting ourselves and others from terrorists and, in the longer term, fostering conditions under which people who at present see their interests as served by committing terrorist acts would in the future be less likely to do so. These are really hard *practical* problems both to frame and solve under any circumstances; but for the life of me I can't see how asking whether people whom you like to call relativists can condemn terrorism gets us any closer to those solutions.

"Relativism" and Status Anxiety

At bottom what the moralists cannot abide is the pragmatists' claim that there can be no freestanding "moral questions"—that is to say, questions that can sensibly be asked independently of practical questions. Pragmatists are not saying that the moral is *reducible* to the practical but rather that practical contexts of action provide the only contexts in which the moral can have any coherent meaning (Fish 1999). The only sense in which pragmatists could be accurately described as relativists, then, owes to their conviction that the moral is always "relative to," by virtue of being contingent upon or constituted by, the particular ways in which practical problems are defined. To act sensibly or practically in the face of terrorism, therefore, requires no prior, and in any case superfluous, "justified" moral judgment about its intrinsic evil.

The fear that, in the absence of such justification, the grounds for practical judgment would surely be undermined mistakenly supposes, as Gunnell suggests, "that practical problems potentially have philosophical solutions, that solving the problem of relativism would be to solve the problem of practical judgment and provide purchase for critical reason" (1993, 565). Because of this mistake, however, moralist philosophers cannot see that relativism is merely a "pseudoproblem conjured up by philosophy" (568) and later appropriated by other moralists, whatever might be their academic credentials, seeking an authoritative standpoint from which to control the terms of public discourse. The pseudoproblem of relativism was generated by the foundationalist aspirations of philosophy (a "second-order discourse"), which, if achieved, would validate its authority to adjudicate not only competing truth claims of other (subordinate) academic disciplines but also competing moral claims made in the wider domain of politics (a "first-order discourse"). What moralists and foundationalist philosophers are really worried about, however, is not "the ability of philosophy to provide substantive transcontextual meaning for . . . [particular truth claims]. The concern is really not about the lack, or dissolution, of the grounds of validity within the universe of first-order [e.g., political] practices but about the ability of philosophy to posit a metatheoretical basis of judgment with respect to such practices. The nervousness is distinctly philosophical, no matter how much that anxiety is projected onto the practical world, and a large part of the nervousness extends even to more mundane issues of professional identity" (567). Because philosophers' arguments concerning relativism's dangers merely mask their field's repressed authority problem, the use of those same arguments by politicians or the public suffers, in addition, from the lack of even an artful disguise. For them, and also for both factions of public administration's standard narrative, the only possible alternative to relativism (in its pejorative meaning) is built upon the doubtful moralist assumption, much like Easton's, that values can be formulated and "allocated" before the business of governing gets started. This is the only way in which the fact/value distinction in the standard narrative can make any, albeit superficial, analytical sense.

Moralism and Rationalism as Parallel Errors

In view of this chapter's brevity, I conclude by noting that I am by no means finished with the fact/value question. Here I have focused on the pseudoproblem of relativism, about which the normativists of public administration's standard narrative have been needlessly concerned. Dissolving the dualism between value and fact reveals a quite different and more pressing problem, namely, moralism, the belief that values, principles, and other philosophical abstractions are needed for defining and engaging with practical problems of action. Pragmatists hold that this belief is logically untenable, and more importantly that it disguises a power play by normativists—even if they do not consciously understand it as such—to define practical problems in ways that further their own interests. On the belief that values and principles are infinitely manipulable, pragmatists prefer to define practical problems—the only kind of problems there are—concretely in terms of what we should do rather than abstractly as questions of what we ought to believe or value.

In the following chapter I address the fact/value dualism from the standpoint of the pragmatists' quarrel with empiricist social science. Whereas normativists commit the moralist error of believing that questions of value logically precede questions of action, empiricists commit the parallel rationalist error of assuming that a predictive, and therefore value-free, social science may and should similarly precede engagement with those practical questions. Both sides accept the fact/value dualism in principle and differ only about which of its two "moments" merits higher priority as a basis for making practical judgments. Both sides therefore construe *practical* as a synonym for *instrumental,* which from a pragmatist point of view constitutes their chief shared failing. Despite the disputes within the standard narrative about the role and importance of values, the problematic virtues the two sides endorse—moral justification for the normativists, instrumental rationality for the empiricists—are simply flip sides of the same misconceived issue rather than genuine alternatives to one another.[9] As we will see in the next chapter, the fact/value dualism, which underwrites the thinking of both factions of the standard narrative, is chiefly an artifact of the equally problematic dualism between thinking and doing. Dissolving that dualism sets the stage for dissolving the related dualisms between ends and means, theory and practice, and ultimately politics and administration.

3
Thinking, Doing, and the Problem of Rationalism

Broadly speaking, dissolving each of the dualisms reviewed in the next three chapters—thinking and doing, ends and means, and theory and practice—entails a restatement of the other two. The separate exercises of dissolving them, however, provide three more or less distinctive angles from which to clarify the idea of governance as the unitary expression of politics and administration. The sequence in which I consider these dualisms refines and expands upon a single core idea—namely, *action*—of which the distinction between thinking and doing provides the most elemental (mis)expression. Next follows *organizing*, including its bifurcation by the ends/means dualism, which connotes the structural, patterned, and (though only sometimes) purposeful character of social action. Finally, *praxis*, the Greek word connoting the fusion, or unification, of theory and practice, highlights organizing's (and action's) reflectively critical dimension.

Each of these dualisms, as we will see, is in turn deeply implicated in the issues raised in the previous chapter about the categorical separation of values and facts, a separation that obscures the unitary character of the moral and the practical. Moreover, in view of the overriding practical intent of this book, I will focus in each chapter upon the ways in which these dualisms promote the misidentification of both the practical purposes ("problematic virtues") and practical problems ("pseudoproblems") of governance that public administration's standard narrative characteristically asserts. I will then identify three generic practical problems of governance, and of action more generally, implied by the dissolving of the dualisms, and in reference to which public administration's final exam ought to be rewritten.

The False Opposition between Reductionism and Holism

The history of the social sciences in the twentieth century was marked by an increasing awareness of the assumptions and methods that ought to ground and guide their inquiries. Any resolution of the disagreements concerning those assumptions and methods that spirited and careful argument might have been expected to provide, however, has yet to materialize. Both within and among the various social science disciplines, disagreement about "method" persists, owing in part to the chronic reluctance of the disputants to address squarely the underlying epistemological assumptions that make their preferred methodologies seem plausible to them and indeed superior to those favored by rival factions or disciplines.

One such persistent disagreement, found in both the natural (Kaku 1994; Gould 2003) and the social sciences, has to do with the appropriate level, or primary unit, to be used as the starting point of analysis. Two commonly opposed positions on this matter are depicted in scientific argot by the labels *reductionism* (representing the micro) and *holism* (the macro). The dispute is complicated by the fact that each term connotes both a positive or at least neutral meaning to its proponents as well as a pejorative meaning to its detractors. In its neutral-to-positive sense, reductionism, as Edward O. Wilson defines it, refers to "the breaking apart of nature into its natural constituents . . . in order to find good points of entry into otherwise impenetrably complex systems" (1998, 58). Reductionism thus indicates a preference, even a quasi-ontological claim, for a microscopic unit of analysis as depicting the most directly observable entity of interest to a discipline and therefore the most "real" or elemental property of its subject matter. Reductionists may and do concern themselves with the analysis of larger (more macroscopic) phenomena, but they insist that their explication build upon the foundation laid by their preferred, microscopic unit of analysis.

Holism claims that "social phenomena may [and, in fact, should] be studied at their own autonomous, macroscopic level of analysis" (Dray 1967, 53). Micro-level entities, therefore, can be understood in terms of their systemic relation to the "whole" of which they are constituent parts. In its mildest form holism reflects the researcher's preference, when stumped in trying to develop cogent explanations at a middle range of analysis, to seek answers by moving to a "higher" rather than a "lower" level. Holists often criticize, therefore, what they construe as the reductionists' implicit claim that macroscopic social entities (e.g., organizations, nation-states, cultures, and other complex social units) consist of *nothing but* aggregations of micro entities. Reductionists, they say, ignore not only the systemic character of the relations *among* those entities but also the more radical claim that these relations *constitute* such "entities" *as* entities to begin with. Holists sometimes depict reductionism more crudely as a misguided tendency to explain complex, multivariate phenomena in terms of a single cause (Donaldson 1985). Cruder still, such a characterization of reductionism thinly masks an accusation of simplemindedness.

Theoretical approaches that employ macro-level primary units of analysis, however, are not immune from falling victim to such oversimplified (i.e., reductionist in the crudely pejorative sense) explanations. Indeed, claims as to the susceptibility of macro-level analysis to just this tendency are implicit in several interpretivist critiques (Berger and Luckmann 1967; Silverman 1971) of functionalist sociology (Parsons 1951) and organization theory (Katz and Kahn 1966), whose reification of societies and organizations by means of an organismic metaphor produce, in addition to other failings, oversimplified and therefore reductionist accounts of their subjects of study.

Similarly, there is also no logical reason why scholars who employ micro units as their starting point for analysis cannot duly consider the systemic, relational character of social phenomena, including those macro-level social collectivities they might ultimately seek to describe. In the discipline of sociology, for example, Berger and Luckmann's (1967) interpretivist account of the "social construction of reality" starts with the face-to-face encounter—in their view, the most elemental social (i.e., relational) unit—as the starting point for constructing, for building up to, a comprehensive picture of social life. Similarly, drawing from the depth psychology of Carl Jung, White and McSwain (1983) posit the relation in a twofold sense—both the face-to-face relation and the relation of the individual unconscious to the conscious ego—as their starting point for grounding eventually macro-level explanations of organizational life.

Whatever objections one might otherwise wish to lodge against these reductionist (in the nonpejorative sense) approaches, any accusation of reductionism in the pejorative sense could be warranted only if these authors were guilty of "reducing" their explanations of more complex phenomena to mere aggregations of micro-level entities, that is, if they had not also introduced (as these authors *have*) additional explanatory concepts uniquely capable of revealing "emergent," as opposed to merely "additive," properties of larger social collectivities. So long as they avoid these important sins of omission, such reductionist approaches, in part owing to their sheer methodological convenience, may provide "good points of entry" to mitigate the tendency—to which macro primary units of analysis are especially prone—to compound micro-level errors in analyzing larger-scale social entities.[1] The upshot of this discussion would appear to be, then, that reductionism, properly conceived as inviting rather than precluding the analysis of uniquely macroscopic (emergent) properties of social phenomena, and holism, when focusing on the constitutive power of relationship rather than on reified social constructs, may be seen as complementary and reinforcing rather than as mutually exclusive. (Voila! Another dualism bites the dust.)

John Dewey and the Concept of the Reflex Arc

In one of his lesser-known articles, "The Reflex Arc Concept in Psychology," John Dewey (1896) illustrates how pragmatism combines the microscopic and the relational in order to convey the unitary nature of human action. Because his critique of the reflex arc may at first seem hardly pertinent to examining contemporary issues of governance, I will start by making explicit the parallel that I wish to expand upon, namely, that the analytical distinction between thinking and doing implicit in the reflex arc concept serves as a micro-level analogue to all of the other dualisms considered in this book, up to and including the distinction between politics and administration in public administration's standard narrative. That is, the conceptual errors of the reflex arc concept illustrate in microscopic form both the analytical and the normative shortcomings of the standard narrative's classic dualism. The reductionist flavor of the argument is thus evident in my working "from the ground up" by starting with the most elemental human act as the primary unit of analysis, while the argument's holistic character derives from Dewey's relational notion of the organic circuit as a preferred depiction of that act.

Dewey's target of criticism, expressed metaphorically by the term *reflex arc,* was the belief, widely shared by American and European psychologists a century ago, that the elemental structure of human mental activity involved a linear, causal sequence consisting of three discrete elements (or "moments"): sensation, which provides a stimulus; idea, the mental product of the stimulus; and action, the response issuing from the idea provoked by the stimulus. In keeping with his habit of questioning and dissolving tacit dualisms and hierarchies, Dewey deconstructed (Menand 2001) the reflex arc by exposing its various elements as constituted by one another rather than existing prior to their "interaction." In Dewey's words:

> [T]he reflex arc idea . . . is defective in that it assumes sensory stimulus and motor response as distinct psychical existences, while in reality they are always inside a co-ordination and have their significance purely from the part played in maintaining or reconstituting the co-ordination; and (secondly) in assuming that the quale of experience which precedes the "motor" phase and that which succeeds it are two different states. . . . The result is that the reflex arc idea leaves us with a disjointed psychology, . . . [which prevents us from seeing] that the arc of which it talks is virtually a circuit, a continual reconstitution. . . .
>
> This circuit is more truly termed organic than reflex, because the motor response determines the stimulus, just as truly as sensory stimulus determines movement. Indeed, the movement is only for the sake of determining the stimulus, of fixing what kind of a stimulus it is, of interpreting it. (1896, 99, 102)

The logical error of the reflex arc concept, variously labeled the "psychological," "historical," or "empiricist's fallacy," entails a confusion of post hoc interpretation with actual description. The fallacy involves the mistaken assumption that "the parts are prior to the whole, when in fact it is the whole that makes the parts what they are" (Menand 2001, 328). That is to say, the reflex arc's parts (elements or moments) are merely, and only sometimes, practical methodological expedients that researchers posit after the fact but which they then "hypostatize" (reify) by falsely attributing to them material existence and thus causal power. Thus, Dewey is not pursuing, as might first be supposed, an inverting strategy by suggesting that the response *precedes* the stimulus, but a dissolving one that depicts, holistically, the most elemental human act as a unitary adaptive adjustment by an organism to its environment.

Dissolving Empiricism's Legitimacy Project

The implications of Dewey's insight for both the empirical examination and the normative evaluation of social life would appear to be far-reaching. The terminology of empiricist social science that was subsequently developed in the twentieth century, in particular the division of the moments of human action into "variables" (which are in turn subdivided into "dependent" and "independent" variables), dismayed Dewey as well as later pragmatists. When an often useful heuristic simplification is translated into a preferred and purportedly scientific program for explaining "the way things really are," more holistic interpretive and structural descriptions of action are either flatly rejected as unscientific or at best condescendingly regarded as possibly enriching supplements to the *real* work of the social scientist. (An obvious illustration of this skewing of epistemological priorities—or, more precisely, of how methodology drives epistemology rather than the other way around—is the almost universal requirement in U.S. public administration and public policy Ph.D. programs of several courses in quantitative methods, with the option of a single qualitative methods course occasionally, though grudgingly, permitted for students weak in math.)

Even more disturbing to pragmatists distrustful of the distortions that dualisms produce, however, is the categorical distinction that mainstream American social science characteristically draws between theory and method. The chief problem is not the priority that quantitative methods have been granted over qualitative methods, but instead the entrenched belief that theory and method (not to mention practice) constitute logically separate enterprises whose connections to one another are made only after the fact. For pragmatism, as well as for other discourses critical of public administration's standard narrative, the problem is not mainly that the theory/method dualism too often privileges its latter element over its former one (a problem of inverted priorities) but rather that the very distinction between theory and method is misleading to begin with. Theorizing *is* a method, in a broad sense of the word, not simply of inquiry but of engagement with a particular subject matter in service of practical and/or critical aims (Morgan 1983). Locked into a dualistic view of the intellectual universe, however, representatives of the social science mainstream hear such arguments from the critical discourses as simply a plea for more qualitative methods courses in their Ph.D. curricula. Just as lamentably, some novices among the critical discourses, blind to their more radical implications, appear satisfied, even grateful, whenever that plea is acceded to.

A standard empiricist response to this sort of critique holds that, notwithstanding its possible merit on epistemological grounds, methodological approaches that divide unitary human acts into parts called variables may nevertheless serve the eminently practical purposes of predicting and even controlling human behavior. Even if the kind of "causal explanation" that enables prediction is based on a methodological fiction, it can nevertheless be a highly useful one, and one that pragmatists, by virtue of their own practical commitments, would be obliged to respect. Despite the formidable difficulties (of which empiricists are usually well aware) in confidently inferring causal influences by means of statistical analysis, their admittedly imperfect attempts to "predict and control" human behavior nevertheless promise a significant practical advantage over the more modest aspirations of either structural or interpretive analysis, whose aim of explaining human action retrospectively makes no claim to predictive power. That empiricists themselves have achieved very limited predictive success simply shows, from their standpoint, that tighter theories, more rigorous methods, additional data, and harder work are needed in the future.

If Dewey's deconstruction of the reflex arc concept is instructive, however, the empiricist's devotion to cause/effect, and therefore predictive, explanation cannot even in principle be vindicated by these measures. Unlike the methods of classical physics, which it purports to emulate, empiricist social science is burdened by the presence of a radical, unbridgeable discontinuity between its purported causes and effects. Anticipating language philosopher John Searle's (1984) later argument as to the impossibility of a predictive social science, Dewey explains that "the reflex arc theory, instead of being a case of plain science, is a survival of the metaphysical dualism, first formulated by Plato, according to which sensation is an ambiguous dweller on the border land of soul and body, the idea (or central process) is purely psychical, and the act (or movement) purely physical. Thus the reflex arc formulation is neither physical (or physiological) nor psychological; it is a mixed materialistic-spiritualistic assumption" (1896, 104). Some implications of this incongruous mixing of the reflex arc's elements have been examined in a related context by Searle, who argues that, logically, social science cannot predict human behavior by emulating the methods of physics or any other natural science. Successful prediction in the social sciences would require that "some systematic correlation between phenomena identified in social and psychological terms and phenomena identified in physical terms" (1984, 81). That is, some principles would need to be established for bridging not only different levels of analysis but also different ontological categories. Even if all the physical laws bearing on the human capacity to act were known in advance, however, social phenomena—for example, money, marriage, revolution, property—could not be systematically connected to physical phenomena, because "social phenomena set no physical limits whatever on what can count as the physical realisation of them. And this means that there can't be any systematic connections between the physical and the social or mental properties of the phenomenon. . . . The attitudes we take toward [social phenomena] . . . are not constrained by the physical features of the phenomena in question. Therefore, there can't be any matching of the mental level and the level of . . . physics of the sort that would be necessary to make strict laws of the social sciences possible" (78–79). Moreover, even if the sought-for connection were narrowed to that between the neurophysiological features of the brain and such basic psychological experiences as "seeing" (e.g., money) or "feeling" (e.g., anger)—as in the reflex arc's sequence of stimulus/idea/response—the same limitation would still apply. Because, as Searle notes, "money can have an indefinite range of physical forms it follows that it can have an indefinite range of stimulus effects on our nervous systems" (80).

Searle's arguments against the possibility of a predictive social science grounded in the principles of classical physics should not be construed, however, as foreclosing the identification of fruitful parallels between the natural and the social sciences. Although important distinctions between them are undeniable—most notably the need, in the latter but not in the former, to account for the fact of human agency—it would be inaccurate simply to characterize natural science as predictive and social science as *not* predictive. In the fields of geology and evolutionary biology, by most reckonings respectable fields of natural science, scientists place slight if any premium on predicting future configurations of rocks or the emergence (or extinction) of particular species, since the contingencies of history that define the subject matter of these fields render such predictions impossible. Rather, it is the identification of meaningful patterns of geological and biological change, determined by chance rather than by either cosmic purpose or eternal laws of nature, that provides the impetus for their investigations. To be sure, the novel and imaginative depiction of these structural patterns can often enable, as well as suggest plausible constraints upon, the identification of possible pathways of future changes, though never to the point of specifying their particulars. In trying to "replay life's tape," to borrow Gould's apt phrase:

> You press the rewind button and, making sure you thoroughly erase everything that actually happened, go back to any time and place in the past. . . . Then let the tape run again and see if the repetition looks at all like the original. If each replay strongly resembles life's actual pathway, then we must conclude that what really happened pretty much had to occur. But suppose the experimental versions all yield sensible results strikingly different from the actual history of life? What could we then say about the predictability of self-conscious intelligence? or of mammals? or of vertebrates? or of life on land? or simply of multicellular persistence for 600 million difficult years? (1989, 48–50)

For Gould the second of these interpretations draws powerful support from, among other sources, his analysis of the decimation of the Permian era's invertebrate marine life, whose fossil remains were discovered, during the late nineteenth century, in the Burgess Shale of the Canadian Rockies. The few surviving orders of marine life, he argues, outlasted their contemporaries, not on the basis of their "superiority of anatomy" but because they happened to be "protégés of Lady Luck or fortunate beneficiaries of odd historical contingencies" (50). Any greater "adaptive capacity" that the surviving orders may have had could only be attributed to them post hoc rather than predicted in advance, even if perfect knowledge of the relevant laws of physics, chemistry, and biology were available for explaining such a capacity. Much like Searle's claim that particular social phenomena, by virtue of having an "indefinite range of physical forms," cannot therefore be predicted from prior knowledge of physical laws, the particular direction and forms of biological life that Gould describes are similarly indefinite, subject only to the proviso that they not violate such laws. (I should add, however, the obvious qualification that physical "laws" themselves must be regarded as contingent in the sense of being subject to revision and outright rejection in the light of new evidence or alternative cosmologies.)

Empiricism's Probabilistic Caveat

Empiricist social science's ostensible debt to classical physics requires a serious (and, as we will see, even crippling) caveat about the meaning of prediction. The empiricist's caveat holds that social science generalizations, unlike those of physics, are necessarily probabilistic rather than strictly lawlike, thus requiring statistical methods rather than axiomatic formulas for explicating causal relationships. (Physicists, it should be noted, hardly ever use statistics. They are seldom interested in making probabilistic statements, but rather in constructing causal explanations derived from mathematical formulas in order, among other things, to predict future events. A formula either works or it doesn't. If it doesn't, it is either rejected or revised, or the observational data are reassessed.)

In empiricist social science, however, *prediction* may be taken to mean either that (1) as-yet-unobserved features or future actions of a given population will, within probabilistic limits, resemble those features or actions of an already-observed sample of that population; or that (2) by using the methods of statistical inference, future events may actually be foreseen. The first of these meanings involves a definitional convention in which prediction—that is, invoking a lawlike generalization *pro*spectively—is simply the logical counterpart of explanation—that is, invoking that same generalization *retro*spectively. The second meaning, of course, matches any non–social scientist's understanding of prediction and would appear to be the basis on which empiricism would have to stake any claim to practical value, and therefore to legitimacy, as a valid and preferred tool for social inquiry. That is, empiricists must show that the second meaning of prediction—foreseeing future events—necessarily follows from the first meaning. Here are some reasons to be skeptical about such a claim.

At the risk of stating the obvious, both social scientists and the public more generally would no doubt agree that human action is predictable in some respects but unpredictable in others. Geoffrey Vickers once observed, however, that when people do act in predictable ways, it is often because they *choose* to do so; for without a substantial degree of predictability in their own and others' actions, social life could not exist.[2] The kind of predictability to which Vickers refers, however, emerges from the contexts within which people formulate both their daily activities and life projects, rather than being "caused" in lawlike fashion by factors extrinsic to those contexts. That is to say, predictability is a constitutive feature of intentional human action. As with Dewey's deconstruction of the reflex arc concept, however, any separation of such action into variables that are accorded causal properties commits the empiricist's fallacy of confusing post hoc interpretation with actual description.

Other features of human action, however, are decidedly unpredictable, making even more dubious the empiricists' aspirations for a social science composed of lawlike generalizations. MacIntyre identifies "four sources of systematic unpredictability in human affairs" (1984, 93) to explain why no genuinely predictive hypothesis in social science has ever been (or ever could be) developed. First, radical conceptual innovation is unpredictable because the very idea of its predictability is incoherent to begin with—a Stone Age man, for example, who "predicted" the invention of the wheel would thereby have already invented it. Second, people who have not yet made up their minds cannot by definition predict which course of action they will take, much less have it predicted by someone else. Third, the "indefinite reflexivity of game-theoretic situations" (97), characteristic of much social behavior, describes action that is intentionally rendered *un*predictable to others. Indeed, organizational "success" often depends upon an ability to mask intentions and thereby to make behavior unpredictable to competitors and adversaries. Finally, there is the sheer contingency of history. Just as replaying the tape of biological evolution described by Gould could never predictably produce the same result in the natural world, so too is predicting the direction of social life similarly rendered impossible by accidents of fate (e.g., "For want of a nail, the shoe was lost").

The predictive generalizations of empiricist social science must, therefore, ignore (or, in the euphemism of statistics, "hold constant") consideration of all four of these indispensable features of social life. Even if this were possible in anything other than a trivial way, the caveat that empiricism's generalizations are probabilistic rather than lawlike sacrifices any meaningful similarity to the predictive power of classical physics that empiricists might claim. The manner in which some branches of physics treat probabilistic (or statistical) generalizations, for example, is far more demanding than that commonly, if ever, found in social science. One example of this difference may be seen in how each variously deals with the criteria for rejecting (or falsifying) generalizations. As MacIntyre notes, generalizations in social science

> do not entail any well-defined set of counterfactual conditionals in the way that the law-like generalizations of physics and chem-

> istry do. We do not know how to apply them systematically beyond the limits of observation to unobserved or hypothetical instances. Thus they are not laws, whatever else they may be. . . . Some social scientists reply: "What the social sciences discover are probabilistic generalizations; and where a generalization is only probabilistic of course there can be cases which would be counter-examples if the generalization was non-probabilistic and universal." But this reply misses the point completely. For if the type of generalization which I have cited is to be a generalization at all, it must be something more than a mere list of instances. The probabilistic generalizations of natural science—those, say, of statistical mechanics—are indeed more than this precisely because they are as law-like as any non-probabilistic generalization. They possess universal quantifiers[,] . . . they entail well-defined sets of counter-factual conditionals and they are refuted by counter-examples in precisely the same way and to the same degree that other law-like generalizations are. Hence we throw no light on the status of the characteristic generalizations of the social sciences by calling them probabilistic; for they are as different from the generalizations of statistical mechanics as they are from the generalizations of Newtonian mechanics or of the gas law equations. (1984, 91)

If the probabilistic caveat cripples rather than salvages empiricism's claim to predictive power—and, further, if the contingencies of social life, like those of evolutionary biology, make the prediction of actual future events impossible in any case—it would seem that the retrospective reconstruction of the "structural" patterns and underlying mechanisms that enable and constrain social life more realistically depicts what is "scientific" about social science. Rather than regarding prediction as the sine qua non of science, as empiricism does, the alternative of retrospective reconstruction and interpretation more closely matches Kaku's (1994) contention that "[t]he purpose of science is to peel back the layer of the appearance of objects to reveal their underlying nature" (vii). By incorporating historical contingency into its research program, evolutionary biology thus appears to provide a more plausible natural science parallel (assuming that one is needed) to social science than does classical physics. In this kind of research, empirical observations are treated as surface manifestations of structural possibilities and constraints interacting with unpredictable accidents of fate. (Under such a view, statistical correlations may thus be regarded as useful supplements to analysis of this kind, often suggesting heretofore unseen or unexpected interpretations. More generally, learning statistics would appear to provide a valuable kind of mental discipline, and, underwritten by the logic of the null hypothesis, can serve as a useful caution against presuming to be certain about anything.)[3]

In social science, the closest approximations to this kind of research would appear to be what are typically called, not surprisingly, *structural* approaches, whose aim is to reveal and explicate the underlying codes, norms, tacit assumptions, and archetypal images of social life that enable, constrain, and regulate empirically observable behavior. Such approaches may be found across a wide range of the social sciences, including, among other fields, structural linguistics, structural anthropology, and depth psychology. Outhwaite (1983), whose "new realism" provides an illustrative example of such an approach in organizational theory, begins by citing Bhaskar's (1978) distinction among three "domains" of scientific inquiry that empiricist social scientists often conflate: the empirical, consisting of observed (both directly and indirectly) experience; the actual, events regardless of whether they are observed; and the real, those underlying mechanisms that generate the events. The real, which in Outhwaite's terminology is virtually synonymous with the structural, describes the "'intransitive' objects of science," that is, those structures that "exist independently of our description of them" (323) and produce the "transitive" phenomena of empirical observation. Much like Darwin's famous assertion that observation is always for or against a point of view, empirical observation, from a structuralist standpoint, is always guided by at least embryonic theoretical assumptions and expectations. The ground for accepting a structuralist theory is its ability to answer the question, "What (relevantly) needs to be the case for a particular set of social relations to appear as they do?" (328).

There are three chief differences between structural and empiricist approaches. First, structuralism (to Outhwaite, "realism") distinguishes the real from the observed, while empiricism assumes that the real *is* what is observed. To the empiricist, that is, "the real world is unproblematically represented in or . . . is identical with the empirical world of our experience [such that empiricist theories] . . . characteristically take the form of stating constant conjunctions between observed events"

(322–23). By contrast, structuralist theory, in the terms of our earlier discussion of the reflex arc concept, avoids the empiricist's fallacy of hypostatizing the methodological fictions called "variables" or of mistakenly assuming that they can be inferred by means of "brute induction." Second, whereas empiricism views prediction as the sine qua non of social science, realists (structuralists) regard "a successful prediction [as] . . . a welcome addition to a successful explanation rather than something intrinsically related to it. This is because . . . explanation for the realist involves the demonstration, *not* of a constant conjunction of events, but of a powerful tendency, materially embodied in a generative mechanism" (324, emphasis in source). Third, unlike empiricism, realism (again, Outhwaite's term for structuralism) enables a plausible accounting of the inherently unpredictable character of human agency, about which the empiricists' constant-conjunction-of-events accounts are necessarily silent. Realists also stress, however, the limitations that social structures impose on the exercise of that agency. Unlike the interpretivists (or "radical conventionalists," of whom Outhwaite is also critical), realists regard human agency not so much as producing the social world but as reproducing and transforming it.

Empiricism as Ideology

Empiricism's failure for more than half a century to produce a single predictive, lawlike generalization has done little to dampen the enthusiasm of its practitioners—or even, it seems, to cause them any noticeable embarrassment. Having so conspicuously failed to satisfy—or even to show any promise of satisfying—the cardinal test of empiricism's legitimacy, why do they persist in claiming its scientific superiority? One plausible answer, I will argue, is that empiricism's commitment to a predictive social science is deeply rooted in a repressed ideological commitment to a particular form and purpose of human action implied by the dualism between thinking and doing (Snider 2000; Evans 2000). That is, empiricism's separation of thinking and doing produces both a "problematic virtue" (instrumental rationality) and a concomitant "pseudoproblem" (irrationality) that, when unmasked by means of dissolving the dualism, reveals a far different generic problem—variously labeled "rationalism" or "scientism."

It should be recalled that claims to legitimacy necessarily entail justifying arguments of an if-then, in-order-to kind in which a particular action is rendered sensible, or at least comprehensible, through reference to a prior rule, standard, or criterion; that is, a justifying argument requires a dualism whose first element logically and temporally precedes its second element. In the dualism between thinking and doing, thinking (which culminates in deciding) provides the criteria for making sense of subsequent doings. In terms of my earlier discussion of social science variables, thinking (or knowing) is the "meta" *independent* variable, while doing is the "meta" *dependent* variable.

The empiricists' aim of predicting particular "doings" (which is to say, empirically observable behaviors), therefore, necessarily presupposes the prior activity of thinking/deciding. Why is it, though, that prediction, assuming it were actually possible in a nontrivial sense, necessarily implies a disguised normative commitment—an ideological bias—legitimating *some* kinds of doings and *de*legitimating others? The very suggestion that prediction somehow implies normative judgment must surely be regarded as incongruous by empiricist social scientists, who, at least since Simon (1947), have issued stern warnings against mixing facts, which are required for prediction, with values, which (or so they assert) provide the criteria for making normative judgments.[4] To say that social science can predict social behavior, therefore, implies no judgment, or so empiricists claim, about that behavior's desirability. Predictive social science is necessarily value-free social science; and normative judgment must be someone else's department.

The empiricists' commitment to a value-free social science draws support from the belief that "ought," or value, statements are logically separate, and therefore cannot be inferred, from "is," or factual, ones. Violating this belief commits what the logical empiricist philosopher G. E. Moore (1903) termed the "naturalistic fallacy," which (broadly construed) formalized the everyday adage that "Just because that's the way things *are* doesn't mean that that's the way they *ought to be*." Without disputing the wisdom of Moore's warning at a commonsense level, it nevertheless provides a questionable basis for grounding a social science that aspires to be free of "contamination" by normative judgments. As Searle has argued, the naturalistic fallacy is itself a fallacy insofar as it ignores the mixture of description and moral judgment that permeates the everyday vocabulary of social life. To say, "factually," that "Jones *owes* Smith five dollars," for example, necessarily implies the value judgment that "Jones *ought* [at least as a general rule] to pay Smith five dollars" (1985, 177). *Owing,* a word depicting the constitution of a particular kind of social relationship, simultaneously connotes both description and prescription. Similarly, as Louch (1969) notes, such commonplace words as *intelligence* and *development,* despite the variety of ways in which each has been defined, necessarily describe qualities—of individuals, organizations, or nation-states—that are *valued.* A value-free definition of either word would not simply be pointless; it is a logical impossibility.[5]

MacIntyre extends essentially the same argument to *any* functional concept. From saying, factually, that a watch keeps accurate time, for example, the value judgment necessarily follows that it is a *good* watch. Similarly, from the factual observation that a farmer whose dairy herd consistently wins all the prizes at agricultural fairs or whose crop-yields consistently surpass those of other local farmers, "the evaluative conclusion validly follows that 'He is a good farmer. . . .' It [therefore] follows that the concept of a watch cannot be defined independently of the concept of a good watch nor the concept of a farmer independently of that of a good farmer" (1984, 58). A similar conclusion must necessarily hold for all other functional concepts as well. Thus, developing and sustaining a value-free social science would require, assuming that other conditions of such an enterprise could be satisfied, the exclusion of functional concepts, which is to say, virtually anything of practical or normative interest about the social world.

In what sense, then, does social science empiricism's logical and temporal dualism between thinking and doing also necessarily contain a commitment to a normatively preferred vision of human action? Why, in other words, does empiricism, to the extent that it grounds its factual explanations in terms of that dualism, also necessarily imply a particular evaluational stance endorsing some kinds of doing and disparaging others? Finally, if the fusion of description and prescription, explanation and judgment, and fact and value in social science is inevitable in any case, how does the empiricists' naïveté about their fusion pose a serious problem?

Key to answering these questions is the particular meaning of *rationality* that empiricists, perhaps most notably Simon and his followers, assume, namely, that action is rational in the most elemental sense of the word insofar as doing corresponds to—that is, serves the intention generated by—the prior activity of thinking (or knowing). Put more succinctly, rationality connotes to the empiricist the idea that doing is the instrument of thought. Deciding, then, provides the fulcrum that links thinking and doing by effectuating and guiding the latter in the service of the former. From the standpoint of this definition of rationality, decision is itself a rationalist notion, irrespective of whether particular doings "maximize" or merely "satisfice," as well as irrespective of any limits that might exist concerning the knowledge required for achieving the decision's intended goals. "Rational decision" is, in this sense therefore, a redundant term (Harmon 1989a).

Construed instrumentally, then, rationality cannot describe a quality of thought itself, nor even a quality of the decisions about the ends that thought produces. Rather, instrumental rationality describes whether or the degree to which later doings are calculated and then undertaken in order to achieve those decisions' objectives, whatever they might be. On this point Simon was clear: decisions about ends (produced by thought) are informed by values; and, as a committed logical positivist, he was firm and explicit in declaring that values can have no rational basis. Although he "rejected" the dichotomy between politics and administration as a valid empirical proposition, he nevertheless insisted on their conceptual distinction by means of the radical epistemological separation of values (whose "allocation," as Easton [1953] said, constitutes politics) from facts (the stuff of administration). The obvious implication of his epistemology, which to his credit Simon did not shy away from, was that politics is therefore irrational, while administration is the domain of the (at least intendedly) rational. In suggesting this distinction, I must emphasize that Simon was not making an empirical claim about the differences between politics and administration; instead, he was asserting a definitional distinction between them dictated by his epistemology.

My purpose here is not to excoriate Simon for characterizing values and therefore politics as irrational, a line of argument, albeit misguided, that the normativists (i.e., the moralists) of public administration's standard narrative sometimes pursue. Rather, it is to show why the preference for instrumental rationality as an empirical assumption conceals an ideological bias by means of which, whether knowingly or not, empiricists smuggle in through the back door normative judgments about their research subjects' behavior. I will state my position as baldly as I know how: Empiricism necessarily suggests that for people to act, either individually or collectively, in an instrumentally rational fashion *is natural and therefore good for them.* Further, the normative bias implicit in the notion of instrumental rationality holds irrespective of whatever "limits" to rationality might constrain people's behavior, however "perfect" or "imperfect" the information relevant to their deciding and acting, or however comprehensive or "bounded" the scope of their deliberations prior to acting. All of these latter considerations bear only on the practical possibilities for and impediments to success in achieving what they purportedly intend. The normative nature of the instrumental rationality assumption may in turn be aptly characterized as "ideological" insofar as its uncritical acceptance either shields from view alternative theoretical viewpoints for explaining action, *or* regards those viewpoints as subsidiary to the core enterprise of social science, *or* depicts particular actions that are revealed by them in pejorative terms, most notably, as evidence of irrationality.

Like *intelligence* or *development, rationality,* as well as much of the empiricist terminology used in elaborating its importance to explaining social life, contains both descriptive and normative connotations. These connotations are implicitly merged or fused with one another owing to the implicit belief that *rationality* describes how and why action *naturally* (another "fused" word) occurs. When, upon examination, observed behavior appears to violate rational expectations—that is, in instances where doing does *not* appear to serve as the evident instrument of thinking—empiricists must choose between two alternatives. The first, which might be called the "emperor's new clothes" strategy, is to invent post hoc interpretations of those observed doings in order to render them sensible in terms of the imputation of a purpose that the prior activity of thinking *must* have decided upon. It is as if to say, "These people can't be totally irrational; they had to have some sort of purpose in mind. Maybe it was this. . . . " The first alternative, then, because it posits that all action must be rational (in the elemental sense), makes the rationality assumption immune to rejection or even serious debate on the basis of evidence. This kind of reasoning raises the hackles of beady-eyed pragmatists, who begin to suspect the germ of an ideological bias.

The empiricist's second alternative is to ascribe a particular generic (though often vague and highly generalized) motive to thought-based decisions (e.g., "people are by nature utility maximizers") to which actual behaviors (doings) may or may not, upon later observation, conform. This strategy, however, may also commit the emperor's-new-clothes mistake unless the researcher clearly specifies in advance criteria for what kinds of behavior count as representing the generic motive and which do not. If "maximizing utility," for example, is not strictly limited in terms of its allowable empirical manifestations, it becomes ubiquitous and therefore meaningless. Even if precautions are taken against defining the generic motive ubiquitously, the elemental assumption of rationality as comprising a sequence of thinking/deciding/doing still remains untested, indeed untestable, by the empiricists' methods. No amount of empirical study, no matter how carefully conceived its methodology or extensive its evidence, can either confirm or refute it. Any argument regarding the superiority of that assumption, therefore, would necessarily have to be made on other—namely, philosophical or epistemological—grounds, rather than by assuming its warrant to be implicit in mountainous, though redundant, factual evidence.

No empiricist, of course, would deny that, from the standpoint of some pre-specified and content-specific motive, people may very often act "irrationally," but in doing so he or she would assert that that conclusion is strictly empirical—which is to say, value-free—rather than normative. Empiricists might well argue, for example, that the thinking/deciding/doing mode of explaining human action can be sustained merely by specifying a different content-specific motive to reveal behavior that they had previously labeled as irrational as now rational. By one light or another, however, all action is nevertheless rational. An instrumentally rational explanation of action in terms of one or another criterion of rationality must, however, implicitly amount to a normative claim as to its desirability simply because any alternative mode of explanation would be "unnatural" (an obviously pejorative word) and therefore virtually unthinkable.

Because the range of possible generic "rational" motives is radically open-ended, however, the selection of one motive as a guiding empirical assumption over other possible candidates constitutes an implicit normative or political choice by the social scientist. No social scientist, empiricist or otherwise, undertakes a research project without at least a nascent sense that someone, somewhere, at some time might either value or benefit from the fruits of his or her research. That is, any research study is motivated by an implicit promise either to illuminate desirable possibilities for action heretofore invisible or unimagined, or to expose the causes or consequences of undesirable ones.

If the normative, practical, or political content of empirical research cannot in principle be divorced from the epistemology that guides it, however, then the meaning of *rationality* and its opposite, *irrationality*, similarly cannot be free of such content. Empiricism implicitly claims, therefore, that to act rationally is therefore good for people—however the particular content of "good" might be defined—and that to act irrationally is, correspondingly, bad for them. Substituting the less obviously pejorative prefix *non* for the more inflammatory *ir* in front of *rationality* merely disguises rather than eliminates this normative stance. In a like manner, to posit "limits" to rationality, or for Simon to observe its necessarily "bounded" nature in administrative decision making, or to note that information relevant to it is typically "imperfect" all imply more than simply soberly scientific descriptions of the real world of organizations; such observations also contain by implication the normative judgment that a perfect world, whether perfect for oneself or for others, is at least worth trying to approximate even though—and by implication, regrettably!—it can never be fully realized. This is what it means to be "intendedly rational," a normative injunction cloaked in the purportedly value-free vocabulary of social science. The meta independent variable of thinking (deciding) thereby provides the standards for making normative and practical judgments about the efficacy of the meta dependent variable of doing. "Factual" social science variables, that is, imply judgments about social values. Empirical beliefs concerning cause-effect or if-then relations between variables convey the hidden admonition: "You ought . . . !" The ideological character of empiricism's commitment to the assumption of instrumental rationality consists in its efforts to conceal that basic truth.

Action as the Fusion of Thinking and Doing

Empiricism's belief that rationality is a virtue and irrationality, therefore, a problem to be remedied or mitigated presupposes that doing is, first and foremost, the instrument of prior thought. The power of this belief owes in part to its seemingly commonsensical appeal as well as to its obvious parallel with the standard narrative's analytical distinction between politics and administration. Public administrators, in the standard narrative, are the "doers," the implementers, the instruments for achieving the purposes previously decided by elected government officials and other political actors. Therefore, revealing instrumental rationality as a problematic virtue, and irrationality (again, in the elemental sense of the word) as a pseudoproblem, requires a radically different understanding of the relation between thinking and doing.

For pragmatists, action connotes the fusion of thinking and doing. Ever since Weber (in Runciman 1978) distinguished behavior (i.e., people's empirically observable doings) from action (i.e., their subjectively constituted and meaningful behavior), the connotative distinction between thinking and doing has weakened to the point of revealing each as constituting, not simply "related to," the other. Beginning with his deconstruction of the reflex arc concept, Dewey and later pragmatists have emphasized thinking, or knowing, as an activity, a process (thus more aptly expressed by a gerund than a noun), as opposed to knowledge, which conveys the meaning of some*thing* that is created, or even discovered, logically and temporally before doing begins. Rather, thinking, for Dewey, *is* a form of doing, connoting a unitary, or fused, conception of action entailed in the human organism's continuous process of adaptive adjustment to contexts that it simultaneously enacts. Similarly, doing, rather than serving as thought's instrument, itself produces ways of knowing that serve the practical aim of action. Rather than being regarded as the vital fulcrum between thinking and doing, decisions are simply objectifications—temporary and artificial stoppages—of action's ongoing stream.

Knowledge, for the pragmatist, can therefore be judged only as either practical or impractical—in terms of its "cash value," recalling William James's metaphor—rather than as truthful or untruthful. The cash value metaphor, however, has proved unfortunate in one sense, conveying upon first encounter a meaning of *practical* quite unlike what James, Dewey's mentor, intended. Taken out of context, "cash value" could seem to endorse a crude reversal of the instrumentalism that pragmatists decry in the rationalist dualism between thinking and doing. Rather than doing serving as the instrument of thought, so this criticism goes, thought—in particular, unreflective thought—serves only the immediate requirements of doing something, and, by implication, anything. As Bernstein has suggested, pragmatists are in part to blame for inviting such a misreading, not only by their critics but, ironically, by some would-be (though misled) allies such as Simon.[6]

> In the opinion of many critics, pragmatism is little more than the pernicious slogan that all inquiry, knowledge, and thought is for the sake of action—where action is understood in some extremely mundane or vulgar manner. Pragmatists have been accused of holding the doctrine that something is meaningful or true only

> if it works or is useful. The reasons and causes for this bias are complex—in part, pragmatists and especially their popularizers are at fault for this caricature. But it is perfectly clear to anyone who reads the pragmatic thinkers carefully that the accusations are false and misleading. (Bernstein 1971, 173)

Practical, to a pragmatist, is best understood not as a synonym for *instrumental* but as an alternative (though not an antonym) to *true.* For knowledge to have practical—as opposed to simply instrumental—value requires that it be regarded as contextual, provisional, and particularistic; that is to say, its "cash value" is necessarily contingent upon its fit with what Follett called "the law of the situation" (1940, 65). As Evans has summarized Dewey on this point, "Inquiry is not a means or method to find the truth; it is the means or method to reduce doubt and to restore balance to a problematic situation, to let us get on with the task at hand. It is the means to the active reduction of uncertainty to such an extent that tentative next steps can be taken" (2000, 313). Unlike the rationalist dualism between thinking and doing, which requires a notion of Truth as independent in order to certify thinking's validity, pragmatism embraces instead "an epistemological stance emphasizing active engagement with nature or experience [from the standpoint of] . . . which problematic situations are resolved through a co-evolution of the situation and the inquirer" (314).

Since Dewey, pragmatists have criticized the idea of truth—in particular, what Rorty (1982) has termed big-T Truth—for underwriting a "spectator" theory of knowledge in which thinking is, first, separated from doing, and then granted controlling status over doing by providing the authoritative criteria for justifying it. The illusion of thinking's temporal separation from doing sustains the companion illusion that knowledge may, ideally, achieve "objective" status. Although the adage that "knowledge is power" might in some respects seem benign (e.g., when power is blandly construed as enablement), knowledge's "Foucauldian" character becomes evident upon recognizing, as Rorty does, "that knowledge is never separable from power—that one is likely to suffer if one does not hold certain beliefs at certain times and places" (1991, 26). The power to determine the operational content of Truth means having not just the power to control action directly but also, though less visibly, the power to control the terms of discourse that make some courses of action imaginable, others unthinkable, and still others seem crazy. Thus, when Thayer (1980) says that epistemology *is* organization theory, he seems to echo Rorty's point by arguing that the rules for determining what counts as valid, or "objective," knowledge can only be sustained through organizational (including political) arrangements in which some people decide and others don't. In contrast to its alternative of intersubjectivity, objectivity is therefore the epistemological expression of hierarchy, a belief as deeply rooted in the ethos of the empiricist research program as in the standard narrative's insistence on administration's subordination to politics.

"Objectivity" (in view of the foregoing argument, always advisedly surrounded by scare quotes) thus presumes a hierarchical separation of thinkers from doers—the meta independent variable from the meta dependent variable. Hilary Putnam (1981) labels this attitude *scientism:* the belief that rationality consists merely in applying criteria. *Scientism* provides a fair synonym for what I have termed *rationalism,* the belief that standards of justification (criteria)—both for knowledge claims derived from research as well as for other warrants for action—must precede action itself.

Toward a Problem-Driven Social Science

The preceding critique of empiricist social science has dropped several hints about what, from a pragmatist standpoint, a preferred conception of social science might consist of. Although shortly I will identify several research (including methodological) strategies that appear to be consistent with that conception, their inclusion depends upon their agreement with the following principles, both practical and epistemological:

1. *A pragmatist social science, including public administration and policy science, is problem-driven*[7] rather than methodology-driven. Form, as it were, follows function. "Problems," moreover, are not defined exclusively by researchers, but necessarily with reference to, and often in collaboration with, the people—the research subjects—who actually experience or are otherwise affected by them. There can be no legitimate "research problem" (or "research question") that does not satisfy this requirement.
2. *The meaning of "rationality" is not restricted to,* although it may occasionally include, *"instrumental" rationality.* As I will explain at

length in chapter 4's discussion of "constitutive rationality" (Tribe 1973) and "practices" (MacIntyre 1984), a richer and more sensible meaning of rationality must take due account of the particular contexts and social processes within which people formulate courses of action.

3. *Pragmatist, problem-driven social science dissolves the rationalist dualisms between thinking and doing, ends and means, and the moral and the practical.* As I will attempt to show later in this and subsequent chapters, the pragmatist commitment to collaborative experimentation, in administrative practice as well as in the conduct of research, presupposes the dissolving of all the principal dualisms that underwrite both public administration's standard narrative and empiricist social science. Such a problem-driven social science committed to such experimentation, that is, necessarily presumes a radically different epistemology—indeed, a radically different worldview—from that implied by rationalist ideology.
4. *Problem-driven social science presumes the priority of the particular over the general.* Local, contextual knowledge—what James C. Scott (1998) has termed *metis*—crucially informs, and indeed is presumed as the logical starting point for, problem-driven research. Generalizability, a key empiricist criterion for judging the adequacy of research, is thus accorded at most secondary importance, giving way to subjective, context-specific judgments about its practical value. Whether a research study might generate wider—or "general"—interest will therefore depend mainly on the researcher's imagination, creativity, and ability to evoke empathic identification among readers rather than on his or her mastery of methodological techniques.
5. Because practical knowledge is necessarily context-dependent, *problem-driven social science takes the "theory/practice" issue seriously in a way that methodology-driven social science typically does not.* The contemporary connotation of *research* in methodology-driven, empiricist social science presupposes an instrumental relation between theory and practice, thus marginalizing "praxiological" approaches that, as I explain in chapter 5, emphasize the interactive relation between theorizing and practicing.
6. In addition to its practical orientation, *problem-driven research also possesses a vital critical dimension.* Although the "positive" commitment needed for practical action may often stand in tension with

the "negative" posture of doubt that critical reflection requires, the latter provides a valuable countervailing force against commitment's tendency to degenerate into impulsiveness, premature certainty, and the exclusion of alternative possibilities. And, although managing the inevitable tensions between commitment and doubt may pose challenges for problem-driven social scientists, such challenges are in principle no different from those confronting natural scientists, whose (often passionate) commitment to confirming their hypotheses has to be checked by their simultaneous efforts to falsify them.

Collectively, these six principles bear a close resemblance to what Bent Flyvbjerg (2001) has termed *phronetic* social science. *Phronesis,* a Greek word whose closest contemporary meaning is "prudence" or "practical common sense," entails the application of practical knowledge coupled with ethical reflection in everyday situations. According to Aristotle, *phronesis* was one of three cardinal intellectual virtues, the other two being *episteme* (in modern parlance, science), which "concerns universals and the production of knowledge which is invariable in time and space" (55), and *techne,* the art or craft of applying knowledge instrumentally in the variable, contingent, and concrete activities of everyday life. Empiricist social science may thus be construed as having *epistemic* aspirations by virtue of its concern with identifying universal (general) causes, and *techne*(cal) insofar as it presumes an instrumental connection between knowledge and practice, thinking and doing. *Phronetic* social science, by contrast, seeks "to clarify and deliberate about the problems and risks we face and to outline how things may be done differently, in full knowledge that we cannot find ultimate answers to these questions or even a single version of what the questions are" (140). Such a social science, then, is variously pragmatic yet critical; action-oriented yet reflective; morally committed yet tentative and open; and rooted in the concrete, everyday experience of research subjects while remaining sensitive to the structural features of human association that might elude their immediate comprehension. Because it embraces (and sometimes dissolves) these seemingly paradoxical oppositions, it should not be surprising that a problem-driven social science is highly eclectic, drawing from diverse sources its characteristic theoretical approaches and methods. Below I briefly describe four "methodological" approaches, which, taken together, serve to illustrate what a problem-driven social science might include. (These four approaches, to be sure, do not comprise an exhaustive list; and, despite their occasional overlap, they can also sometimes conflict with one another.)

1. *Case studies* provide excellent illustrations of multiple "rationalities" among various actors in the same situation, including the manner in which historical context and social process affect their development and expression. Instead of analyzing relationships among variables, cases focus upon problematic situations in order to glean instructive lessons—typically in the form of maxims rather than lawlike generalizations—that are simultaneously practical and normative. Unlike empiricism, which regards the value of case studies as limited to generating subsequently testable, generalizable hypotheses, a problem-driven social science sees particular kinds of cases as being "generalizable" in a practical (and admittedly looser) rather than a technical sense. Flyvbjerg, for example, defines as *critical* cases those "having strategic importance in relation to . . . [a] general problem" (78), and as *paradigmatic* cases those that suggest novel metaphors around which new theoretical perspectives might be developed, both of which may produce knowledge that "enter[s] into the collective process of knowledge accumulation in a given field or in a society" (76). Studying cases, especially those that explicitly raise "public interest" issues, can for similar reasons provide valuable training for administrative practitioners. White and McSwain (1990) note in this regard that the pedagogical value of such cases lies in their ability to reveal to practitioners the overall patterns—"the essential and underlying form or structure" (32)—of administrative situations, enabling a deeper understanding of those situations than that provided by observational "data," which can only categorize and organize surface appearances. "True expertise," as Flyvbjerg concludes, "is based on intimate experience with thousands of individual cases and on the ability to discriminate between situations, with all their nuances of difference, without distilling them into formulas and standard cases" (2001, 85).
2. Problem-driven social science often relies upon one or another variant of the *interpretive* method, including phenomenology (Berger and Luckmann 1967; Schutz 1967; Hummel 1982), ethnomethod-

ology (Garfinkel 1967), hermeneutics (Gadamer 1975), and what Silverman (1971) calls the "action frame of reference." The generic question posed by these approaches is: "What is going on here" from the standpoint of the actors involved in the situation? Like Flyvbjerg's phronetic researchers, interpretivists begin by asking "'little questions' and focusing on what Clifford Geertz (1973, 6) . . . calls 'thick description'" (Flyvbjerg 2001, 133). Such "thick descriptions," especially those involving the everyday lived experience of research subjects, are compatible with several of the principles of problem-driven social science suggested earlier. First, "rationality" is presumed to be a function of the actors' subjective viewpoints rather than defined in terms of a priori (usually instrumental) criteria such as efficiency, effectiveness, or goal attainment. Second, by studying particular contexts (as with case studies), interpretivists feel obliged only to say something novel or interesting that might encourage readers to rethink their taken-for-granted beliefs about the social world rather than to make formal generalizations about it. Finally, and in keeping with a basic ethnomethodological assumption, the skills required to conduct such research are in principle "just as situational, just as dependent on the context, as the interpretations of the people whom the researchers study" (Flyvbjerg 2001, 33). That is, problem-driven social scientists cannot presume a privileged, more "objective" claim to valid or useful knowledge than anyone else.

3. Problem-driven social science also necessarily includes a *critical* dimension by virtue of its concern with uncovering hidden dynamics of power. People's ability to perceive alternative possibilities for practical action are both enabled and constrained by their historically conditioned beliefs about what is "real" as well as by entrenched modes of communication and forms of social relationships that frame, but also distort, public discourse (Habermas 1970, 1971). Some of the critical discourses often disagree with one another concerning both the meaning and the practical value of rationality in serving an "emancipatory" critical interest. But, notwithstanding the seriousness of their differences, both Habermas's theory of "communicative interaction" and Foucault's (1997) "genealogical" and "archaeological" critiques of history and social institutions, for example, variously affirm the idea that *praxis,* construed as theoretically informed and reflective practice, requires

an essentially critical attitude.[8] This critical attitude, among its other benefits, mitigates the tendency of some interpretivist approaches either to ignore a consideration of structural sources of political domination or to accept at face value social actors' unreflective accounts of why they do what they do.

4. Perhaps the paradigmatic approach to problem-driven social science is *action research*. Despite the legitimate concern that action research may lack a sufficiently critical attitude in view of the way it is often conducted, it is nevertheless the most explicitly "problem-driven" research approach discussed thus far, as well as the most characteristically pragmatic approach by virtue of its dissolving the empiricist dualisms between thinking and doing, ends and means, and theory and practice. In dissolving these dualisms, action research takes most seriously the long-standing pragmatist commitment to collaborative experimentation. Although both pragmatists and empiricists avow a commitment to experimentation, they differ sharply on its meaning and about the kinds of contexts within which it is relevant. To pragmatists like Dewey, *experimentation* is a virtual synonym for *action,* which involves the fusion of thinking and doing, and in which action and knowledge simultaneously inform one another in novel and unpredictable ways. For empiricists, by contrast, the most highly valued, most prestigious research model is the controlled experiment, although they must often settle for field studies, in which "control" takes the form of statistical tests for manipulating data *about* research subjects, as opposed to literally controlling (or manipulating) the subjects themselves.[9] In either case, the posture taken by researchers toward both their subjects and those who could later benefit from their findings is one of distance, of separation (McSwite 1997). Criteria for judging the success, and therefore the legitimacy, of empiricist research include, among others, "rigor" and "objectivity."

   Although Dewey did not coin the term, action research would appear to provide a research model that affirms his conception of experimentation. In action research, the relation between researcher and research subjects is one of mutual engagement and collaboration, in which the latter perform, simultaneously, the roles of knowers, deciders, and doers, but who sometimes want or need "professional help" in clarifying the connections among those three roles in action contexts that they find especially problematic.

> Resistance to the action research model from social science empiricists and public administration's standard narrative, however, is both clear and easily anticipated. Action research violates the empiricists' subordination of doing to thinking, thus producing at best a condescending attitude toward it; while the fusion of thinking and doing leaves both the rationalists and the normativists of the standard narrative at a loss about whom to hold accountable, to blame, if something goes wrong. Both the rationalists and the normativists strongly suspect—correctly, as it turns out—that the very distinction, both conceptual and practical, between policy and administration would be jeopardized were the promise of action research to be fully realized.

Pragmatists often differ among themselves about whether empiricism's virtual hegemony over administrative and policy research ought chiefly to be regarded as dangerous or as merely futile. Although empiricism's futility is clearly evident in its failure to deliver on its promise of predictive, lawlike generalizations, pragmatists of a more doleful bent detect in addition a sinister double meaning in *control,* which empiricism tries to pass off as a value-neutral methodological principle. If the power to control rests chiefly in determining the content of knowledge and its uses, empiricism's continuing efforts to redeem past predictive failures while at the same time denying their inevitability may constitute the source of its hidden, though paradoxically ineffectual, political power. That power, it would appear, closely resembles that of the emperor's tailors, worried about losing their jobs, to deceive and confound both the emperor and his subjects—and, in the bargain, themselves.

4
Ends, Means, and the Problem of Managerialism

I hope by now to have made plausible the conceptual connection between the thinking/doing and politics/administration dualisms as well as the politically problematic nature of scholarly stances toward them. In this chapter I will argue that the dualism between thinking and doing that underwrites contemporary empiricist social science mirrors almost precisely the analogous dualism between ends and means that has dominated public administration's standard narrative for at least a century. That is, the standard narrative's commitment to ends/means logic recapitulates empiricism's epistemological error by uncritically embracing the otherwise problematic principles of effectiveness and efficiency, and therefore the equally problematic assumption that instrumental rationality is synonymous with, or at least a privileged variant of, the more generic notion of rationality itself. Insofar as an uncritical acceptance of the ends/means dualism shields from view alternative conceptions of organizational rationality and alternative normative images of governance, that acceptance also qualifies as ideological—in particular, an ideology of *managerialism.*

My critique of managerialism consists in an effort to expose that ideology by using two related strategies to undermine the ends/means dualism. The first strategy draws from empirical evidence in neurophysiology, social psychology, and organizational behavior revealing that the two moments of that dualism may more sensibly be construed as inverted (reversed) in sequence. The second, more radical strategy *dissolves* the dualism, and other related dualisms as well, by reinterpreting selected contributions to the public administration and management literature. The practical payoff of this effort—in William James's phrase, its "cash value"—is twofold: first, to introduce a "unitary," or "process," conception of governance based on the notion of collaborative experimentation; and second, to make plausible an alternative view of rationality that I have chosen to label "intelligent vetoing."

The connection between the thinking/doing and ends/means dualisms may be briefly summarized as follows: *thinking* culminates in people's decisions about *ends* (or goals or objectives), about which they then *do* something by selecting and then executing the *means* for their accomplishment. In addition, and like any notion involving functional relationships, ends/means thinking has both descriptive and evaluative connotations. Decisions about ends not only "naturally" precede the selection and implementation of means, but the former also provide an ostensibly sound basis for making evaluative judgments about the latter. The generic (but, as I will argue, problematic) virtues of ends/means logic and action are the twin notions of effectiveness and efficiency, while the generic (albeit pseudo-) problems that such logic seeks to solve or ameliorate are simply those virtues' opposites, ineffectiveness and inefficiency.

The task of criticizing the ends/means dualism—of exposing its concealed ideological assumptions—is made somewhat easier by the fact that cases illustrating its limitations can be drawn from people's everyday experience.[1] Everyone "knows" what ends and means are and can therefore readily identify the distinction between them with case examples. That same advantage, however, can also be turned against itself. Ends/means logic may be so deeply embedded in people's commonsense thinking that they may simply reinterpret purportedly *counter*examples as being, instead, confirming ones by ascribing the status of "ends" to what the researcher intended them to regard as a "means." Ends/means logic thus suffers from the dual liability of being both overly commonsensical and yet so pliable in its application as to be analytically meaningless unless care is taken. In addition, if effectiveness and efficiency are *problematic* virtues, does that therefore mean we should all strive to be *in*effective and *in*efficient? The answer is certainly "no"; but explaining why the question is beside the point—the wrong question to ask—poses a difficult challenge.

Later in this chapter I will be concerned with dissolving the ends/means dualism by drawing from insights from three landmark contributions to the literatures of policy analysis, management, and public administration. The purpose of that exercise is explicitly normative and political. Specifically, I hope to explain why an uncritical acceptance of the ends/means dualism conceals an ideological bias that not only perpetuates disparities of political and organizational power but also precludes an alternative vision of personal development and social relationship upon which a more practical and humane conception of governance might be grounded. Normative and political critique can also profit, however, from insights that are chiefly descriptive and analytical, for the reason that any normative image of governance presupposes certain empirical conditions needed for its practical realization.

Six Eccentric Insights about Ends and Means

What I described in chapter 1 as "inverting," or "eccentric," strategies for dealing with the dualisms of public administration's standard narrative are typically found in academic disciplines (including neurophysiology and social psychology) whose research agendas are at most only minimally political. Such strategies, it will be recalled, invert the commonsense assumption that ends precede means by suggesting, counterintuitively, that the reverse is typically, perhaps always, the case. Insights based on such strategies reveal reasons for doubting the factual plausibility of the more commonsense (which is to say, rationalist) view, thus opening the space for an alternative normative conception of governance *not* predicated on the standard narrative's dualisms. (My purely intuitive sense, in addition, is that inverting strategies often consist of nascent or disguised dissolving strategies.)

The six examples of "inverting" (eccentric) insights summarized below assume a somewhat relaxed interpretation of these dualisms by subsuming the parallel dualisms between "problems and solutions" and "experience and belief." Although each of these insights conveys a certain irony by virtue of reversing the commonsense beliefs of instrumental rationality, none implies that human action should thereby be deemed *ir*rational. What they collectively suggest, rather, is an alternative conception of rationality.

1. In experiments he conducted in the 1970s, neurophysiologist Benjamin Libet (in Nørretranders 1998) found that people's conscious initiation of voluntary acts lags behind (by about half a second) their unconscious mental experience of "deciding," or preparing to decide, to perform those acts. Action, that is to say,

originates in the unconscious, and the subsequent role of reflective consciousness is chiefly to *veto* some, but only some, of those impulses. In the terms of the last chapter, doing (at least the *impulse* to act) precedes thinking (in the sense of consciously deliberating). Moreover, Libet says, people usually don't enjoy exercising consciousness's veto power; they prefer simply to act.

2. In the 1950s social psychologist Leon Festinger and his colleagues (1956) infiltrated a religious cult whose leader had convinced the members that, on a specified date, God would unleash a reprise of the great flood, wiping out the earth's human population. The cult's leader, however, promised her followers that their (and *only* their) salvation—in the form of divine rescue by flying saucers—could be assured if they accepted her spiritual guidance. Festinger wanted to know how the cult would react once the appointed day uneventfully came and went (which, no doubt to his and his colleagues' relief, it did). Although many of the cult's members initially felt betrayed by their leader, they soon thereafter accepted her explanation that, owing to their steadfast devotion, God had decided to spare humanity by postponing the deluge. Festinger cites this "failed prophecy" as an extreme example of what is in fact a natural human proclivity, namely, that people typically interpret their experience to fit their prior beliefs, on the basis of which they have already formed their commitments to act. Rather than the evidence of experience providing the basis for belief, just the reverse is more often the case. The reason, he concluded, is that evidence which might otherwise prompt people to revise their beliefs creates "cognitive dissonance" between what they already "know" and what they "see," which they reduce to tolerable levels by adjusting interpretations of their experience to fit those beliefs. If the failed prophecy of the flood might seem too bizarre to serve as a plausible ground for Festinger's conclusion, consider how reluctant much of the American public was to withdraw its earlier support for the U.S. invasion of Iraq once the original reasons offered in support of it were contradicted by the evidence (Kull 2004).
3. Karl Weick devotes much of his classic work, *The Social Psychology of Organizing,* to explicating a single sentence: "How can I know what I mean until I see what I say?"[2] (1979, 133). According to Weick's "natural selection" theory, organizing consists of four stages: (1) *ecological change:* events that provide the highly "equivo-

cal" (i.e., ambiguous and unfiltered) raw materials of the environment with which people may engage; which leads to (2) *enactment:* the preliminary "bracketing" or focusing of attention upon some of those events; thus leading to (3) *selection:* imposing structures of interpretation on those enactments; which then culminates in (4) *retention:* storing the products of successful sense-making of previous enactments and selections. Retention—the products, that is, of what people "know" (or think)—is the culmination of, rather than the prelude to, the act of "saying" (or doing). Saying/doing precedes knowing/thinking, suggesting to Weick this reversal of an everyday maxim: "I'll see it when I believe it" (135).

4. In their notorious "garbage can" model, Cohen, March, and Olsen (1972) define *organization* as "a collection of choices looking for problems, issues and feelings looking for decision situations in which they might be aired, solutions looking for issues to which they might be the answer, and decision makers looking for work" (qtd. in Weick 1979, 21). A cautious reading of this definition might suggest that its authors' seemingly whimsical reversal of commonsense (rational) beliefs about organizations is simply intended to show the interactive rather than the unidirectional relation of thinking and doing, ends and means, and cause and effect. My own hunch is that Cohen, March, and Olsen pretty much mean just what they say inasmuch as their definition of organizations as garbage cans simply extrapolates to a macro-organizational level the micro-level insights of the kind that Libet, Festinger, and Weick provide. (One quick and sure way to spot a rationalist, incidentally, is to notice if he or she chuckles condescendingly at the supposedly "irrational" behavior that the garbage can model describes.)
5. Harold Garfinkel (1967), the founder of ethnomethology, offered two insights directly on point of this discussion. First, from his eccentric "breaching experiments" (observing how research subjects behave in experimental situations that breach, or violate, their normal social practices and expectations), Garfinkel concluded that people's actions are not governed or even greatly influenced by prior-held rules of conduct. Rather, he found, rules (the products of thought) chiefly rationalize decisions about action after the fact. Second, and reversing the rationalist assumption that values precede, determine the relevance of, and thus provoke stronger dis-

agreement than facts, Garfinkel discovered that people's moral attachment was far greater to their interpretations of facts than it was to their values. People readily tolerate value differences, but they experience discrepant versions of the "factually normal" as profoundly unsettling.

6. In distinguishing "tame" from "wicked" problems, Rittel and Webber (1973) describe the latter as "malignant," "vicious," and "tricky" because, among other reasons, they resist any definitive formulation or purely technical solution; their proposed solutions determine rather than follow from the problems' definition; there are no ultimate tests for gauging the efficacy of the problems' solutions; and those solutions may unintendedly create or exacerbate other problems. Policy makers and public administrators are routinely called upon to contend with wicked problems, but they run into trouble when they either mistake them for tame problems or *try* to tame them by applying technical fixes.

Taken together, these six eccentric insights challenge all three of the principal dualisms considered so far, providing strong, perhaps even compelling, reasons for reconsidering the epistemological assumptions upon which both public administration's standard narrative and social science empiricism depend. An easily anticipated rationalist rejoinder to these insights, however, might assert that the research on which they are based provides interesting but nevertheless perverse evidence of widespread irrationality (or nonrationality). The presence of that irrationality is thus a problem that needs to be ameliorated by training policy and administrative professionals chiefly in, and otherwise institutionalizing, methods of rational analysis and decision making.

The difficulty with this rejoinder lies in its conflating the more generic notion of rationality with the more restricted idea of *instrumental* rationality, implying that any act that contradicts the latter is therefore irrational in a generic sense. The standard English dictionaries I have consulted, however, include in their definitions of *rational* such everyday synonyms as *sane, sensible,* or *reasonable,*[3] with only secondary, if any, references to or connotations of *instrumental,* as in (to invent one such definition) "the quality of action taken in service of a predefined end." In view of the more commonplace synonyms for *rational* noted above, empiricists who associate it with *instrumental* would appear to face an uphill struggle in explaining why it is sane, sensible, or reasonable for people to act just the reverse of how they normally act, *or* why the empirically more persuasive "inverted" sequence of action's moments should necessarily be characterized as irrational or nonrational.

In reply, empiricists might say that despite its descriptive shortcomings, instrumental rationality nonetheless permits a post hoc basis for judging the efficacy of particular actions in a way that inverting its dualisms does not. Even if the six eccentric insights might supply a more descriptively accurate account of people's typical mode of acting, it doesn't follow that particular actions fitting that alternative description are therefore sane, sensible, reasonable, or rational in any other praiseworthy sense of the word. To this I would certainly agree: *rational* does in its everyday connotation imply a normative judgment of praiseworthiness, and that normative connotation needs to be retained. *Rational,* however, ordinarily connotes a praiseworthy quality of a particular sort, namely, deliberate and reflective as opposed to impulsive and capricious. The question, therefore, would appear to be: What could rationality—in the sense of sane, sensible, reasonable, deliberate, or reflective—plausibly consist of if, as a factual matter, the relation of ends to means is the opposite of what the empiricists assume?

My short and still preliminary answer, suggested in part by Libet, is that *rationality entails the intelligent or sensible vetoing of particular impulses and action plans. Intelligent* and *sensible* require no advance specification of criteria for making these judgments (e.g., about an action plan's effectiveness or efficiency). Such criteria would necessarily presume the prior identification of ends, goals, or purposes, which, if Weick and Cohen, March, and Olsen are correct, are constructed either retrospectively or during the process of formulating action plans. Criteria that *are* selected would necessarily be local, context-specific, and flexible. Acting rationally in such contexts essentially means adopting a critical and tentative attitude toward one's own or others' embryonic plans. Intelligent vetoes require seeking answers to such questions as the following: "Plan A certainly feels like the right thing to do; but, can we think of good or compelling reasons *not* to carry it out? Can we construct plausible alternative definitions of our present situation that might suggest acting differently? Are we so emotionally attached to our current understanding of the 'facts' of the situation (à la Festinger and Garfinkel) as to be blind to other equally sensible accounts of those facts? Are we so committed to our solution (Rittel and Webber) that we have ignored other problem definitions? Have we carefully considered the perverse and unintended consequences that might result from following Plan A? How self-aware are we (and *can* we be) of our reasons for wanting to pursue Plan A in the first place? Might we be seeing only what we want to see?"

This portrait of rationality as consisting of a critical and tentative attitude will undergo later revision in the light of the following section's dissolving of the ends/means dualism. Because that attitude's essential features will be largely retained, however, a few stipulations about them are in order here. First, the "we" referred to in the previous paragraph made no mention of who was, and who was not, included in it, a subject that I will return to later. Second, if ends and means are more typically inverted in sequence (or if they are more sensibly seen as fused with one another), we should be forced to admit that no clear line of demarcation can be drawn between "giving reasons" for our actions and "rationalizing" them. Knowledge of ends or goals typically presupposes an already (if only partially) imagined course of action that, as Rittel and Webber suggest, embodies both the problem's solution and its definition.

Third, and perhaps most importantly, this alternative conception of rationality is, although necessary, still insufficient for depicting the normative vision of governance to which I have thus far only briefly alluded. The new primary moment in the inverted dualism—which is to say, the unconscious origin of people's impulses to act—should not be paired invidiously as rationality's evil twin, and thus ever needful of control by the "better nature" of our conscious deliberation, but instead acknowledged as a fully equal partner in action. Unconscious impulses to act, although some of them will sensibly be vetoed as impractical, nevertheless provide the wellspring of imagination, energy, and commitment without which rational analysis, even in this revised sense of the term, could have no raw materials, no real-world contexts, with which to engage. That is, even intelligent vetoing may be so overdone that the virtues of doubt and tentativeness degenerate into cynicism and a failure of nerve.

Notwithstanding the value of neurophysiological and social psychological research for destabilizing the ends/means dualism, it is tempting to regard the alternative conception of rationality suggested by such research as a grudging admonition to put the best face possible on our eccentricities. That is surely too harsh a judgment; but intelligent vetoing, whatever might be its appeal on practical or prudential grounds, still seems unsatisfying, or at least incomplete, as a foundation on which to erect a new normative conception of governance. Rationalism's priority of ends over means, by contrast, produces the idea of political and bureaucratic accountability as *its* normative foundation, one that, though rife with paradoxes and contradictions (Fox and Miller 1995; Harmon 1995), is in principle clear and easily grasped. Seeing those paradoxes and contradictions as genuinely crippling rather than simply as irritants to be coped with or brushed aside, however, requires a more affirmative vision in which moral value and democracy are conceived as emerging from social interaction itself. To be rendered plausible, that vision requires the more radical strategy of dissolving, rather than merely inverting, the ends/means dualism.

From Inverting to Dissolving the Ends/Means Dualism: Michael Oakeshott on Rationality

If, as I have suggested, eccentric strategies often imply (or are disguised forms of) dissolving strategies, it is important to consider how the characteristically "rationalist" view of rationality in public administration's standard narrative might be altered by questioning the distinction between ends and means at the micro level of human conduct. Such an exercise would appear to be important, because the distinction (or dualism) between ends and means directly parallels the analytical distinction between politics and administration still retained by both of the standard narrative's opposing factions. Eventually, dissolving the standard narrative's originating dualism, rather than superficially "rejecting" Wilson's hoary dichotomy, requires questioning both the conceptual coherence and the practical possibility of separating ends from means. In this section I will employ Michael Oakeshott's (1991) critique of rational*ism* (which I take as a rough proxy for the standard narrative's implicit conception of rationality) as a bridge from Dewey's dissolving of the thinking/doing dualism, discussed in chapter 3, to the following section on "process" theory, in which I dissolve the ends/means dualism at the institutional (macro) level. The plausibility of the arguments developed in the following section, that is, requires an alternative conception of rationality to that presumed by the standard narrative.

Oakeshott's central claim is that rationalism, the prevailing mind-set of politics in the modern era, has misconstrued the nature of rationality by assuming both an impossible conception of human conduct (or what

Dewey would term *action*) and a profound misunderstanding of the role knowledge plays in generating and guiding it. The logic of rationalism, Oakeshott says, assumes that the ends of human conduct precede and are then linked instrumentally to subsequent choices of the means for their accomplishment. The character of the rationalist is that of a well-trained engineer (rather than that of an educated mind) whose "assimilation of politics to engineering is . . . what may be called the myth of rationalist politics" (9). The politics of engineering, optimistically motivated by visions of rational control in order to achieve utopian purposes, combines two essential characteristics: the impulse toward perfection (certainty) and the demand for uniformity. "[E]ither of the characteristics without the other," Oakeshott says, "denotes a different style of politics. The essence of rationalism is their combination" (9–10). Such a politics, it need hardly be said, is therefore uncomfortable with, indeed it abhors, uncertainty and variety, which are the enemies of orderly and purposeful control.

The combination of perfection and uniformity as defining attributes of rationalist politics springs from its conception of the nature and role of knowledge. To the rationalist all genuine knowledge is *technical* knowledge, susceptible to formulation according to universal principles, rules, and propositions. By contrast, *practical* knowledge—that is, knowledge derived from people's actual and varied lived experience—is incapable of being so formulated and is therefore, to the rationalist, not really knowledge at all. "The heart of the matter is the pre-occupation of the Rationalist with certainty," writes Oakeshott. "Technique and certainty are, for him, inseparably joined because certain knowledge is, for him, knowledge which does not require to look beyond itself for its certainty" (16). Because such knowledge *cannot* look beyond itself, Oakeshott says, it therefore lacks any "homeopathic" capability of self-correction.

The ends/means dualism is implicit in every notion of technical knowledge, which consists of "a set of rules of universal application; it is a true technique in that it is an instrument of inquiry indifferent to the subject-matter of inquiry" (20). By "indifferent," Oakeshott means, first, that such knowledge is neutral with respect to the particular ends or purposes in whose service it might be applied. But more importantly, technical knowledge is indifferent, even oblivious, to the variable and unpredictable contexts that might otherwise invite its revision or rejection. Universality, in short, implies uniformity.

For my present purpose, Oakeshott's reasons for judging rationalism to be politically obnoxious are less significant than (although they are partially implied by) his explanation of why "rational conduct," the kind ostensibly informed by technical knowledge, does not exist. And if it does not exist, then the dualism between ends and means—in Oakeshott's terms, the selection, first, of a premeditated purpose, and second, of the separate, similarly premeditated selection of the means for achieving it—is itself exposed as a fiction. The fictitious distinction between ends and means, he says, commits the same sort of logical error that Dewey (1896) earlier attributed to the reflex arc concept's contrived distinction between thinking and doing, namely, of hypostatizing (reifying, or attributing thing-like status to) what is in reality an activity or process. For Oakeshott, the rationalist's hypostatized activity in question is an initially empty human mind, which, like Locke's tabula rasa, supposedly has imprinted upon it facts, sensory observations, and various bits of (technical) knowledge, which are later called upon in deciding what to do and how to do it. Oakeshott objects, however, that "You do not first have [such] a mind, which acquires a filling of ideas and then makes distinctions between true and false, right and wrong, reasonable and unreasonable, and then, as a third step, causes activity. Properly speaking the mind has no existence apart from, or in advance of, these and other distinctions. These and other distinctions are not acquisitions; they are constitutive of the mind" (109). If what we think of as the mind is constituted by our conduct (the "unitary," or "fused," activity of thinking/doing) rather than preexisting as an (hypostatized) object, then the knowledge that the mind acquires or generates similarly cannot be meaningfully distinguished from that conduct. It is only the separation of the notions of mind from knowledge, and then of knowledge from conduct, that provides the illusion of universal technical knowledge and therefore of the purported distinction between ends and means. Moreover, even if the instrumental mind of the rationalist *did* exist, Oakeshott says, it could give no coherent account of how choices about ends, or purposes, are made or of how rational (or indeed any) conduct is generated: "Activity springing from and governed by an independently premeditated purpose is impossible; the power of premeditating purpose, of formulating rules of conduct and standards of behaviour in advance of the conduct and activity itself, is not available to us. . . . To speak of such conduct as 'rational' conduct is meaningless because it is not conduct at all but only an emaciated shadow of conduct" (120).

Just as, for Dewey, *action* conveys the unitary idea that replaces the contrived dualism between thinking and doing, for Oakeshott, a similarly unitary conception of *conduct* replaces the parallel dualism between ends and means. The question arises, then, as to how such conduct—in particular, *rational* conduct—might accurately be depicted in the absence of the dualistic conception of human activity that construes "rationality" as the calculated adjustment of means, informed by technical knowledge, for achieving preconceived ends or purposes. What might it mean, in other words, to assert rationality as a quality that inheres in, is "internal" to, that activity (conduct) itself? Oakeshott's answer begins by noting that all human activity originates within "an already existing idiom of activity," which is to say, "a knowledge of how to behave appropriately in the circumstances" (121). Learning how to behave appropriately, how to perform the idiom's characteristic form of activity, can only be attained by actually practicing it, thereby gradually accumulating, and occasionally discarding, practical knowledge uniquely suited to the historically situated context at hand. Rational conduct, then, may be said to consist of "acting in such a way that the coherence of the idiom of activity to which the conduct belongs is preserved and possibly enhanced. This, of course, is something different from faithfulness to the principles or rules or purposes . . . of activity; principles, rules and purposes are mere abridgments of the coherence of the activity, and we may easily be faithful to them while losing touch with the activity itself" (122).

Perhaps the key insight provided by Oakeshott's ideas about rationality is that judgments concerning the degree of its presence or absence are more appropriately local, and thus informed by practical knowledge, than subject to instrumental determination in terms of universal rules, principles, or external criteria of correctness. My objective in the following section is to examine how this insight implicitly underwrites what I term a "process" conception of governance. Process theory, I will argue, replaces the standard narrative's traditional concern with effectiveness and efficiency with a primary concern for promoting collaborative interaction in public institutions, thus dissolving at a practical level the rationalist distinction between ends and means.

Process Theories of Governance and the Ends/Means Dualism

Collectively, the three works reviewed in this section suggest a conception of governance, organizing, and social interaction for which the rationalist distinction between ends and means is neither necessary nor illuminating. Owing to its double meaning, however, the label I have selected—the process approach (or process theory)—may provoke some misunderstanding that needs to be addressed early on. Rationalists typically construe *process* as a synonym for *procedure,* which in turn is virtually synonymous with *instrument* or *means,* thereby reinforcing their taken-for-granted distinction between ends and means. To rationalists, moreover, it is ends that embody the values from which moral or political purposes must derive, while processes, in view of their instrumental connotation, are concerned with the "factual" domain and are therefore morally indifferent about ends. Indeed, preoccupation with process (construed as procedure) issues may, to some rationalists, discourage appropriate concern with normative, or value, issues.

Process theorists are guided by a wholly different intuition about the meaning of the word. For them *process* connotes *interaction* and *relation,* in the context of which people form action commitments and in reference to which they make value judgments that are local and context-specific rather than general and abstract. Although some process theorists provisionally retain a nominal distinction between ends and means, Gregory Bateson's paraphrasing of Margaret Mead's warning about the dangers of taking that distinction too literally provides a helpful clue as to the direction of my argument.

> "We have learnt, in our cultural setting, to classify behavior into 'means' and 'ends' and if we go on defining ends as separate from means *and* apply the social sciences as crudely instrumental means, using the recipes of science to manipulate people, we shall arrive at a totalitarian rather than a democratic system of life." The solution which . . . [Mead] offers is that we look for the "direction," and "values" implicit in the means, rather than looking ahead to a blueprinted goal and thinking of this goal as justifying or not justifying manipulative means. We have to find the value of a planned act implicit in and simultaneous with the act itself, not separate from in the sense that the act would derive its value from reference to a future end or goal. (Bateson 1972, 160–61, emphasis in source)

The remainder of this section draws out some implications of the Bateson/ Mead paragraph for a process theory of organizing and governance.

Laurence Tribe and the "Fourth Discontinuity"

In his critique of rational policy analysis, Tribe argues that its key underlying assumption of instrumental rationality—that is, "*the selection of efficacious means to previously given ends*" (1973, 617, emphasis in source)—produces a deeply alienating "discontinuity" (his word for *dualism*) "between man and his machines . . . which must be bridged if man is to live in harmony with his tools, and hence with himself" (617).[4] Building upon Weber's (1954) classic distinction between *Zweckrational* (purposeful/instrumental rationality) and *Wertrational* (value rationality), Tribe derives from the latter a conception of "constitutive rationality" in which social processes, rather than being seen as isolated from value considerations, are acknowledged as shaping the value commitments embodied in policy preferences. By focusing exclusively on ends rather than on the social processes that generate those ends, rational policy analysis necessarily fails to appreciate how existing policies and institutions constitute people *as* citizens and thus determine how they come to prefer some policies over others.

> Even more fundamental, perhaps, than the tendency of the policy sciences to reduce complex structures and dwarf soft variables, has been their almost universal tendency to focus on "outcomes," "impacts," "end results," and the like, while largely ignoring—or relegating to the realm of politics—the questions of process that bear not on *where one ends up but on how one gets there*. . . . [I]n many cases it is the process itself that matters most to those who take part in it. By focusing all but exclusively on how to optimize some externally defined end state, policy-analytic methods distort thought, and sometimes action, to whatever extent process makes—or *ought* to make—an independent difference. (Tribe 1973, 630–31, emphasis in source)

Constitutive rationality requires, Tribe says, abandoning three interconnected assumptions of instrumental rationality on which mainstream policy analysis is based. The first is the conceptual separation of the choosing subject from the objects of his or her choices. Rational policy analysis assumes an already constituted (pre-formed) chooser who determines by autonomous acts of will the content of the latter. The choosing individual may, for example, be postulated to be a "utility maximizer," someone who conceives of the objects of his or her choices independently of any prior association with other choosers. This assumption necessarily fails in either of two ways: by ignoring how prior social choices (e.g., policies and accepted social practices) shape and alter the choosing individual, or by yielding a conception of choosers as people "profoundly isolated, sharing nothing truly personal and yet enduring with one another" (618). Constitutive rationality, by contrast, entails "a fluid and reciprocal notion of personal and communal identity and of the subject-object relationship in which the act shapes the actor no less than the actor chooses the act" (653–54). By dissolving the temporal distinction between means and ends—by regarding each of the dualism's moments as mutually creating the other—constitutive rationality thus seeks to dissolve the psychological and moral distance among citizens as makers of policy choices.

The second assumption of rational policy analysis is that choices about ends, in addition to preceding action, are necessarily subjective and arbitrary. Any evaluation either of the ends themselves or of the social processes that affect choices about them is thus beyond the scope of the rational policy analyst's concern. Instrumental rationality's separation of ends from means presupposes the radical separation of value issues from factual concerns, such that the former are taken as givens that in theory have been settled in advance of analysis by aggregating individual preferences through market or political mechanisms. Judgments about "how one gets there"—about how social and political processes shape both individual identity and communal values—are necessarily beyond the scope of rational policy analysis.

In discussing rational policy analysis's third assumption—"that of morally significant reason as necessarily universal to all of humanity and invariant through history" (653)—Tribe makes clear that constitutive rationality's alternative to the moral vacuity of subjective and arbitrary will is anything but Kantian. Just as his critique of the second assumption by implication distances him from the rationalist (Simon) wing of public administration's standard narrative, he also separates himself from those normativists of the standard narrative whose moral conception of governance is rooted in an appeal to universal, abstract reason. Rather (and dissolving yet another dualism), constitutive rationality promotes "a vision of human existence in which wanting and knowing—desire and reason—present integrated facets of a common reality rather than opposing poles of an inexorable dichotomy" (654). The combination of desire and reason—more prosaically, of feeling and thought—requires, moreover, a continuing process of negotiation in which thinking and doing, ends and means, and value and fact mutually inform and continually reconstitute one another. In constitutive rationality there are, and can be, no end results.

Alasdair MacIntyre and "Practices"

MacIntyre's (1984) critique of the ends/means logic of mainstream management theory closely parallels Tribe's critique of rational policy analysis. Like Tribe, MacIntyre also faults the two chief post-Enlightenment moral philosophies that underwrite modern institutions' efforts to justify particular policies and social practices. What Tribe depicts as the morally vacuous and isolated decision maker, MacIntyre describes as the product of "emotivism" (chiefly utilitarianism), a philosophy that conceives the individual as devoid of any moral compass. To the emotivist, morality is reducible to mere preference; and because individuals' preferences will vary, no common moral ground is possible for adjudicating conflicts that arise between them. MacIntyre also regards, as does Tribe, the Kantian appeal to abstract principles revealed by "universal reason" as similarly unsatisfactory. When put to the test, pairs of competing principles such as justice and survival, individual rights and universal obligations, and equality and liberty cannot resolve moral conflicts, because their premises are conceptually incommensurable. Moreover, any single principle, when applied to a moral or political controversy (e.g., abortion, affirmative action, capital punishment), can be used to defend with equal plausibility diametrically opposed positions. As a result, moral arguments that are supposed to be resolved by such principles are inevitably inconclusive and interminable.

MacIntyre claims that moral argument might actually produce agreement if it were instead grounded in a shared tradition of social practices that constitute citizens' identities and conceptions of morality. Much of his analysis (some of whose features I am not especially eager to defend) has been embraced by conservative communitarians and "virtue ethicists," and predictably decried not only by the two mainstream philosophical camps but also, though sometimes ambivalently, by more avant-garde (and typically left-leaning) poststructuralists (Mangham, 1995). Rather than commenting on the controversies surrounding Mac-

Intyre's broader contribution, I will limit my focus here to a single feature of his theory that bears directly upon dissolving the ends/means dualism, namely, his concept of practice.[5] Formally defined, a practice consists of "any coherent and complex form of socially established cooperative human activity through which goods internal to that form of activity are realized in the course of trying to achieve those standards of excellence which are appropriate to, and partially definitive of, that form of activity, with the result that human powers to achieve excellence, and human conceptions of the ends and goods involved, are systematically extended" (MacIntyre 1984, 187). The crucial term here is *internal good.* Paralleling Tribe's notion of constitutive rationality, for MacIntyre a good is internal insofar as it can be evaluated only in terms of the social processes, including the norms and "standards of excellence," that make it meaningful to those "practicers" who cooperatively produce it. "Where one ends up" and "how one gets there" are, if not one and the same, functionally inseparable. Each not only reinforces but also transforms the other. Ends, that is to say, are both produced by and, at the same time, alter the practices that generate them.

The notion of external goods, by contrast, presupposes a radical distinction between ends and means by regarding management processes as instruments for achieving pre-given, and typically authoritatively determined, purposes. From the standpoint of external goods, managing involves manipulating people's actions in order to achieve those purposes. Successful managers seldom resort to blatant coercion, although its implied threat hovers in the background. Armed, at least ideally, with scientifically validated principles and knowledge, managers manipulate (although they prefer "motivate") subordinates by offering them inducements and inspiring or cajoling them into compliant forms of behavior—all in an effort to achieve ends effectively and/or efficiently. The very coherence, but also the epistemologically suspect character, of the "problematic virtues" of effectiveness and efficiency presuppose the ends/means logic of external goods.

MacIntyre is skeptical, to say the least, about the scientific validity of the expertise that is supposed to enable managers to manipulate people effectively. In view of the severe limits to the predictive power of the social sciences reviewed in the previous chapter (several identified by MacIntyre himself), the most that managers can hope to achieve is a skillful impersonation of the manipulative expertise that the social sciences purport yet inevitably fail to provide. The best manager, he concludes (either dolefully or whimsically, it's hard to tell which), "is the best actor" (107).

Quite apart from whether managers *can* employ expertise (or its skillful impersonation) effectively, the more crucial question is whether to endorse an epistemology of organizing that regards effectiveness as a meta-criterion for assessing organizational performance. It might be claimed that MacIntyre's distinction between internal and external goods suggests that the ends/means logic of effectiveness may be appropriate for the latter but not for the former. Defining goods as external or internal, however, is itself a function of the epistemology of organizing, and of action more generally, that one already prefers. Goods are, intrinsically, neither external *nor* internal, but only "become" one or the other as a result of epistemological commitments that mirror, and in fact may influence, political choices about how to organize and structure authoritative relationships.

By accepting as given—rather than the product of an openly problematic political choice—the predominantly external character of goods, the standard narrative's commitment to an epistemology of ends/means logic would thus appear to qualify as ideological. The ideology of ends and means is clearly evident in the literatures of program evaluation/performance assessment, strategic management, and leadership (to mention just three staples of the standard narrative), in which analysts typically take for granted the factually and normatively settled character of ends' priority over process. What might otherwise be interpreted as the internal character of goods, and thus properly subject to evaluation from the standpoint of the social and organizational processes that produce them, are construed as regrettable yet persistent anomalies that impede rational analysis. They provide yet further evidence to the standard narrative's proponents of what Simon called the "limits" of rationality—unfortunate reminders of the need for analytic modesty—rather than of the need to reconsider their beliefs and assumptions.

The practical value of highlighting the ideological hegemony of the ends/means logic lies in its suggestion of a plausible diagnosis of "implementation" problems in public agencies as involving a collision of two competing vocabularies. The "official" vocabulary of external goods holds that ends, goals, and objectives provide prior and ostensibly stable standards against which administrators' actions can later be judged. By implication, the vocabulary of external goods conceives of practices as means to implement "programs," a word whose technicist connotation radically divorces substance (the ends to be attained) from process (the fabric of social relationships within which those ends might be deemed contextually appropriate).

The alternative vocabulary of internal goods, by contrast, would appear to capture more accurately both the "motivational" and "organizational learning" aspects of management practices. The notion of internal goods embodies the widely accepted maxim that people will be committed to achieving, as well as to making sensible adjustments to, courses of action in those contexts about which they have intimate knowledge and in which they are personally invested. From the standpoint of internal goods, the generic question is not "Is (or To what extent is) this program effective?"—as if the "program" were somehow constituted independently of the practices and commitments of those whose actions produce it. Rather, the generic question implied by the logic of internal goods might be stated as follows: "What actions and norms should we either embrace, alter, or discard in order to both realize our commitments to those whom we serve *and* assist us in further developing those 'standards of excellence' that constitute us, in this unique context, as public servants and citizens?"

In proposing the latter as the more sensible question to ask, I do not mean to suggest that the standard narrative's ends/means vocabulary of external goods should be eradicated (as if that were possible in any case). Rather, the presence of the alternative vocabulary of internal goods reveals an epistemological/political choice as to the preferred relation of those two vocabularies to one another. Selecting one of the vocabularies as prior, that is, would set the terms under which the other might, if cautiously, be resorted to on occasion as a practical expedient. That choice, however, is not simply about a preferred vocabulary but also one of deciding who should decide. If dissolving the dualism between ends and means implies that the *what* is inseparable from the *who,* then a consideration of who is (or ought to be) the *who* can no longer be deferred.

O. C. McSwite and "Collaborative Experimentation"

Toward the conclusion of *Legitimacy in Public Administration,* McSwite says that "an essential requirement for a theory's being considered fundamentally new is that it implies a restructuring of power relationships" (1997, 180). Dissolving the dualism between ends and means, by implication, cannot succeed without addressing squarely the question of who should determine "what to do next." To separate, as public administration's standard narrative does, the question of "what we should do" from the question of "who should decide" is tantamount to accepting the dualism between ends and means. The ends/means and what/who dualisms precisely parallel one another. Thus, although McSwite's pragmatic alternative of governance—a continually iterative and collaborative process of experimentation—finds some echo in Tribe's idea of constitutive rationality and in MacIntyre's notions of practices and internal goods, neither Tribe nor MacIntyre directly comes to terms with the import of that parallel.

Tribe skirts this issue in his (otherwise commendable) argument that questions of "how one gets there" and "where one ends up" are inseparable. In order to deal with the still-submerged issue of power relationships, however, Tribe's "process" question of *how* begs more explicit comment on *who* ought to participate in those processes. Because he directs his critique to methods of policy analysis rather than to administration and governance, his silence is perhaps pardonable. The silence on the part of MacIntyre, however, is more conspicuous owing to his direct concern with administration, for which the issue of citizen involvement—the "problematic who"—has long been prominent and controversial. In an earlier critique, McSwite (1995) concludes that despite the cogency and elegance of his argument, MacIntyre ultimately retreats to the sober judgments of "Men of Reason" for settling differences among citizens and, more broadly, for constituting practices. If this is what MacIntyre intends, then the initial promise of practices, as he describes them, for truly "internalizing" public goods cannot be successfully realized.

McSwite's conception of democracy as involving citizens in direct daily relationship with government grows out of their[6] pragmatist critique of public administration's "legitimacy project." That project, they suggest, was and continues to be misconceived, owing to its origin in the Federalists' victory in establishing America's form and philosophy of government, and in the subsequent acclaim of Woodrow Wilson's (1887) essay, published a century later, as the founding document of American public administration. McSwite's pragmatist alternative draws support from the (alas, losing) anti-Federalist view that governance should be founded in the related notions of communal association and public virtue, in contrast to the (winning) Federalist principle that government's proper role is to protect and, when necessary, manage the competition among private interests. The guiding Federalist principle is essentially instrumental inasmuch as interests are synonymous with preconceived ends (whether of individuals or of groups), which require later aggregation and protection by governmental means.

The (belated) influence of Wilson's essay advocating a science of administration stemmed chiefly from its compatibility with the Federalists' instrumental conception of government. "[Wilson's] idea of using techniques for good purposes has the effect of establishing not only the assumption that means and ends are separate but the assumption that purposes can be taken as givens, making their realization a matter of the correct use of instrumental power" (McSwite 1997, 149). Public goods are therefore, in MacIntyre's terms, necessarily external in the sense of existing prior to either their aggregation (which is what markets are for) *or* their programmatic implementation (which is why we have bureaucracies). Much of the current controversy within public administration regarding the relative merits of bureaucracies and markets—as in, for example, the debate between public administration traditionalists and proponents of the New Public Management—simply conceals their underlying agreement.[7] Both sides of that debate embrace an instrumental, ends/means conception of governance, and disagree only on the details concerning *which* means might more efficiently or effectively achieve political ends.

The belief that ends and means are separate is indispensable to the standard narrative's quest for legitimacy. Recalling the terminology introduced in chapter 1, the standard narrative's rationalist wing seeks to "split" politics, the arena in which public ends are "democratically" determined, from administration, which is supposed to implement the most effective and efficient means for their attainment. If splitting strategies could succeed, however, they would shield administration from having its legitimacy "*called into question at all.* By invoking the symbols of science and technique, Goodnow [Wilson's contemporary] was bootlegging into his argument the idea that because it was grounded in science, administration should be considered beyond controversy, or even inadvertent question. Administration, defined as scientifically based efficiency, provides the ultimate device for finessing the possibility of criticism or 'interference': criticism can only be about *what* is being done, not *how* it is being done—namely, efficiently" (McSwite 1997, 163–64, emphasis in source). The standard narrative's normativist wing, dubious about the likely success of splitting strategies, tries to reconcile the tensions between politics and administration and, by extension, between ends and means. Both sides agree, however, that politics and administration—democracy and effectiveness—may often oppose one another. As fundamentally different forms of activity, they are guided by different values, methods of analysis, and parochial interests. Where the rationalists finesse the legitimacy question by asserting that the political (the *what*) isn't their department, the normativists finesse it by eliding the distinction between reconciling administration *to* politics and reconciling it *with* politics, the former suggesting administration's subordination to politics, the latter connoting a negotiation between equals. The question of power relationships, and therefore of what "legitimacy" might really mean depending on how they are configured, is effectively sidestepped.

Returning to the "problematic who," the stances of both wings of the standard narrative on the question of *participation—citizen* participation as well as participative *management*—are predictably linked to their bifurcation of ends from means. In fact, little disagreement can be found within the standard narrative on either of these issues. Both wings, though with little evident enthusiasm, are willing to tolerate participative management practices so long as they are restricted to the means for effectively attaining political ends. Normativists (Mosher 1968), however, sometimes worry (and with good reason, as it turns out) that participative means might alter or undermine those ends, and thus recommend vigilance against that possibility.

From the standpoint of the standard narrative, citizen participation in the governance process is, again, tolerable if it is limited to decisions about political ends, but not about means. In order to have any concrete meaning in their daily lives, however, citizens' decisions about those ends require their active involvement in the processes—the means—through which ends are mutually created and accomplished, raising the (dangerous) possibility that those ends might thereby be transformed. The fluid and unpredictable nature of this kind of citizen involvement, then, serves to confuse and undermine the fundamental administrative aims of effective implementation and control. Two ways to prevent this sort of contamination of ends by means are, first, to manage citizens' participation carefully by creating formal "mechanisms" through which their voices may officially be "heard," and second, to keep citizens' participation in public discourse at a high enough level of abstraction (e.g., by encouraging talk about "values") that citizens' concrete, practical concerns remain unconsidered. If, predictably, citizens end up unhappy with either of these tactics, it only goes to show that "citizen participation just doesn't work"; and politicians and administrators can safely return to business as usual, still confident about the efficacy of their ends/means logic.

McSwite's pragmatist alternative addresses the issue of citizen involvement in governance (and by implication of participative management) by collapsing the philosophical oppositions that have traditionally underwritten the standard narrative's conception of public administration's legitimacy project. Extending the anti-Federalist principle of communal association through the ideas of early-twentieth-century pragmatists such as John Dewey (1976–83) and Herbert Croly (1963), McSwite's process alternative of collaborative action reveals the standard opposition between democratic participation and efficiency as misconceived.

> Whereas traditional [citizen] participation founders on the question of fitting means to ends, which demands that ends be defined and judged as "good" in both a moral and a practical sense, collaborative action, by denying the validity of abstractions, combines ends and means into the same question—"What do we want to do?"—addressed iteratively, continuously, and permanently. The question of efficiency [and, by extension, of effectiveness] is entirely finessed, since it is contained in the one summary question that is to be collectively addressed. Most important, the question of legitimacy is avoided completely because there is no agent acting on behalf of others. (McSwite 1997, 149–50)

Most striking about this brief paragraph is how many of the standard narrative's dualisms the idea of iterative, collaborative action dissolves. The ends/means dualism (and by implication the thinking/doing dualism) is dissolved by focusing entirely on the generic question of action: "What do we want to do?" Action simultaneously embodies "ends" and "means," rendering any distinction between them as retrospectively contrived. The problematic relation between "what" and "who" is dissolved by eliminating the distinction between principals and agents, because there are no longer agents or leaders to act—to decide about "what" or "how"—on citizens' behalf. Finally, the dualism between effectiveness/efficiency and democracy—the source of the standard narrative's legitimacy problem—is dissolved by regarding questions about the former as wholly internal (in a stronger sense of the word than MacIntyre perhaps intended) to the collaborative—which is to say, democratic—process. "Any procedure for experimentation that we decide to follow is, therefore, a matter of efficiency or convenience rather than a basis for coming to any authoritative conclusion independent of our collaborative dialogue" (133).

Governance and Vetoing Managerialism

It might seem that I have lost sight of a chief subject of this chapter—organizing—amid my later discussion of the traditionally "political" concerns of democracy, citizenship, legitimacy, and power. I have also yet to address what I identified in chapter 1 as the generic problem of organizing—managerialism—which requires at least brief comment once the ends/means dualism is dissolved and ineffectiveness and inefficiency are exposed as pseudoproblems. The link between organizing and politics becomes clearer if the latter is seen as simply a special case of the former, suggesting that any strong distinction between them has little if any theoretical or practical value. With a mixture of temerity and acuity, Frederick Thayer (1972) has claimed that organization theory is *the* "grand theory"; that is, organizing provides the starting point from which all social phenomena—political, economic, and cultural—historically derive. What we now think of as politics, for example, must have been preceded by (initially, micro-level) "patterned decision making practices," which might serve as a fair definition of organizing. Politics, to Thayer, refers to a particular type or refinement of what are, generically, organizational practices. Although political theory long predated organization theory as an academic pursuit (Aristotle wrote more than two thousand years before Weber, after all), the practices that these two fields focus chiefly upon originated in inverted order of their scholarly exposition.

The question of which of these two types of practices emerged first, or of which type is the more generic, however, is less important than noting how trivial are the differences in the core themes with which both bodies of theory are concerned. The distinction between politics and organizing as separate subjects of academic study may itself be a product of, and still appear tenable only in terms of, the legacy of the ends/means dualism—with politics the domain of ends and organizing the domain of means. Pragmatism's chief contribution to American public administration may lie in its challenging that distinction by insisting that democracy, citizenship, legitimacy, and power are as much "administrative" as "political" issues, or, and more to the point, that they are generic issues of governance.

The blending of the organizational and the political is especially evident in the writings of public administration's first and greatest pragmatist and process theorist, Mary Parker Follett (1918, 1924, 1940), whose chief contributions anticipate (and, in the case of McSwite, have directly influenced) much of the preceding discussion. The integration of "where one ends up" and "how one gets there" in Tribe's notion of constitutive rationality, for example, closely parallels Follett's belief that purposes emerge from social relationships and that these relationships, including the purposes they produce, in turn reconstitute and transform the people who participate in them. Allowing for some latitude in interpretation, MacIntyre's concept of practices echoes Follett's "law of the situation" (1940), in which both superiors and subordinates are internally guided by their shared experience rather than by externally sanctioned "performance evaluation" criteria. And at almost every turn one can detect traces of Follett in McSwite's proposal for iterative, collaborative experimentation: in, for example, her distrust of philosophical abstraction as opposed to the lived experience of workers and citizens; in her belief that the individual's freedom is realized *through* organized relation, not independent of it; in her unifying what others would regard as the distinct ideas of experimentation and collaboration; and in her conviction that democracy's principal task is to promote collective action within what she terms "socially valid" relationships (1924, 211).

Follett's management philosophy is at the same time her political philosophy; she assumed, in effect, no difference between the two. Whether its focus was vocational education, social work, labor relations, industrial management, or administering the League of Nations—irrespective, that is, of her scope or level of analysis—Follett's message was always consistent: that democracy in its best and truest sense has little if anything to do with perfecting the mechanisms of voting and representation, and everything to do with facilitating cooperative, experimental action. Opposing her conception of democracy is managerialism, which conceives of public administration's proper role instrumentally as "implementation," the paradoxical effect of which is to conceal the power of instrumental means to legitimate some, while discouraging other, kinds of social practices, and to determine the content of, not simply to achieve, public ends. Managerialism is not an espoused philosophy (no one actually calls him- or herself a "managerialist") but rather a cluster of taken-for-granted beliefs whose implicit ideology undermines the pragmatists' vision of democracy. Managerialism is, in a word, "irrational" in the ordinary sense of being neither sane nor sensible nor reasonable—and so it qualifies as an excellent candidate for intelligent veto.

5
Theory, Practice, and the Problem of Technicism

The distinction that American universities characteristically draw between academic disciplines and professional fields, and by implication between theoretical and practical (or applied) knowledge, has generated both ambivalence and defensiveness about public administration's proper designation. At the same time, however, that distinction has provided a convenient pretext for celebrating the field's virtual uniqueness as a subject of academic study. The ambivalence stems in part from public administration's variable location either in schools of business and management, in which case it is labeled a professional field, or in departments of political science, paradoxically designating it as an *applied* subfield within an academic discipline. Some universities, especially during the past two decades, have established freestanding schools of public administration or public affairs, often in league with public policy programs, thus finessing to some extent the profession/discipline distinction. Deciding whether public administration is a profession or a discipline is also a matter of some delicacy, owing to the loftier intellectual status (though often diluted by lower faculty salaries) that universities typically accord the latter. Worries about intellectual respectability thus often infect the subtext of discussions about where public administration and public policy properly fit within the academic structure.

In partial defiance of these conventional designations, public administration scholars, like their colleagues in urban planning and social work, often assert that the field is both a profession *and* an academic discipline: the former, owing to its commitment to training for professional practice; and the latter, because, like other disciplines, it can boast of a long tradition of scholarly theory and research. Having it both ways, moreover, need not be construed pejoratively as either ambivalence or academic gamesmanship, but more hopefully as a modern-day extension of Aristotle's ancient concern with the linkage between theory and practice. You can't appear much more respectable than citing Aristotle as an intellectual forebear, even if that connection might seem a bit strained by the passage of more than two millennia.

Despite the impressive intellectual lineage it occasionally claims, however, public administration has failed, or so I will argue in this chapter, to connect theory with practice in a coherent way, owing to its entrapment in the conceptual dualisms that ground its standard narrative. Drawing from insights of pragmatist and other scholars, I will explain how the dissolution of those dualisms reveals a radically different understanding of the relation of theory—or, more precisely, theorizing—to practice. Following the convention of previous chapters, the argument claims that the standard narrative's theory/practice dualism conceals what is in fact a unitary idea (expressed by the Greek word *praxis*), a generic pseudoproblem (uncertainty), and a problematic virtue (expertise), and it concludes by identifying the "real" problem (technicism) made evident by the dualism's dissolution.

Rationalism and the Instrumentalizing of Theory

On superficial inspection it might appear that public administration is already securely grounded in, at least loosely speaking, a pragmatic spirit honoring the practical value of theory. "Does this (or that) theory work?" is probably asked more often by the field's academics than by those in most other disciplines; and the maxim "There's nothing so practical as a good theory" has long been a staple of introductory lectures in MPA courses. Appearances, however, can be deceiving; both the question and the maxim, when examined more closely, take for granted the rationalist dualism between thinking and doing, thus dividing the enterprises of theory and practice to such a degree that their "integration"—that is, using theory as a practical guide to action—is precluded.

"Does this theory work?" might seem to be just the kind of question that pragmatists would ask, given their practical commitments and their aversion to abstract, metaphysical concerns. For academics to ask whether a theory works, however, is quite different from what it might reasonably mean for administrative and policy practitioners to ask whether a theory works. When it is assumed that the question of a theory's workability can mean the same thing to practitioners that it typically means to academics, theory is instrumentalized and the oft-noted gap between theorizing (thinking) and practice (doing) becomes unbridgeable. Miller and King concisely summarize the logic implicit in conflating the problems of the two groups in their description of "rationalistic theory," which,

> in its ideal, is composed of systematically related statements organized into lawlike generalizations. In this perspective, theory is made relevant to practice through the transfer of theoretical knowledge to practitioners who are expected to improve administrative effectiveness by applying such knowledge to practice. In other words, theorists "make" theory and then teach (transfer) it to practitioners who then, assuming they accept the theoretical notions, take it upon themselves to apply theory to practice. . . . The belief that government can play a positive role as the progenitor of progress, science, and reason led to an administrative apparatus of expert technicist administrators informed by the academy who are charged with generating the science and reason that guide administrators' expert actions. (1998, 45)

Miller and King are rightly dubious about the purported connection between rationalistic (or what I call instrumental) theory and the notion of administrative expertise; and my interpretation of their and others' reasons for skepticism about that connection comprises the central thrust of my argument in this chapter. The belief that social science theory can be applied instrumentally commits, I will contend, two related errors: first, it assumes a conception of theory that is problematic in terms of its own aims and standards of evaluation; and second, even if it is "successful" in the insulated world of academic research, particular theories that satisfy its requirements could be of little value in informing administrative practice or policy making. Clarifying the nature of these errors, then, serves to undermine the credibility of claims to administrative or policy-making expertise grounded on an instrumental conception of theory, opening the way for considering an alternative, pragmatist conception of the theory/practice relation grounded in the idea of praxis.

A preliminary indication of how these two errors are related can be inferred from the different meanings of the question "Does this theory work?" When a research economist, for example, asks whether one or another theory of rational choice works, his "practical" concern is only indirectly, if at all, with the consequences of later action predicated on the findings that the theory generates. Rather, his chief concern about the theory's workability is whether it can produce valid generalizations that enable successful predictions. That is, criteria of practicality are internal to the research enterprise, and judgments about the wisdom of policies or programs that might be enacted and implemented in the light of the theory's findings come later and are made by someone else. Setting aside for the moment the question of whether such generalizations are possible or likely, the meaning of the question to the economist is very different from its meaning to a public administrator who wants to know whether, say, a new "applied theory" of organizational development will work—that is, prove effective—in her organization. In this latter instance, judgments about the practical success of the theory in a particular action context cannot be separated from the personal commitments, interests, and talents of the administrator who "uses" it; nor can the theory's practical value be assessed independently from an account of how the cultural norms and political climate of her organization might affect the theory's workability. Theory (thinking) and practice (doing) are inextricably "fused" for the administrator contemplating a new organizational development strategy, unlike the case of the economist, for whom a theory's development and validation is logically distinct from its practical application. For the administrator, "Does (or will, or can) this organizational development theory work?" is precisely the wrong—and conspicuously *un*pragmatic—question to ask. Even to ask the question with any seriousness, in fact, virtually guarantees "its" (the theory's) failure. I will explain the reasons for this assertion later when I examine the related notions of theory's reification and the role that responsibility necessarily plays in determining its practical success.

Theories and Clocks

Before discussing why theory doesn't work "instrumentally" for practitioners—and why, therefore, expert knowledge cannot be derived from it for application in practical contexts—preliminary mention should be made of the paradoxes encountered by academics in evaluating the explanatory power, as opposed to the practical value, of their theories about human behavior. Expanding on Thorngate's (1976) "postulate of commensurate complexity," Weick (1979) illustrates how the three principal criteria typically used to evaluate such theories—generality, accuracy, and simplicity—work at cross-purposes with one another. Any two of the criteria can be satisfied, he says, but not the third.

To visualize the relation among generality, accuracy, and simplicity, Weick asks us to imagine a clock face in which the word *general* is located at twelve o'clock, *accurate* at four o'clock, and *simple* at eight o'clock. Three kinds of theories are thus suggested, each combining two of the criteria. What he calls "two o'clock theories" are both general and accurate, though far from simple, as with, for example, psychoanalytic theory, which is notoriously complex and difficult to understand, not to mention hard to apply. Case studies provide the most obvious example of "six o'clock theories," which are (or, if done well, can be) accurate and simple, but at the sacrifice of generality. Given the premium that empiricist social scientists typically place on general(izabil)ity, six o'clock theories rank lowest in their preference among the three kinds of theory, although they often concede that case studies may be useful supplements to the other two kinds. "Ten o'clock theories" (Weick's favorite) combine simplicity and generality, but at the expense of accuracy. Such theories are easy to understand and remember and are applicable across a wide variety of situations and contexts. Weick includes Hirschman's (1971) theory of "exit, voice, and loyalty" in this category, along with aphorisms, which Ravetz defines as "an expression of a deep personal understanding of [a theory's] . . . objects in a condensed and communicable form" (1971, 375). The accuracy of ten o'clock theories may often be quite low, however, owing to the numerous amendments and qualifications needed to compensate for their imprecision about particulars.

Of the three criteria, generality appears to be the one valued most highly by empiricist social scientists, who then "select" either accuracy (usually) or simplicity as their preferred "supporting" criterion. In contrast, practitioners, because they typically deal at the level of the particular, are (if they consider theory at all) likely to value generality least among the three criteria, preferring instead the combination of simplicity and accuracy that defines six o'clock theories. Already, the tensions between the two groups start to become apparent, owing to the differing interests that guide them. Those differing interests reappear in somewhat different guises when considering each criterion separately.

Accuracy and the Problem of Representation

The criterion of accuracy would appear to have at least two distinct meanings, which should not be confused with one another. One can either speak of a particular theory's ability to generate accurate *predictions,* or one can ask whether the theory provides an accurate image of the phenomena that it purports to *describe.* The predictive accuracy of theory (which is closely related to the criterion of generality) is the empiricist's "practical" test of its workability. In his classic essay "The Methodology of Positive Economics," for example, Milton Friedman (1953) urges that accurate prediction, rather than what he dismisses as unnecessary philosophical concerns about the "truthful" accuracy of a theory's description, is what really matters in evaluating it.

Because chapter 3 has already commented on the limits to the predictive power of social science research, I will focus here chiefly on the problematic character of theoretical claims to descriptive accuracy. Accuracy in this sense might be provisionally defined as the faithful representation, or mirroring, of observed phenomena. This definition seems reasonable enough, even innocuous, until one asks what, precisely, the "phenomena" consist of that one is trying to describe. Two quite different possibilities are suggested by the following question I pose to students during the first meeting of my doctoral seminar on organizational theory:

> Of the following two statements, which makes more sense to you?
> a) Some languages (which is what theories consist of) describe organizations more accurately than do other languages (other theories); the best theory, therefore, is the one that most accurately describes either a particular organization or organizations in general.
> b) Because organizations are *constituted* by languages, when we describe organizations, we are really using one kind of language (which we call a theory) to describe another kind of language, or set of language games or practices (which we call an organization).

Predictably, most students, at least initially, say that a) is the more sensible statement, not only because it matches closely their understanding of what theories and organizations *are,* but also because most of them aren't quite sure what b) means. They readily accept the idea that theories are languages (ways of talking), but they typically ascribe, in a commonsense way, an ontological status to organizations that is separate from either the formal theoretical or everyday languages they and others use to describe them. Organizations, the students assume, possess a nonlinguistic essence; and the function of language, theoretical or otherwise, is to describe their essence accurately. Using a professorial trick, I ask if any of the students has ever actually seen (or felt, heard, tasted, or smelled) an organization, in an effort to shake their confidence in statement a). Except for the more perverse among them, most concede, if grudgingly, that in fact they *haven't* seen one.

My question's preliminary purpose is to make students receptive to an interpretivist (Berger and Luckmann 1967; Silverman 1971) view of organizations, which regards social phenomena as products of language rather than as existing independently of language. From an interpretivist standpoint, organizations are languages no less than are theories. My longer-term purpose, however, is more subversive, namely, to make plausible the more radical notion, perhaps most influentially (in the United States) advanced by Richard Rorty (1979), that language does not and cannot describe, in the sense of faithfully mirroring or representing, *any* phenomena (or ideas or concepts) whatsoever, whether "socially constructed" or material. Owing to what the poststructuralists call the "arbitrariness of the sign," all that language can "describe" (refer to) is other language; and thus it cannot mirror—in the sense of providing possibly truthful (*non*arbitrary) descriptions of—anything. Thus, where the interpretivists sought merely to unseat structural functionalism from its position of undeserved prominence in twentieth-century sociology, Rorty's aim is somewhat grander: to expose the fallacy of the still-dominant Platonic philosophical tradition that conceives of the human mind's relation to language through the "metaphors of vision, correspondence, mapping, picturing, and representation" (1982, 164). An important consequence of Rorty's project is to reconfigure our understanding of the relation of theory to practice by showing how the dubious notion of descriptive accuracy—that is, the notion of objective truth—prevents rather than enables their connection.

Rorty labels his chief target of criticism the "ocular metaphor," which conceives of the human mind as a kind of mirror, an accident of intellectual history dating back to the ancient Greeks, without which "the notion of knowledge as accuracy of representation would not have suggested itself" (1979, 12). The ocular metaphor of language as a (if not *the*) means of accurate representation promises the possibility of "objective" knowledge, whose discovery and contemplation is therefore presumed to be logically and temporally separate from action.[1] The Platonic separation between "representing the world and coping with it" (11) simply expresses, in a slightly different way, the dualisms between thinking and doing and between theory and practice. To pragmatists like Rorty, the question of whether truth does or can exist—whether, in his later terminology (1989), "truth" is *found* or *made*—is inseparable from the question of whether knowledge precedes or, alternatively, is produced by action. Preferring the latter view, Rorty in virtually all of his writings treats the matter of truth whimsically and ironically in making his point that the word could well be dispensed with so that we might move on to more edifying subjects.

In view of the widespread attention paid to metaphors in social science theory during the past quarter century, it might at first appear that alternatives to the ocular metaphor could remedy the latter's effect of splitting knowledge and action, theory and practice. Sabatier (1999) and Allison (1971), among many others, depict metaphors as "lenses" through which analysts can observe indirectly what they cannot observe directly. The more metaphors one has available from which to choose, the less the likelihood of being misled by the "biases" implicit in one's preferred or sole metaphorical lens. According to this view, the expertise of practitioners could then be said to consist of, in addition to whatever repertoire of technical skills they might possess, the cognitive capacity to pick and choose among a variety of metaphorical lenses on the basis of which to define and solve problems. Indeed, it might be that some metaphors could prove more useful than others in connecting theory and practice, thus mitigating the problem that bothers Rorty.

It is doubtful, however, that Rorty would be satisfied in the least by such an approach, since it conceals rather than solves the problem he identifies. First, the problem is not *which* metaphorical lens, or lenses, that analysts or practitioners ought to choose, but with the metaphor of "lens" itself for understanding theory's function. In view of how people use actual lenses for everyday purposes (e.g., to improve their eyesight or to bring the heavens into closer view), the lens metaphor implies that particular theories might, by "refracting" the objects of analysis in a particular way, reveal essences or truths about the objects that have heretofore been obscured either by their inherent complexity or by distortions of them that other, inferior metaphorical lenses have produced.

The lens metaphor, however, rather than dissolving the subject/object dualism as Rorty recommends, retains the dualism and inserts an intermediary between its two elements. When the dualism is retained in this way, as Kochis (2005) notes, the metaphor of theories as lenses simply promises a more sophisticated, though still problematic, pathway to accurate (truthful) description. In order to make any judgment that one lens is better at this than another presupposes the ability of the analyst "to critique it from an objective point of view, that is, with no lenses or filters inhibiting the analysis" (35). But, if the analyst already possesses such an "objective" (*pre*metaphorical) point of view, it is hard to see what purpose could be served by using a metaphorical lens in the first place. Why not, in other words, just let the "brute facts" speak for themselves?

Simplicity

Most empiricists acknowledge, however, that there are no brute facts, that "facts" themselves always presuppose theories that constitute shared observations *as* facts. Thus their response to the preceding question might hold that social reality is so complex that metaphorical lenses may serve the practical purpose of simplifying reality in order to clarify, to bring into sharper relief, its essential aspects. But this response meets the same objection that Rorty lodges against the notion of representational accuracy. The ocular metaphor is still at work here. *Social* reality, because it is constituted by language (including, inevitably, metaphors themselves),[2] is intrinsically neither complex nor simple; rather, that reality appears (and thus becomes) simpler or more complex, depending on the features of the metaphors by and through which its members simultaneously constitute, perceive, and act, and according to the interests and beliefs of analysts who "observe" it. Moreover, members (insiders) and analysts (outsiders) may have widely differing practical interests, suggesting that simplification, even if both groups in principle regarded it as a virtue of theory, will have very different operational meanings to them. What might appear to the outsider/analyst to be an illuminating theoretical simplification might well appear to the insider/member as either beside the point or even paralyzing when he or she attempts to act in its light.

Quite apart from such varied operational meanings, simplicity may in many instances be precisely what the insider—the practitioner faced with the question of what to do next—does not need or want. As Weick has suggested, the impulse toward simplification itself, while helpful in some contexts, might be harmful in others. The removal of blockages to action *could* result, not from finding better ways, theoretical or otherwise, to simplify our understanding of a situation, but from deliberately complicating it. Practical suggestions implied by Weick's general admonition to "Complicate yourself!" (1979, 261) include, for example, "discrediting" standard operating procedures originally designed to simplify (by routinizing) organizational functioning, as former U.S. National Park Service director George Hartzog did in the 1960s when he ordered the burning of park superintendents' operating manuals. Randomizing (by, to cite one of Weick's examples, "reading" the cracks of dried caribou bones) is another good way to complicate through discrediting. Among its many benefits, randomizing can confuse competitors, it's fun to do, it introduces genuine novelty, and it requires no storage files. Chiefly, though, randomizing, much like spontaneous action informed by intuition, hunches, and experience, complicates situations in the sense of generating new information on the basis of which previously unimagined courses of action become apparent.

Generality

Like its companion virtues of accuracy and simplicity, generality (more technically, generalizability) is similarly linked to the representational ideal of the ocular metaphor such that the relation between theory and practice is instrumentalized. In the next section I will examine how the claim to administrative expertise critically depends upon this questionable notion. For the present, however, I will confine my focus to the limits of generality as an aspiration of empiricist theory and its inevitable disconnect from the standpoint of administrative practitioners.

In its strongest sense, *generality* refers to a theory's ability to reveal invariant, lawlike causal relations between variables. These lawlike relations are "generalizable" in the sense that they apply uniformly across all cases of the same class. In the social sciences, however, generalizability has taken on the softer meaning of statistical probability; that is, generality is always a matter of degree in the social sciences, owing either to their methodological imperfections or to the complexity or sheer perversity of their subject matter. The purportedly practical value of social science theories' having a high degree of generalizability is their ability to predict, even if imperfectly, either future or previously unobserved instances of human behavior.

Setting aside for the moment chapter 3's arguments about the doubtful possibility of a predictive social science, what would it mean to say that such theories, including the predictive statements and findings they might produce, could have practical value for the practitioner? If Weick is correct that the three virtues of theory cannot all be satisfied simultaneously, it would appear that generality (prediction) can be achieved only by sacrificing either accuracy or simplicity. Both simplicity and accuracy, from a practitioner's standpoint, involve features of a theory that appear relevant to the unique features of the action or knowledge projects that he or she pursues. The fit between the general claims of the theory and the specifics of the practitioner's particular context, however, will always be imperfect. General and simple (ten o'clock) theories, for example, will necessarily fail to describe accurately the complexities and subtleties of particular situations. The best one can hope for from such theories are, as MacIntyre (1984) has suggested, generalities that take the form of proverbs and folk maxims, a far cry from the lawlike generalizations originally promised by empiricist social science. And general and accurate (two o'clock) theories, owing to their complexity and difficulty of application, may fail to engage the practitioner's highly particularized and localized interests. Practitioners may well regard research findings of two o'clock theories as interesting by virtue of their suggesting clues as to what kinds of strategies formulated in their light might or might not work, but beyond this modest possibility they are unlikely to be much impressed with the virtue of theoretical generality, irrespective of whether it is coupled with simplicity or accuracy. Their indifference is likely to be especially pronounced when they experience what Rittel and Webber (1973), discussed in chapter 4, call "wicked" problems, that is, problems that are unique and contextual and whose very definitions presuppose particular rather than general solutions.

The criterion of generality suffers from the further liability of implicitly presupposing a static conception of knowledge, which is to say, a conception of knowledge as existing prior to and independent of action.

In contexts of practical action, however, relevant knowledge is necessarily not only idiosyncratic to a large degree but also continually altered and transformed by the actions of those engaged in those contexts, further accentuating mismatches between "local" knowledge and purportedly general knowledge. That is to say, the criterion of generality presupposes an epistemological dualism between thinking and doing (knowledge and action) whose first "moment" not only precedes but authoritatively determines its second moment.

The Problematic Virtue of Expertise

What I have referred to as an instrumental relation between theory and practice underwrites the notion of professional—and therefore politically neutral—expertise upon which the rationalists of public administration's standard narrative ground the field's claim to legitimacy. Hardly anyone now holds that the ideal of neutral expertise (or neutral competence) can be fully realized in practice; however, pragmatists, unlike rationalists, argue that that ideal is in principle unrealizable and, more importantly, that efforts to approximate it in practice misconceive the relation between theory and practice. Several assumptions follow about the theory/practice connection on which the rationalist conception of expertise is based.[3]

1. Expertise is a special form of generalized knowledge that has been validated by widely accepted systematic procedures. Experts are people who either possess generalized knowledge produced by such procedures, as in the case of expert practitioners, or are skilled in using the systematic procedures that produce such knowledge, as with expert analysts. Implied here, therefore, is a categorical (as well as an invidious) distinction between expert knowledge and knowledge based on "mere" opinion or experience.
2. As a foundation of expert knowledge, "theory," broadly speaking, provides the means for generalizing knowledge about cause/effect relations, which can lead to confidence in predicting its success when applied to future action contexts. That is, contexts of action are regarded as particular cases of the general.
3. Expert knowledge presupposes the dualism between thinking and doing inasmuch as the situations in which it is applied will not materially affect, or be affected by, the knowledge itself. Concomi-

tantly, experts who apply such theoretical knowledge of cause/effect relations are themselves "in theory" immune to the causal influences that such knowledge reveals. Their "objective" standpoint, conferred by training in systematic procedures of formulating and applying theoretical knowledge, provides them that immunity.

4. Theoretically grounded expert knowledge is in principle indifferent to the practical and political values or ends in whose service it is later applied. That is, the instrumental dualism between theory and practice presupposes the parallel dualisms between values and facts and between ends and means.

A careful reading of prior chapters should already have made clear some of the shortcomings of the rationalist ideal of expertise, while other of its limitations will become apparent later when it is explicitly counterposed against the pragmatist conception of the relation between theory and practice. My earlier critiques of the value/fact, thinking/doing, and ends/means dualisms provide some hint, however, as to what that pragmatist alternative might consist of, namely, an iterative and experimental (in Dewey's sense of the word)[4] approach in which the distinction between expert and lay judgment is collapsed and in which theory and practice are seen as mutually constitutive rather than instrumentally connected with one another (Snider 2000).

Owing to Dewey's influence, the pragmatist conception of theory's relation to practice is one in which experts are denied the privileged status as the principal creators—and arbiters of disputes about the validity—of knowledge whose practical use is certified in advance (Evans 2000). A chief impediment to a wider acceptance of the pragmatist conception of theory and practice (and indeed to pragmatism more generally) was the enormous influence of Simon's *Administrative Behavior* on public administration. As Snider explains:

> For though the field never embraced pragmatism, it had maintained throughout its early years a strong practitioner orientation. This continuing emphasis on practice gave the field at least a flavor of pragmatism in that it emphasized administrative experience. *Administrative Behavior* practically erased this vestige because it made the formation of theory the province of academicians inves-

> tigating value-free, factual administrative decision making. Thus, Simon reinforced not only the fact-value split but also the theory-practice split. Under Simon and, more generally, behavioralism, pragmatism in public administration had come to stand for precisely that which Peirce, James, and Dewey had opposed, namely, the separation of thought and action. (346–47)

Since the publication of *Administrative Behavior* in 1947, public administration's standard narrative has been often sharply divided over the question of what kind of expert knowledge properly commands respect as the field's primary source of legitimacy. Despite their undeniable differences, the two chief contending factions—the managerialists, following the Simon tradition, and the administrative legalists, represented chiefly by Lowi (1969), Rosenbloom (1983), Moe and Gilmour (1995) and, to a degree, Rohr (1986)—both assert claims to expertise setting them apart from nonexpert knowledge based on experience and intuition, or (and, for them, more importantly) knowledge guided by parochial or partisan ends. As we have already seen, the claim to managerial expertise founders on the spurious idea that social science is capable of producing the lawlike generalizations needed to ground that expertise. As MacIntyre (1984) has suggested, and by implication hoisting Simon on his own petard, the best that empirical social science can offer in the final analysis are folk proverbs of the sort that, ironically, Simon had disparagingly attributed to Gulick. Miller and King neatly summarize MacIntyre on this point, noting that "instead of scientifically managed social control, we have witnessed the dramatic reenactment of social control, an imitation of the real thing (in which the real thing is actually the imagined thing: expertise at management)" (1998, 45).

From a pragmatist standpoint, administrative legalists would appear to fare no better than the managerialists in their claims to privileged expertise. Richard Posner (in Menand 1997), a pragmatist scholar as well as a sitting judge for more than a quarter century, baldly asserts that "there is no such thing as 'legal reasoning.' Lawyers and judges answer legal questions through the use of simple logic and the various methods of practical reasoning that everyday thinkers use" (423). Rather than consisting of a set of formal concepts privy solely to members of the legal fraternity, the law is instead merely what judges say it is, "the scope of their license being limited only by the diffuse outer bounds of professional propriety and moral consensus" (421). Posner, it should be stressed, is anything but cynical in characterizing the law this way. Applying (general) legal rules to particular cases is always murky and ambiguous, a fact complicated by the presence of multiple, competing, and incommensurable legal as well as other principles relevant to those cases. Nor is he the first to proclaim such views, sharing, no doubt, in Justice Holmes's droll satisfaction of nearly a century ago in explaining to his colleagues on the Supreme Court how any legal principle they might identify could with equal plausibility be used to support *both* sides of whatever case lay before them (Menand 2001).

The Pseudoproblem of Uncertainty

Why should we want to have expertise, or want analysts and professional public servants to have it, in the first place? To what generic category of problems might expertise in its broadest connotation provide solutions? Or, to invert the question, in view of the preceding effort to demystify expertise as a unique and privileged form of knowledge, are we as either citizens, analysts, or professional public servants any worse off as a practical matter for having our illusions about it shattered? I hasten to note here that my critique of administrative, legal, and policy analytic expertise does not entail a blanket indictment of the notion of expertise itself or, in all cases, of instrumentalizing theory's relation to practice. In many fields—for example, medicine, dam construction, or elevator repair—biological and physical laws and processes may be sufficiently well known and stable that it seems fair to demand in advance a high degree of certainty about the consequences of applying expert technical knowledge to a clearly defined problem. Even for these fields, however, the distinction I am suggesting between "social" and "technical" practices should not be overdrawn. Through their own attitudes about illness, health, and their relationship with their physicians, for example, sick people may in myriad ways either perpetuate their illnesses or, alternatively, participate in curing them. Similarly, Mary Schmidt (1993) describes the importance of intuition in the profession of dam building in making sensible judgments about the best combination and positioning of cement, gravel, and water needed to prevent the catastrophic breakage of earthen dams. And readers of Colson Whitehead's (2000) fine novel *The Intuitionist* will recall that his "intuitionist" hero, Lila Mae Watson, chalked up a perfect record for elevator safety, a feat unmatched by any of her rival "empiricists." Technical problems, it seems, are seldom purely technical.

Instrumentalizing theory's relation to practice in administration and policy making, however, exacts a far greater cost than it does with respect to mainly technical tasks, for which intuition and experience may rightly be seen as supporting rather than primary considerations. It may indeed be sensible to demand a high degree of certainty about the consequences of applying technical knowledge; but it is altogether another matter when that same demand is made of knowledge about social processes such as administration and policy making. Rationalism's belief in an instrumental relation between theory and practice in matters of social conduct produces its implicit conception of the generic problem with which it must contend, namely, uncertainty. Indeed, if one regards doing (practice) as simply the servant of prior thought (theory), then the identification of uncertainty as a problem to be solved or mitigated does, it would seem, logically follow. If, for example, people *are* utility maximizers, then surely (especially if they are "fully rational") they would cherish valid theoretical knowledge in order to reduce, if not eliminate entirely, uncertainties about the consequences of their choices. Similarly, managers who believe in the myth of management as a form of social control will also be attracted to an instrumental conception of theory's relation to practice. Rationalist scholars and practitioners alike know, of course, that some uncertainty is an inevitable feature of social life, but they believe that its reduction to the fullest practical extent is a worthwhile pursuit.

For reasons already discussed, pragmatists harbor strong doubts about the possible success of rationalism's aspiration of reducing uncertainty. But more crucially, they are dismayed by the normative image of social life that such an aspiration implies. For pragmatists, the belief that uncertainty is the generic problem that social theory does or should address contradicts their own image of social life as consisting of the mutual and inevitably fluid creation of shared projects in which thinking and doing, ends and means, and thus theory and practice are fused with one another. Mutual commitment and action in the service of those projects therefore requires a commitment not simply to tolerating uncertainty, as the rationalists regretfully concede, but to actually embracing uncertainty as a vital principle of social existence. Embracing uncertainty means thinking, talking, and acting in a spirit of tentativeness and even permanent doubt as to what the future might hold, finding solace and indeed inspiration from the conviction that the processes of discourse and collaborative experimentation will reveal sensible and mutually fulfilling courses of action.

Against Theory

Early in this chapter I asserted that "Does this theory work?" is a conspicuously unpragmatic question to ask and that the maxim "There's nothing so practical as a good theory" is not only bad advice but is in fact incoherent on closer examination.[5] My misgivings about both the question and the maxim were prompted in part by reflecting on Weick's (1979) reason for titling his classic work of a quarter century ago *The Social Psychology of Organizing*. His choice of the gerund *organizing* was a pointed wordplay on the title of Katz and Kahn's (1966) *The Social Psychology of Organizations,* which for more than a decade preceding the publication of Weick's own book was widely regarded as the magnum opus of the then-dominant structural functionalist approach to organization theory. Weick preferred *organizing* over *organizations* because "Whenever people talk about organizations they are tempted to use lots of nouns, but these seem to impose a spurious stability on the settings being described. In the interest of better organizational understanding we should urge people to stamp out nouns. If students of organization become stingy in their use of nouns, generous in their use of verbs, and extravagant in their use of gerunds, then more attention would be paid to process and we'd learn about how to see it and manage it" (1979, 44). If, as Weick claims, the noun *organization* "impose[s] a spurious stability on the settings being described," consider the possibility that the noun *theory* functions in an analogous manner, namely, by being implicitly conceived as having intrinsic and stable properties, and thus value, independent of any human activity undertaken in its light. Such a conception has the consequence of instrumentalizing theory by reifying "it" as an object or tool, as when, for example, one speaks of theories as metaphorical lenses "crafted" by the theorist. As Kochis explains, reifying theory not only removes the theorist (or "theorizing subject") "from the activity to be studied . . . but removes the human from the intellectual enterprise in general. In short, theories do the theorizing and humans just use them. The 'lens' becomes the agent of theorizing" (2005, 40), thus concealing the researcher's interests and biases.

It might appear, then, that a first step toward making theory truly practical for guiding conduct—for solving, as it were, the "theory/practice problem" of administration or governance—would involve conceiving of theory *non*instrumentally, as something other than a "tool" (or any other metaphor) that implicitly reifies the word. Such a strategy, however, somewhat misstates the problem. Recalling Dewey's epigraph with which this book began, the theory/practice problem should be "gotten over" rather than directly engaged, dissolved rather than solved. The instrumental connotation of *theory* inheres in the word's nominal form (the noun) itself rather than in particular metaphors that are sometimes used to depict it. That connotation, therefore, cannot be eliminated, at least entirely, so long as the noun is retained. The noun simply reinforces the tacit belief that some*thing* called a "theory" stands separate and apart from the purposes and actions of moral agents. That is, there can be no *de*reifying (or "deinstrumentalizing") of theory in administrative, policy, or any other form of social practice short of discarding, discrediting, or, at a minimum, discouraging the use of the word's nominal form. The pragmatist alternative of *praxis,* as I will later develop the idea, entails a dissolving of what might be called the "theory/agent dualism," a feat that can be accomplished by using instead the verb *theorize* and the gerund *theorizing.*

Readers already steeped in the pragmatist tradition should not be at all surprised at this suggestion (despite the fact that many, myself included among them, persist in the hard-to-break habit of talking about theory or theories). Skepticism about theory, as Rorty reminds us, can be traced back to the writings of pragmatism's founders: "As long as we see James or Dewey as having 'theories of truth' or 'theories of knowledge' or 'theories of morality' we shall get them wrong. We shall ignore their criticisms of the assumption that there ought to *be* theories about such matters" (1982, 160, emphasis in source). To these early pragmatists, theory seemed remote from practical discourse about action in the context of which truth, "theoretical" or otherwise, is created by *doing,* by engaging in action, rather than by observing passively and from afar. Theory's frequently alleged impracticality thus stems not chiefly from the (admittedly irritating) esoteric vocabularies in which it is often presented but from the disconnect of the aims and hidden normative agendas of those who create it, from the action contexts of those who are supposed to use or otherwise benefit from it. Repairing or reestablishing that connection, however, should not be seen as the main task at hand, as, for example, by urging theorists to become more sensitive, more attuned to the problematic situations that practitioners experience. This not only risks sacrificing the important critical function that those who call themselves theorists might perform, but, and more importantly, it still reserves to the theorist or outside analyst a prior and therefore privileged role of expert advice giver.

The chief difficulty with such expert advice as it bears on administration and policy is that it just doesn't work. Like MacIntyre's claim that management expertise is nothing more or less than a myth sustained by the masquerades that managers perform, administrative theorists and policy analysts participate in what might be called a "masquerade of legitimacy" by providing analysis and advice that, if not rejected or simply ignored, are invoked as justifications for what the manager or public official wanted to do anyway. If my calling this the "masquerade of legitimacy" seems overly cynical, it is not because of any cynicism about the personal motives of theorists, analysts, or practitioners; rather, the masquerade is a predictable outcome of the belief that something called objective knowledge—expertise—could in principle mirror the "real world" of policy making and administration and later be "applied" or "used" for practical purposes.

To say that knowledge cannot be objective or neutral means that "expert" knowledge conceals both judgments about value and implied prescriptions for action. This observation (by now rather commonplace among leftist critics), however, may nevertheless misrepresent the real but still-submerged issue by giving the false impression that it is experts who, by virtue of their possession of or ability to generate such expertise, wield inordinate though hidden political power. The notion of a masquerade, however, points toward a different conclusion, namely, the futility rather than the hidden power of expertise. Orion White has recently commented in this regard on the irony that an emerging acceptance of the "relative," as opposed to the objective, nature of knowledge has produced a powerful conservative effect by transferring decision-making power from experts back to officials (who, to be sure, never entirely lost it in the first place) in positions of political or bureaucratic authority.

> This conservative effect was to legitimate further the idea that policy cannot be based on knowledge, but must be based ultimately on the judgment of men in positions of power. In this fashion, academics and intellectuals are accorded a role in the world

> of affairs, and are thus placated, but it is a role that is only apparently meaningful. In fact, because all knowledge is now seen as paradigmatically biased [and thus inherently "relativized"], it cannot be trusted and instead the personal judgment of leaders must be the final arbiter of policy. Intellectuals and academics are thus neutralized. Over time, such a system of policy setting induces those who create knowledge to do so with less and less concern for its "objective validity" and more and more openly adhere to the methods of knowledge in form only, following instead the more substantive lead set by those with money or power. (This I take to be a pretty close description of what is already going on, as the role knowledge plays in policy is as fodder for interest-laden debate, and it is difficult to find policy that is set clearly on the basis of knowledge.) (White to author, September 10, 2004)

White's comment points toward what I earlier referred to, but did not fully explain, as the real but submerged issue that the "theory/practice problem" represents. I argued in chapter 4 that the ends/means dualism merely disguises what I called the "who/what" dualism, which implies the dubious separation of *what* should be decided from *who* should decide it. My argument held that answering the question of who should decide—that is, including those who, on an ongoing basis, are most directly affected by the consequences of decisions—obviated the need for general, a priori, and authoritative criteria (chiefly, effectiveness and efficiency) for determining the efficacy of the what. Criteria, if any are needed, should emerge on a situational basis from action contexts as defined by those most directly involved in and affected by them.

By extension, if theorizing (as yet still undefined) can be seen as a way of thinking to inform and provide alternative perspectives on contexts of practical action, then the relevant, and closely related, questions would appear to be, first, "Who should theorize?" and, second, "What might 'theorizing' mean or entail in a *non*instrumental sense?" The answer to the first question is essentially identical to that provided in chapter 4, namely, that the thinkers (theorizers) should be the doers (practicers), including both citizens and administrators, who are most directly engaged in action projects. This answer should not be interpreted, however, as simply an egalitarian judgment, as a sort of power-to-the-people moral injunction; instead, it should be understood as following directly from my earlier claim that theory is almost inevitably reified when the word is used in its nominal form. In and of themselves, that is, theories are and can be neither practical nor impractical; rather, "theoretical" insights are *made* practical (or not), and thus rendered as "true" (or not), through practitioners' and citizens' morally committed actions, through their acceptance of responsibility for the consequences of actions that are informed or inspired by those insights (White 1973).

From this it seems fair to conclude that although theory and practice cannot be connected in the instrumental sense of being "applied" or "used" (the assertion itself, in fact, is incoherent), *theorizing* and *practicing,* as mutually constitutive activities, can be thought of as inherently unified or fused. The distinction suggested here might initially appear either obscure or overly precious, but it bears directly upon what Knapp and Michaels (1997) describe as the impossible task that theory (construed, as I understand their argument, in its nominal form) presumes to undertake.[6]

> The theoretical impulse . . . always involves the attempt to separate things that should not be separated: on the ontological side, meaning from intention, language from speech acts; on the epistemological side, knowledge from true belief. Our point has been that the separated terms are in fact inseparable. It is tempting to end by saying that theory and practice too are inseparable. But this would be a mistake. Not because theory and practice (unlike the other terms) really are separate but because theory is nothing else but the attempt to escape practice. Meaning is just another name for expressed intention, knowledge just another name for true belief, but theory is not just another name for practice. It is the name for all the ways people have tried to stand outside practice in order to govern practice from without. Our thesis has been that no one can reach a position outside practice, that theorists should stop trying, and that the theoretical enterprise should therefore come to an end. (380)

What I take Knapp and Michaels to mean by theory's attempt to "escape practice" is that theory, in its nominal form, falsely implies, even promises, the possibility of an objective accounting of the social world that is separate and distinct from—and thus "outside"—its ongoing production by moral agents. If the theoretical aspiration of objectivity could be achieved, then the practices of those agents (including their own "theorizing" activities) in creating, sustaining, and transforming the social world would be revealed as purely illusory, as mere epiphenomena produced by determinate, causal forces knowable only by theorists. Moreover, *as* outsiders, theorists, as well as other experts knowledgeable about those causal forces that theorists seek to discover, are themselves presumably immune to their influence, a necessary precondition of theory's subsequent instrumental application. If, however, Knapp and Michaels are right about the futility of the "theory enterprise," then the variant of it that has informed public administration's final exam for the past seventy years provides a dubious starting point for ever answering its sole question successfully. The rationalist ideal of management or policy expertise requires that theorists as well as practitioners "stand outside" practice rather than (or before) engaging in it. Theory and practice cannot be "connected," however, because the very distinction drawn between them presumes their instrumental rather than mutually constitutive relation.

Pragmatism, Praxis, and Technicism

What practical benefits might dissolving the theory/practice dualism—that is, viewing the activities of theorizing and practicing as mutually constitutive—provide for professional theorists and practitioners? One such benefit is to demystify theorizing (as well as *theory,* on the assumption that the word's nominal form will persist) by revealing it as a way of thinking and doing in which everyone, to some degree and in some form, already engages. As we saw with Posner's claim that what passes for "legal reasoning" is no different from the everyday logic that everyone uses, so too there is no such thing as "theoretical reasoning" as a distinctive and superior form of thinking performed from a standpoint outside practice, and therefore free of normative commitments and practical interests. Normative judgments about ends and social processes, even if partially concealed, always drive the activity of theorizing. As C. I. Lewis summarizes the pragmatist view of the matter, "all judgements are implicitly judgements of value, and that, as there can be ultimately no valid distinction of theoretical from practical, so there can be no final separation of questions of truth of any kind from questions of justifiable ends of action" (qtd. in D. J. Wilson 1995, 135).

Those (including the present author) who call themselves theorists would therefore be obliged to come clean, insofar as they are able, about what their interests and normative inclinations are. Especially those who regard their intellectual orientation as chiefly "critical" would have to concede that criticism cannot issue from an objective point of view; "objective criticism" is a contradiction in terms. To do criticism, rather, is to engage *in* or *with* practice from a somewhat eccentric, though provisional, point of view, in the hope of saying something novel or interesting that might prompt practitioners, citizens, and other theorists to rethink some of their taken-for-granted beliefs (Foucault 2000). All three groups thus might consider adopting White and McSwain's epistemological principle—that "Something is true to the extent that it is interesting" (1983, 298)—in order to reduce the arrogance that can accompany the pose of objectivity. A salutary side effect of taking such an epistemology seriously might be to revive for academic theorists the role of public intellectual, a role steadily relinquished as empiricism began to dominate the social sciences a half century ago.

Praxis is commonly taken to mean "theoretically informed practice," or, still more succinctly, "practical theorizing." Although various refinements of this general meaning could be added, I will not provide much in the way of definitional precision, nor will I discuss the word's historical origin and subsequent theoretical development.[7] Rather, I see the word as useful, in part owing to the looseness of its connotation, for subsuming an already abundant supply of insights about practical theorizing for administrative and policy practitioners. Practical theorizing—a "praxiological" attitude, to use a fancier term—would start with what Schön has described as the practitioner's willingness to engage in "reflective conversation with the situation" (1983, 165). Miller and King cite Schön in support of their own view that theory, or what I prefer to term *theorizing*, "amounts to potential action under consideration" in which practitioners perform the role of "social action theorists" (1998, 54). Also consistent with this general notion of praxis is Kochis's contention that "theorizing (the verb) is an ongoing activity in which the human mind constructs a 'social reality' in an interactive way, constantly modifying both the theorizing and the 'reality' in the process" (2005, 39).

Practical theorizing might be further condensed by defining it as *thinking differently from how one usually thinks*, or, to invoke somewhat reluctantly a currently overused idiom, as "thinking outside the box." This definition oversimplifies what I am getting at, but it has the virtue of capturing the idea's essential ordinariness. Although practical theorizing would appear in principle to be simple and ordinary, it is nevertheless, judging from my own experience as a teacher, extremely difficult to render meaningful to many public administration students at both the master's and doctoral levels. Their typical (and, to me, discouraging) reaction to McSwite's "Theory Competency for MPA-Educated Practitioners" serves the dual purposes of illustrating what practical theorizing might involve as well as explaining why what I label *technicism* poses the "real," or generic, problem that needs to be confronted once the theory/practice dualism has, in concept, been dissolved.

McSwite (2001, 112–13) begins by defining practical theorizing as "a kind of systematic reflection and analysis . . . [that enables] richness of perspective, flexibility of attention, and modesty." Six dimensions illustrate what is involved in such analysis: (1) an inclination to look for hidden "linkages and interconnections" among seemingly unrelated events or phenomena; (2) a "structuralist attitude . . . [consisting of] the ability to search out and understand the underlying codes that govern situations"; (3) an awareness of the "social fields of interpersonal energy" in organizations and groups, and being able to maintain a "nonanxious presence" within those social fields; (4) looking, at least mainly, "for 'general causes' represented by the characteristics of the organizational system rather than the 'specific causes' represented by the people who make up the workforce"; (5) thinking dialectically and paradoxically, that is, being aware "that actions will always tend to have an effect or effects that neutralize, overturn, or deny the original purpose of the positive action"; and (6) given the inherent limits on what one can understand, being tentative and experimental in deciding and acting.

I should preface my discussion of students' typical reactions to McSwite's article by noting, first, that it is very short (only four pages), it provides clear examples to illustrate the six dimensions, and its quite minimal "theoretical" terminology is explained in language that lay readers should easily grasp. Still, the article does require readers to think counterintuitively, to look "beneath the surface" rather than "at" it, to set aside some old habits of observation, and to think *more* abstractly and *less* concretely. Moreover, because many of the students are pre-service, they often lack the kind of work experience in large organizations that may be needed to identify readily with the points the article raises.

When, as often happens, students "just don't get," or resist getting, the article's message, more appears to be involved than simply the intellectual disorientation they might experience when reading it. Sometimes they sidestep this problem by "glossing" the article's message as little more than a recommendation to "look at the big picture," or they miss the point entirely by construing its message as a preachment that learning the content of particular theories is somehow good for them. And some even claim that the article is "too theoretical," although its title clearly indicates that theory itself is the principal topic. To be fair, the article is, in perhaps several senses, difficult, but no more difficult, surely, than multiple-regression analysis or the perverse logic of the null hypothesis, which students are required to learn in their statistics course. Students might find statistics *hard* to master, but they seldom *resist* mastering it, accepting whatever difficulties they might experience as *their* problem rather than the professor's, unless of course he or she is utterly incompetent.

The chief difference between finding statistics hard to master and resisting theory, it seems, is that asking students to think theoretically, even in the practical sense that McSwite describes, profoundly violates an unstated and not fully conscious expectation that what they learn should provide them with a feeling of certainty about, and ultimately enable them to control, the situations they will later confront as administrators. Because theory and theorizing, however, destabilize their thinking about organizations—and therefore promise to destabilize the very situations in which they will later act—students are asked in effect to trade the illusion of possible certainty (or more precisely the possibility of reducing *un*certainty) for a form of knowing that is inherently uncertain, relativized, and contingent.

A more important, though related, difference between technical knowledge and theorizing is that the latter dissolves the distinction between knowing and acting, whereas the former sustains it. From the standpoint of practical theorizing, uncertainty is not chiefly an empirically certifiable feature of a world "out there" but is instead a product of dissolving the distance between oneself and that world, of seeing oneself and others as mutually constituting and reconstituting each other in radically unpredictable, uncertain ways. Practical theorizing engages the individual *in* the world, committing him or her to let the chips fall where they may, so to speak, rather than seeking safety in the emotional distance provided by what the philosopher William Barrett (1978) calls the "illusion of technique." Practical theorizing, then, accepts the idea that knowledge is irreducibly personal because it cannot in the final analysis be separated from the actor's responsibility for the consequences of acting upon it.

To mistake the personal and the practical for the technical—which is what I take the word *technicism*[8] to mean—is a morally dangerous illusion because it lodges responsibility, and thus the justification for action, outside the domain of the personal and the social. The quest for certainty, undertaken in the mistaken belief that *un*certainty is the generic problem with which social theory should contend, itself entails therefore an avoidance of the theorist's responsibility and a tacit invitation to practitioners to avoid theirs as well. The complaint, therefore, that this article or that book is "too theoretical" and thus insufficiently "practical" masks the real complaint that it fails to relieve the anxiety of accepting the responsibility that is part and parcel of coping emotionally with radical uncertainty. The technicist attitude, in mistaking the technical for the practical, thereby distorts the practical by divorcing it from the personal and the moral.

To claim that technicism is the generic problem revealed by dissolving the dualism between theorizing and practicing is not to suggest by any means that government or social institutions overall are caught in the dangerous grip of technical control, especially control by experts. Technicism is problematic, rather, by producing the illusion, dangerous in its own right, that "practice" conceived *as* technical control is "theoretically" possible and in principle a good thing. Technicist thinking is thus an avoidance—albeit a very costly and time-consuming avoidance—that prevents responsible and flexible engagement in the human experiment of governance.

6
Rewriting Public Administration's Final Exam

A rough measure of the reliance of public administration's standard narrative on dualisms for grounding its legitimacy project is their sheer number (a total of twenty-two by my retrospective count).[1] These dualisms are, to put it cautiously, intimately interconnected, although with perhaps greater accuracy one might insist more strongly that they entail restatements of one another. The separate exercises of dissolving them simply expose from differing angles the underlying unity of human action that John Dewey described a century ago. The dualisms' interconnectedness thus obviates the possible objection against dissolving any one of them on the ground that its dissolution would contradict the already secure acceptance of another. All dualisms commit the same basic errors and are thus dubious for the same reasons; dissolving one implies dissolving the lot.

A final issue, however, still needs to be addressed in order to anticipate the most strenuous objection that my argument is likely to provoke, namely, that the unitary conception of governance implied by the dissolving of these dualisms poses a serious challenge to—and indeed may directly violate—the unquestioned and unquestionable sovereignty of the People, whose collective will can only be expressed by and through their elected representatives. In order to stake a rightful claim of legitimacy, public administrators, as secondary agents, must faithfully re-represent the representations of the People's will initially articulated in law and policy by their primary, democratically elected agents. Whatever sympathies, therefore, that readers might have generated to this point for such notions as action research, collaborative experimentation, constitutive rationality, and praxis inevitably find their limit if and when the pragmatist conception of governance implied by them begins to run up against, or simply takes with insufficient seriousness, the sanctity of the popular sovereignty.

The remainder of this chapter directly addresses this objection. I acknowledged in chapter 1 that a unitary, pragmatist conception of governance challenges the standard narrative's beliefs concerning administration's accountability to politics, but I asserted that any tensions implied by that conception of governance with respect to the traditional authoritative relation between these two spheres should not be regarded as a *normative* problem. To be sure, the legal and otherwise official subordination of administration to politics often generates *practical* problems concerning compliance with political, legal, and bureaucratic edicts, which administrators flout or ignore at their peril; but to qualify as a grand normative, or legitimacy, problem, the practical issue of administrative accountability requires a more compelling justification. Specifically, the standard narrative would have to provide not simply defensible criteria and means for determining whether particular discretionary acts by public administrators either violate or, alternatively, faithfully represent the popular will; but, and more importantly, it would have to explain theoretically how that "will," if it existed, could in principle be represented. Such a justification, that is, would have to show, not just rhetorically assume, that the notion of the popular will can or could provide a coherent point of normative reference for judging whether this or that discretionary act either represents or contradicts its authentic expression. If the popular-will-to-be-represented is itself a theoretically problematic notion, however, then the issue of administrative discretion—that is, whether administrative judgments accurately reflect legislative intent or some other purported expression of the popular will—becomes secondary, if not entirely irrelevant, to the question of whether legislative intent, even if it were perfectly known, could in principle express the will of an entity, the People, whose very existence is in question.

I intend in this chapter to show that these requirements cannot be satisfied. My argument is not guided, I hasten to add, by an insouciant disregard for the virtues of civic duty, moral rectitude, and devotion to the public interest (which, for the record, I heartily affirm). Rather, my critique of the related notions of political representation and administrative accountability that ground the standard narrative's legitimacy project is motivated by the same deep skepticism about dualistic thinking that informs the arguments of earlier chapters. At issue is not any particular justification of public administration's normative legitimacy within a system of democratic governance, but instead the standard narrative's belief in the possibility of justification, and thus moral innocence, itself and its conception of democracy as a "means" of representation. In order to show, from a pragmatist vantage, why those beliefs are problematic, I need to introduce, and then dissolve, two more dualisms.

Two Variants of the "P/A" Dichotomy

The standard narrative's founding dualism—"Wilson's dichotomy"—comes in two variants, which are sometimes construed as more or less interchangeable: *politics*/administration and *policy*/administration. The two variants are interchangeable insofar as politics is equated with, or defined loosely as, the activity of policy *making*. I will argue later that politics, as a generic idea, need not be construed in so limited a fashion, that it is in fact a more protean term. Pragmatist conceptions of both politics and democracy, and thereby the unitary notion of governance they suggest, derive directly from initially inverting and then dissolving the conceptual dualisms implicit in both variants of the originating dichotomy. Policy, I will suggest, is properly regarded as a limited feature (in a sense, a regrettable necessity) of politics, in which "good" policy as a practical matter is provisional and experimental rather than a definitive and visionary expression of the popular will.

The first dualism, the policy variant, implies a conceptual distinction between the *general* (although occasionally the universal) and the *particular;* while the second, the politics variant, connotes the distinction between *expressing* and *executing.*[2] Examining the asymmetry, or logical disconnect, between these two dualisms helps in drawing out the implications of a pragmatist conception of governance (including both its "policy" *and* "administrative" dimensions) for citizens—the "problematic who" discussed in chapter 4.

Policy might with only minimal objection be defined as an authoritative and general course of government (but also corporate or institutional) action or conduct that subsumes, regulates, and guides the disposition of cases of a purportedly similar kind. An "informal policy," although not quite a contradiction in terms, nevertheless conveys the irony of constituting an exception to the rule. A "formal policy," there-

Table 6.1: The "P/A" Dichotomy and Its Dualisms

Variant of the Dichotomy	*Dualism*
Policy/Administration	General/Particular
Politics/Administration	Expressing/Executing

fore, is almost (though, again, not quite) a redundant term. This definition of policy appears flexible enough to absorb the commonplace insights that policy is invariably altered by the experience of implementing it and that policies (in the formal, authoritative sense) often consist of the codification of prior informal, but nevertheless generalized, practices.

Administration, by extension, involves the application of policy rules, regulations, or guidelines to particular cases "covered" by the policy. Policy application (or implementation) necessarily implies substantial uniformity in applying rules, because they are intended, after all, only for "authoritatively similar" cases. (In the absence of such similarity, the very idea of policy as general authoritative practice would therefore be nonsensical.) Shafritz and Russell's definition of public administration as "putting into practice legislative acts that represent the will of the people" (2003, 18) provides a typical contemporary example of such a view. Also worthy of mention at this point is the parallel, albeit an imperfect one, between the general/particular dualism and ends/means dualism discussed in chapter 4. The instrumental logic of ends and means is clearly implied in the distinction between policy as the domain of the general and administration as the domain of the particular; that is, administration is usually thought of as an instrumental means for achieving policy (political) ends. Ends/means logic, however, does not in itself necessarily presume the general/particular distinction, since it is possible to decide and act instrumentally entirely within the domain of the particular, and thus independently of "general" policy.

Turning now to the "politics" version of the "P/A" dichotomy, Redford (1969) has described the distinction between politics (as opposed to policy as I have defined it) and administration as consisting in the functional distinction between *expressing* (either the popular will or public ends) and *executing* (it or them). The expressing/executing dualism might at first glance seem to replicate almost precisely the general/

particular dualism that conceptually grounds the policy/administration dualism. I will argue, however, that politics, as the name for this expressive function, finds its generic form in policy as a generalized statement of public purpose. Administration, by combining the latter "moments" of both dualisms, would therefore appear to connote (though darkly) something like the "execution of particulars."

Thomas Catlaw and "The Fabrication of 'the People' "

Viewed separately, but especially when they are conflated, the two dualisms that ground the standard narrative's legitimacy project have produced a distinctive understanding of the generic problems with which the profession and the discipline must perennially contend, as well as of the overarching principles needed for guiding efforts to solve them. As in earlier chapters, I will clarify the "pseudo" character of those problem definitions and principles by dissolving their underlying dualisms; and, from the standpoint of the unitary ideas heretofore concealed by the dualisms, I will identify the repressed ideological issues thus exposed that constitute the principal challenges confronting public administration practitioners and academics. (Table 6.2 includes the latter portion of Table 1.1 as a capsule summary of this chapter's argument.) My argument is drawn chiefly from Thomas Catlaw's (2003) recent critique of the related notions of popular sovereignty, political representation, and what he terms "the fabrication of 'the People.' " The remainder of this section summarizes Catlaw's argument from the standpoint of, and with a view toward destabilizing and dissolving, both variants of the "P/A" dichotomy. My purpose is to make plausible a conception of democratic governance based on the inherently political character of administration, but in a form that is not hostage to the impossible and unnecessary requirements of justification that public administration's final exam takes as given.

The United States' more-than-two-century-old tradition of representative government, Catlaw says, has always taken for granted the "sovereignty of something 'out there' called 'the People' " (2003, 2), whose "universal" will it is government's ultimate purpose faithfully to mirror, or represent. Ever since Wilson's announcement of a dichotomy between politics and administration, debate has centered on whether, or the degree to which, public administrators can or should act as strictly

Table 6.2: Dualisms, Problematic Virtues, and Pseudoproblems of the "P/A" Dichotomy

Dualism	Problematic virtue implied by the dualism	Pseudoproblem produced by the dualism	Unitary activity/ idea concealed by the dualism	Problem revealed by dissolving the dualism
6. General (*Policy*)/ Particular (Administration)	Social equity (Fairness)	Inequality	Universal equality as "infinite difference"	Presupposition of sameness (Homogeneity)
7. Expression (*Politics*)/ Execution (Administration)	Representation	Threats to the popular sovereignty	Administration as "a politics of the subject"	The *myth* of representation

secondary agents (legal and/or technical "executors," so to speak) of that will, *or* whether, along with the people's elected representatives, they also play, and ought to play, a direct role in discerning, interpreting, and expressing its content. In accepting the analytical distinction between politics and administration, the rationalist faction of public administration's standard narrative brackets the executing function of administration from the representative function of politics. Insofar as such bracketing is possible as a practical matter, administration would not have to "concern itself with the status of the sovereign to whom . . . [it] is beholden" (Catlaw 2003, 2). Holding a contrary view are the idealists of the "unified sovereignty" movement (similar to the normativists of the standard narrative described in chapter 1). Unified theorists regard public administrat*ors,* in concert with elected political representatives, as primary agents in discerning the popular will, but they nevertheless differentiate between administration and politics as functional categories. However, for unified theorists, just as for rationalists, "the sovereignty of the People is asserted above [both] politics and administration" (17).[3]

Entailed in the idea of popular sovereignty are two closely related yet problematic beliefs on which public administration's legitimacy project depends. The first is the "presupposition of homogeneity" (or sameness), that is, the assumption that the People universally share identical, preconstituted ends.[4] The category of the People, however, requires another (and in this case, a directly opposing) category to designate those who are "constitutionally excluded" from membership among its ranks. "That is, the 'inside' is given content solely by virtue of some element being excluded" (8). This opposing category of the excluded consists of those who seek to define for themselves unique expressions of citizenship or personal development "outside"—that is, different from—the People's presumably universal identification of them. The question here is not an empirical one of whether citizens in fact either share or don't share these homogeneous identifications; rather, homogeneity is presupposed by the category of the People, and thus by the idea of the popular sovereignty itself.

This presupposition, however, produces "a dilemma because categories tend to enforce identifications that restrain both the production and recognition of difference by imposing a set of criteria through which judgments about inclusion are made" (7). Catlaw's target is not particular *types* of judgments—whether legal, technical, bureaucratic, or sober assessments of what the public interest might require—but instead the generic notion of authoritative judgment according to general criteria of correctness. Catlaw is not referring to the everyday exercise of what Vickers (1995), for example, calls the "art of judgment," the subjective sizing up of situations of the sort in which everyone engages. Rather, judgment in an authoritative sense requires stable and universally accepted standards of similarity in terms of which proposed exceptions—that is, those based on assertions of difference—are adjudicated. Thus, despite liberal democracy's avowed commitment to the toleration of individual differences, the popular sovereignty's presupposition of homogeneity ultimately takes priority as the People's trump card. Difference demands special justification, while homogeneity is granted, a priori, the benefit of the doubt. As with the conceptual dualism that underwrites the *policy*/administration variant of the "P/A" dichotomy, the general necessarily precedes the particular by providing the standards against which the People reluctantly consider(s) the always tenuous, contingent claims of difference. In administration, for example, the priority of the general over the particular informs the logic of managerial expertise (discussed in chapter 5), which judges particular cases against uniform criteria of positive knowledge. Local, idiosyncratic, and contextual knowledge is presumed to be suspect, and thereby subject to judgments about whether it conforms to universal tenets of correctness.

Readers might be tempted to interpret Catlaw's argument as summarized to this point as mainly affirming a liberal/pluralist conception of democratic politics that tips the balance between "collective" values (e.g., of order or security) and "individual" values (e.g., of liberty or maximizing individual utility) in favor of the latter. Such an interpretation would commit a serious error, for his project is far more radical than this. The power of the category of the People to "restrain the production and recognition of difference" is profoundly troublesome because it contradicts Catlaw's conviction that "*absolute difference* and not presupposed sameness . . . constitutes the basis for less violent, more cohesive social worlds" (8, emphasis in source). At stake are the very conceptions of politics and administration that, in the guise of simply representing a unitary popular will, in fact *constitute* citizens, and thus constitute their interests as well, so as to deny the legitimacy of meaningful differences between them.

In place of judgment, Catlaw proposes a conception of democratic governance committed to enabling *collaborative interaction,* which not only respects expressions of difference but positively enables them. The notion of representation, the second core belief grounding public administration's legitimacy project, impedes such collaboration to the point of effectively denying its practical possibility. Catlaw introduces representation, not as a straightforward empirical question of whether this or that system of governance does or doesn't accurately mirror the popular will, but as an idea whose underlying epistemology—or, more accurately, its belief *in* epistemology as a set of rules for judging the representational accuracy of knowledge claims—is itself disputable. He is therefore unconcerned with whether the U.S. system of government, for example, is less or more democratic—by faithfully mirroring the popular will—than other "representative" democracies (see Dahl 2002). Instead, his concern is with the assumptions about knowing and doing (the principal dualism dissolved in chapter 3) that the notion of representation takes for granted. The possibility of making positive *political* judgments about the accuracy of purported representations of the popular will presupposes what is most dubious, namely, the disguised ideological belief that nonarbitrary rules of knowledge can in principle adjudicate competing political claims. His political critique presupposes an epistemological critique.

Representation as Model and Copy

Catlaw's discussion of representation builds upon Rorty's (1979, 1982) critique (discussed in chapter 5) of the "ocular metaphor," which depicts the human mind as a kind of mirror. From the standpoint of this still-dominant Platonic conception of objective knowledge, the purpose of language is to "*re*-present" phenomena already present in nonlinguistic or prelinguistic form. The ocular metaphor of representation, Rorty says, thus bifurcates the activities of knowing and doing—"of representing the world and coping with it" (1979, 11)—leaving the false impression that objective, and therefore authoritative, knowledge precedes and may even determine the content of action. Catlaw extends Rorty's epistemological critique of representation as objectivity to a political critique of representation. "Representation," he begins, "entails a relationship of [an epistemological dualism between] model and copy. . . . That is, a model is posited that expresses a generality connected with the real or objectivity of the world. In representation's relation of model-copy, the relationship of a general to the particular, or more specifically, a general which grounds and forms the particular, is encountered. The particulars . . . are . . . manifestations of the general and are related to one another based upon their relationship to the general" (2003, 58–59). Politically, representation denies difference by conceiving of "social relations in terms of sameness, as representations of the model" (177), which means that "correct" action in dealing with particular cases is that which functionally replicates the model. "Incorrect" action, of which administrative discretion would seem to qualify as a paradigmatic case, therefore entails "a personal, subjective breakdown" (188). For reasons similar to those I proposed in chapter 1, the notion of "justifiable administrative discretion" is therefore paradoxical because *justification* connotes, in Catlaw's terminology, a *correspondence* between model and copy (the reconciling of the particular *to* the general), while *discretion* entails the very denial of that correspondence. Particular discretionary acts, therefore, might well be regarded as sensible on practical grounds, but they cannot, strictly speaking, be justified in the sense of satisfying the sterner requirements of "legitimacy" that the standard narrative's final exam assumes.

Political representation further presupposes that the objects to be represented—either the will of the People *or* their particular interests—already exist in preconstituted form. If this were true, it might indeed be sensible to think of politics and administration as mutually compatible means for, first, identifying what those objects "really" are and then achieving them efficiently and effectively. Such a suggestion, however, immediately encounters the objection that the category of the People itself, abetted by authoritative judgments based on the presupposition of homogeneity, shapes the constitution of interests in particular ways and prohibits their constitution in other ways. The presumed givenness of those interests would obviate the need for, and would in fact prevent, acts of collaboration through which citizens constitute and continually reconstitute them. "What is impeded in representation and reproduction," Catlaw says, "is the act of collaboration, which is fundamentally concerned with the generation of a solution in the situation rather than preserving the integrity of the model. . . . [T]he grounds for a universal political transformation that locates itself distinctively such that a new mode of governing and living itself might be postulated. The universal struggle is against not a model but the *very idea* of a model that authoritatively grounds the judgment of copies" (233–34, emphasis in source). Like Tribe's notion of "constitutive rationality" (reviewed in chapter 4), the "matter of how we shall live together" (1973, 231) necessarily precedes the ends-driven questions of what we ought to do. Rather than serving as a (manipulative) means for achieving already constituted ends, collaboration forms the matrix of social interaction within which difference, rather than homogeneity, is honored as the guiding presupposition of a radically new politics.

Administration as a "Politics of the Subject"

As I suggested earlier, the politics/administration variant of the "P/A" dichotomy presupposes the conceptual dualism between expression (as the generic function of politics) and execution (the generic function of administration). In performing *its* generic function, politics "expresses" by means of "representing" the content of the popular will in homogeneous terms, which administration then "executes" by making authoritative judgments in order to ensure that the disposition of particular cases conforms to uniform criteria of correctness. To be sure, actual politicians and administrators perform other roles as well and often violate these "ideal" (in Weber's sense of the word) descriptions of their generic functions. Because these functional descriptions flow directly from a "universal" conception of the People, however, any departures from them in actual practice pose possible threats to their purported sovereignty and thus, as anomalies, require special justification. "Micromanagement" by politicians and "arbitrary" acts of administrative discretion are frequently cited examples of such anomalies. Their pejorative labeling, in fact, is itself predicated on functionally distinguishing between politics and administration in terms of the expression/execution dualism.

Public administration's standard narrative has historically interpreted the widespread presence of these anomalies as evidence of the "breakdown" of the politics/administration dichotomy, while at the same time leaving intact its underlying conceptual dualism. What I have termed the standard narrative's chief problematic virtue of faithfully representing the popular will, and its chief pseudoproblem of guarding against threats to that will, both presuppose its homogeneous identification. By contrast, Catlaw's critique of representation and homogeneity suggests a far more radical rejection of the old dichotomy by first inverting and then dissolving the dualism between expression and execution. The key to that radical rejection is what Catlaw terms the "presupposition of infinite difference" (2003, 243).

Catlaw's reconception of politics and administration builds upon two related propositions. First, the expressive function of politics chiefly involves the processes by which citizens' interests are simultaneously constituted and acted upon, rather than the means by which they are represented and later executed. Second, in view of the impossibility of representation, and therefore in the absence of a homogeneous popular-will-to-be-represented, the constitutive function of politics necessarily assumes the a priori legitimacy of individual differences. That is to say, the constitution and expression of these differences are taken as the primary material of politics rather than judged as either more or less faithful "copies" of a prior and homogeneous "model" of the popular will. This presupposition of difference finds its expression (and its execution), moreover, at the level of the particular, the level of "administration," where constitutive acts of collaborative interaction can only occur. With quotation marks to signify their conventional meanings (and levels), "administration" thus *precedes* "politics"—thus inverting the conventional priority between them—in the sense that the particulars of social interaction precede later, and necessarily provisional, generalized statements of public purpose.

With the quotation marks removed, however, administration (as collaborative interaction) *is* politics—in Catlaw's phrase, "a politics of the subject"—in which the functional distinction between expressing and executing, and therefore between ends and means, is dissolved at the "administrative" level of the particular.[5] *To dissolve that functional distinction between ends and means is to dissolve the dichotomy—indeed, the very analytical distinction—between politics and administration.* The "expressive" function of politics is no longer conceived as that of representing either preconstituted interests or the popular will but rather as "the expansion of *subjective* capacities to engage and interact collaboratively with others" (241, emphasis in source). As a politics of the subject, then, administration "is not the execution or actualization of the representation" (247), as assumed by the epistemological dualism between model and copy, but is instead concerned with the processes by which the Good is constituted—that is, simultaneously expressed *and* executed—through collaborative interaction. The myth of representation itself, deeply ingrained both in the public consciousness and in mainstream political and administrative discourse, is therefore exposed as the repressed ideological barrier to the Good's ongoing constitution.

Universal Equality as "Infinite Difference"

If collaborative interaction dissolves the *politics*/administration dichotomy's dualism between expression and execution, then the general/particular dualism that grounds the *policy*/administration dichotomy is rendered similarly vulnerable. Conflating *politics* and *policy*—the standard narrative's assumption, that is, that the two variants of the "P/A" dichotomy are roughly interchangeable—by implication affirms the priority of the general over the particular. The preceding analysis, however, reveals two quite distinct conceptions of politics: first, a politics of *policy* (making), in which the general (policy) precedes the particular (administration); and, second, a politics of the *subject*, in which the priority between the general and the particular is inverted. The question, then, is which of these two conceptions of politics, along with the differing roles for public administrators they imply, ought to be granted primary status. Answering this question is vitally important because it determines how policy as a generic idea ought to be conceived and then integrated within a conception of democratic governance.

Having in effect already dissolved the dualism between expression and execution, Catlaw not surprisingly endorses the latter of these two conceptions of politics. If it is only at the level of the particular that a politics of the subject may be realized, then policy, along with the effective execution of programs mandated by it, can at most be accorded secondary or derivative status. In a politics of the subject, he says, "administrative action is not the execution or actualization of the representation but . . . [action] that reconfigures the matrix of the model itself at the level of the subject or subject-group. . . . The operation is not executive in any sense of carrying out, but is transformative. . . . by reconfigur[ing] the situational matrix within which Good is constituted. It cannot construe the 'successful' administrative program or act in terms of fulfilling some programmatic goal or target. . . . [P]ublic administration is [thus] not concerned with distribution, coordination or production of goods and services" (247). In a perfect world—that is to say, a world of governance in which a politics of the subject held exclusive sway—there would be no need for, indeed no possibility of, policies as generalized statements of public purpose.

Under the justifiably cautious expectation that the "real world" will neither soon nor fully accommodate this more radical conception of governance, those who support it will have to be content in the near term with achieving more modest aims. One such aim is to clarify a more practical and cautious way to think about policy. Rather than presuming to represent a positive, normative vision of the popular will, policy might be regarded as a "regrettable necessity," an always tentative expedient made necessary when the demands that a politics of the subject will surely prove to be overly burdensome.[6] I make such a concession with regret because decisions about the degree of its burdensomeness are, within the context of current governmental institutions, themselves "policy" decisions over which citizens, alas, can seldom exert much influence. Policy makers, those who *do* make such decisions, might do so with greater reluctance, however, if they understand that policy itself constitutes evidence of, as it were, a *failure* of politics rather than the principal instrument of its expression.

Policy's secondary status within a politics of the subject may account for Catlaw's refusal to consider public administration as being fundamentally about the distribution of goods and services, and thus concerned chiefly with the normative distributional principle of social equity embraced by some members (Frederickson 1997) of the standard narrative's normativist wing. The presupposition of difference that grounds a primary commitment to collaborative interaction means that any criteria for authoritatively judging how goods are to be distributed—even criteria such as equity and fairness—necessarily presuppose homogeneity at the expense of difference and are therefore problematic. In a politics of the subject, moreover, the Good is constituted through interaction and in always uniquely different and unpredictable ways, and therefore it cannot be "distributed," equitably or otherwise, as if it were a preconstituted entity. A politics based on the presupposition of difference must, in short, be about people's development, not about the things they get.

Because the general and the particular are virtually binary opposites, any possibility of dissolving the distinction between them, as I have attempted to do with respect to the other principal dualisms in this book, would appear to be absent in this final instance. A politics of the subject and a politics of policy making are committed, or so it would seem, to irreconcilably opposed positions as to the primary moment of the general/particular dualism. Readers would therefore have to choose one side or the other, with the author nudging them to invert rather than accept the conventional priority between them. If mainly for the aesthetic reason of hoping to sustain to the end the symmetry of my argument's architecture, however, I was on the alert for hints from Catlaw as to how the general/particular dualism might also be dissolved, and finally I found the solution (more or less) on his last page: "The core of democracy," he writes, "is infinite difference, for only infinite difference, which suspends representational judgment, can ground universal equality. Democratic equivalence has no measure" (2003, 249). To count this statement as implying the dissolution of the dualism, I have taken the minor liberty of construing *universal* as an emphatic synonym for *general*. If this is allowed, however, from the presupposition of infinite difference—of "radical particularity"—*equality* no longer risks being construed pejoratively as *sameness,* which the presupposition of homogeneity implies. Rather, infinite difference suggests a truly universal conception of equality that transcends any representational categories, which paradoxically both "constitutionally exclude" (designate as *un*-equal) members of *other* categories and reduce to sameness the interests of those who *are* included. Equality in this alternative sense presupposes a universal entitlement to be different, to trust the variable and idiosyncratic products of collaborative interaction, rather than adjusting to the uniform categories that policy and bureaucratic rules establish. It must be freely admitted that, in dissolving one set of problems, the presupposition of difference reveals and generates other problems of a practical nature that cannot be avoided or glossed over. As I will explain in the next section, however, these problems are more real and thus more tractable than the "theoretical" problems contrived in terms of the presupposition of homogeneity. Because that presupposition is so deeply entrenched in these categories, and thus taken for granted as an inevitable feature of them, it persists as the primary ideological and practical problem with which a politics of the subject will have to contend.

Conclusion

Introducing his edited volume of essays on the subject, Menand summarizes pragmatism as an account of how people think. This raises the obvious question of why anyone should want to read such an account; perhaps pragmatists believe there is something wrong with how people think, and that, if set straight about their failings, they could then learn to think in a new and better way. "But," Menand says, "pragmatists don't believe there is a problem with the way people think. They believe there is a problem with the way people think they think. They believe, in other words, that other accounts of the way people think are mistaken; they believe that these mistaken accounts are responsible for a large number of conceptual puzzles; and they believe that these puzzles, when they are not simply wasting the energy of the people who spend their time trying to 'solve' them, actually get in the way of our everyday efforts to cope with the world" (1997, xi). Following Menand's lead, I have attempted to show how standard ways of "thinking about how we think" about governing have produced a distinctive set of problems that defy solution. Trying to solve those problems—for example, trying to answer public administration's final exam question—has not only wasted intellectual energy but has hampered efforts to cope sensibly with other, more pressing concerns. The chief reason for that wasted effort lies in the misplaced and unstated assumption that practical problems require a prior theoretical basis from which to address and solve them.

The manner in which the standard narrative has traditionally thought about problems of governing has been crucially influenced by the conceptual categories it uses to distinguish among them. Especially when these categories are predicated upon the dualisms between value and fact, thinking and doing, ends and means, and theory and practice (or indeed any of the other dualisms discussed here), particular problems that are defined in terms of those categories remain permanently unsolvable. From a pragmatist point of view, public administration's legitimacy project is a "problematic problem" of precisely this sort. For pragmatists, *all* problems, in order to qualify *as* problems, necessarily entail practical concerns about "what we ought to do." Therefore, to characterize a particular problem as a practical one is quite superfluous, because there can be no opposing category or set of categories to differentiate practical problems from problems of other kinds. Just as there can be no freestanding normative (or value) problems that exist independently of action considerations, neither can there be freestanding theoretical problems that require resolution before action is taken. Recalling Gunnell's (1993) explanation of why "relativism" is a pseudoproblem invented by philosophers in order to mask their status anxiety, "theory," as a "second-order discourse," cannot set the terms for judging either the cogency of "first-order" problem definitions or the efficacy of action taken in their light. (Practical) problems do not admit theoretical solutions. The standard narrative's assumption that administrative discretion requires or admits a prior theoretical justification makes its final exam question unanswerable.

In formulating that question, I posed the standard narrative's legitimacy problem as the normative (theoretical) requirement to justify administrative discretion from the standpoint of democratic principles, and then to defend the use of administrative expertise as a valid instrument for its exercise. As I have already suggested, however, the question imposes a paradoxical, self-contradictory requirement. If to justify means to reconcile particular decisions in terms of general rules of correctness, and if discretion means making exceptions to those rules, then "justifiable discretion" is a contradiction in terms. Particular acts of administrative discretion are, and no doubt will continue to be, contestable on legal, bureaucratic, or other grounds, but their resolution and adjudication are practical matters, not theoretical ones. Inverting and then dissolving the dualisms of the standard narrative, moreover, not only renders the issue of administrative discretion immune to the kind of justification that the final exam question demands but also reveals as beside the point the discipline's long-standing theoretical preoccupation with it. The political and legal subordination of administration to politics is simply a fact of life rather than an embodiment of high principle in terms of which administrative discretion has to be reconciled. Administrative discretion is here to stay, made necessary, among other reasons, by the inevitable mismatches between politically authoritative "models" (problematic in their own right) and the imperfections of administrative "copies."

Public administration's historical claim that its legitimacy depends on its unique expertise founders on the dubious belief that those imperfections in principle may and should be eradicated. In a politics of the subject, however, there is no administrative expertise qua administrative expertise.[7] (Nor should anyone be surprised or alarmed by this assertion. Real-life administrators are, after all, often described as experienced, wise, or flexible, and sometimes as rigid, authoritarian, or even clueless; but I have yet to read or hear of an "expert administrator." Eyebrows would no doubt rise reflexively at the suggestion.) By connotation, expertise, as an ostensibly practical form of objective knowledge, adjusts particulars to the general (copies to models) in the expectation of reducing the uncertainties produced by the former's "failure" to correspond to the latter. By thriving upon rather than suppressing difference, however, collaborative interaction forsakes the rationalists' aspiration of reducing uncertainty and instead embraces it. No longer armed with its traditional claim to expertise, "A public administration as a politics of the subject," Catlaw concludes with a flourish, "knows nothing. It is not a practice constructed upon the foundation of knowledge-based authoritative judgment or its possibility. . . . Administration as a politics of the subject . . . proposes a politics that is not based on any positive knowledge at all" (2003, 247–48).

Dwight Waldo (1968) was once rebuked by a colleague (V. Ostrom 1974) for expressing more mildly much the same view when he proposed that although public administration is not a profession, it ought to *act* like one. Ever sensitive to nuances of language, Waldo knew, as his critic evidently did not, that *profession* and *professional* have multiple and opposing connotations. As a social process rather than a technical activity, administration, he held, defies designation as a profession that claims to possess a unique kind of knowledge. Moreover, if "all professions" (as once, in conversation, he approvingly quoted George Bernard Shaw) are indeed "conspiracies against the laity," such a status is hardly one to which public administration ought to aspire. Waldo also realized, however, that *professional* (as an adjective) carried the positive connotations of *conscientious* and *dedicated* and served therefore as a fair antonym for *venal* and *self-serving.* At least in this sense, both pragmatists and contributors to the field's standard narrative could agree that acting "professionally" is a good idea.

If there is no positive knowledge for public administrators to learn, nor any for academics to discover and teach them, what *should* administrators learn and master? Important as this question is in view of the critique of expertise presented here, it can nevertheless be posed only as a subquestion within a new, rewritten examination that is more broadly cast. Among the features of the new exam are, first, that it is far briefer than its predecessor (albeit still multifaceted), coupled with the expectation that it can admit no single or conclusive answer. As a "process" question, it achieves importance from continually being asked, suggesting that any answers to it would have to be regarded as provisional. Even the question itself invites ongoing revision, and for this reason it cannot accurately be termed a *final* exam question. Second, because it would not impose a requirement of theoretical justification, it is self-evidently a *practical* question, which no one, including academic theorists, can claim a privileged standpoint from which to answer it. Everyone is entitled to an opinion.

The question's initial form is not restricted to administrative concerns, or even to governance more broadly, but is instead a generic *public* question. At its most general level, the public form of the question might be posed as "How shall we live together?" while at the level of the particular it asks: "What should we do next?" In both its general and particular variants, the question is distinctively pragmatist by virtue of its implicitly dissolving the dualisms that inform the standard narrative's legitimacy question.[8] The new question is obviously normative, but the answers it asks for cannot be found—much less justified—by appeal to or analysis in terms of a priori values, principles, or other abstract criteria; instead, it can only be answered through reference to the concrete "factual" contexts in which administrators and citizens become morally invested, though on occasion committed to contest. By focusing on courses of action and ways of relating, the question also dissolves the dualisms between thinking and doing and between ends and means. Ends, goals, purposes, or objectives are not presumed to precede action; instead, they are formed and continually re-formed through social interaction, through doing. The question, in other words, is not an instrumental one that invites, at least chiefly, programmatic answers and solutions. Finally, the new question undermines the standard narrative's dualism between theory and practice because it demands engagement, albeit *critical* engagement, by academics ("theorists") in practical problems of action as experienced by the people—citizens and administrators—whose lives are affected by them. There can be no research questions that are not, by some plausible interpretation, also public, and therefore practical, questions.

In then addressing directly the subject of governance, the question would regard issues such as public accountability, effectiveness, social equity, or the *size* of government as always subsidiary to what *kind* of government can best contribute to the development of its citizens (Wamsley et al. 1990). The governance question is intimately connected with the earlier public questions, because "how we govern," rather than passively reflecting an already constituted social world, actively shapes and determines "how we live."

At least in general terms my own answers to these questions should be easy to anticipate. They would envision a generic kind of social process chiefly characterized by experimental and collaborative interaction, with government's chief responsibility being the promotion of a conception of citizenship that extends and develops that social process. Those technical, distributional, and authoritative functions that government additionally performs must ultimately be judged in terms of their contribution to fulfilling that primary responsibility. Because administration, the domain of the particular, engages with citizens at the most intimate levels of government, it is therefore involved most directly with their day-to-day development *as* citizens. What administrators "ought to learn and master" are therefore, above all others, the skills and personal dispositions needed to perform such a role. The knowledge required for its performance, however, is not a new form of expertise, if expertise is construed as *positive* knowledge. The latter reinforces the illusion of control, while facilitating citizen interaction and development requires abandoning that illusion.

In the absence of positive knowledge to guide the performance of the administrator's role, proverbs appear more and more attractive as fertile sources of practical wisdom about it. If Alasdair MacIntyre is right in saying that proverbs are the best kind of knowledge social scientists have to offer, then no apology is needed in recommending them. One proverb of particular relevance to collaborative interaction is the old organizational development adage "Trust the process."[9] Wise practitioners of organizational development know from experience that administrators' efforts to control social interaction, rather than allowing its products to emerge organically, are really ways of avoiding rather than honestly confronting their anxiety. If that is indeed the case, then learning to perform a facilitative role in engaging with citizens and one another would require that administrators attend to their own development as well, rather than hiding behind the illusion of technique.

As a last comment I will highlight the chief practical conclusion that public administrators might draw from the cancellation of their original final exam. Whether that conclusion mainly signals to them the benefit of a more liberating and creative role or serves as a caution about risks to be prudently avoided is, of course, for them to judge. On the assumption that they might regard *both* interpretations as to some degree plausible, that conclusion could be stated as follows: Because the old exam's question cannot and therefore need not be answered, administrators no longer need to justify their "mature" participation in democratic governance. To dissolve the dualisms that have made that justification appear necessary is to dissolve public administration's adolescent dilemma of having to assert a spurious form of independence—the claim to expertise—from a one-down position of political dependency. The conventional claim that administrators "speak truth to power" via the language of expertise has seldom been politically persuasive, and in any case it was always dubious as an intellectual proposition. In public administration as a politics of the subject, speaking truth to power assumes a more radical dimension, aptly expressed in what David Farmer (2003) has termed the "Great Refusal."[10] What public administrators need to refuse, he says, are all forms of oppression or domination that produce "power over" rather than, in Follett's term, "power with." Knowing the difference between the two, however, is chiefly a matter of expanding the ways in which we think about government and ourselves. Thus, for Farmer, refusal "includes overcoming traditional PA's tendency to one-dimensionality in privileging speaking-from-power, or system-affirming, frameworks and action. Refusal includes aspiring to PA thinking/practice that is radically multi-dimensional, radically human" (2003, 173). These are strong, and to some even provocative, words, which if acted upon may portend greater personal and political risks than even the most courageous (or the most adventurous) administrator might anticipate. And the practical problems they may produce for public administrators, it must be conceded, are not the kind for which theory can provide solutions or against which it can offer protection.

An Epilogue on Maturity

A unitary conception of governance provides an alternative way of thinking about governing to that grounded in the dualisms of public administration's standard narrative. I should stress "alternative" rather than "new" or "radical" because several of its core ideas predate the new millennium by more than a century; and many of the insights that inspired it have for decades appeared in the literature of management theory, a discipline not widely suspected as a font of revolutionary ideas. With their theoretical guard down, even contributors to the standard narrative might endorse, if only by way of lip service, some aspects of it. That its pragmatist origins reveal such a conception of governance as neither new nor radical may thus disappoint some, comfort others, or encourage skeptics to discount it as merely old wine in new bottles. My purpose all along, however, has been chiefly to clear away the theoretical and ideological debris that has obscured an already present, though only partially articulated, conception of governance, which from pragmatism's alternative vantage has long been visible and compelling.

In this epilogue I hope to end on a more positive note by commenting briefly on why the cultural, political, and economic conditions that for a century have marginalized long-familiar pragmatist ideas about governance no longer exert the force they once did, and why the changing demands upon government generated by the emergence of the "global era" will prove auspicious for reinvigorating pragmatist thinking. Pragmatism is, quite literally, an idea whose time has finally come, even if some might regard the new time itself as disorienting and even frightening. One consolation deriving from pragmatism's relevance for contending with globalization's often unwelcome challenges, however, is its promise of a more mature approach to governance that dissolves the modern era's adolescent paradoxes.

As my introductory sentence also noted, pragmatism's unitary conception of governance is just that: a conception, a way of thinking, rather than a program of structural or procedural reform, although various candidates for such reform might plausibly be inferred from it and others excluded as incompatible with it. Its key features include the following:

1. *Collaborative experimentation* involving policy makers, public administrators, and citizens in which ends and means are regarded as interactive and subject to continual revision.
2. *Practical theorizing* (praxis) in which the conceptual separation of thinking from doing—and thus the institutional separation of thinkers from doers—is minimized, if not dissolved.[1]
3. Embracing *uncertainty* as a cardinal feature of social life rather than a condition to be eliminated or controlled in the ostensible interests of managerial effectiveness and efficiency.
4. *Facilitating*—and finding value in—the *processes of social interaction* that expand citizens' capacities to engage in collaborative action.
5. A conception of democratic equality that, in presupposing the *legitimacy of individual differences,* regards citizens' development in diverse and idiosyncratic ways as its primary normative commitment.
6. A conception of *rationality as the intelligent vetoing* of embryonic action plans rather than the instrumental adjustment of administrative means to policy ends.
7. And finally, a profound *distrust of any and all conceptual dualisms* that impede the realization of that unitary conception of governance.

Globalization and Its Cognates

Globalization now appears to be "the epithet of choice" (Himmelfarb 1995, ix) for describing modernity's successor era. *Postmodernism,* in addition to evoking disagreeable connotations for many, also inadequately describes the new age by remaining ever hostage to, owing to its connotation as a permanent reaction against, its predecessor, *modernism.* Other cognate terms, however, serve well in fleshing out globalization's general meaning. Mulgan (1997), for example, uses *connexity* (an old English word, not a fancy new one) to describe a worldwide interdependence no longer manageable by social, political, and economic institutions associated with the predominance of the nation-state. Rosenau's (1997) neologism *fragmegration* denotes the emergence of new institutional processes for managing the fluctuations between the fragmenting and integrating forces at play on the frontiers of increasingly obsolete national boundaries. And James C. Scott (1998) extends the agricultural term *polyculture* to describe metaphorically social practices informed by local and context-specific experimental knowledge to replace the rationalistic technologies spawned by what he terms the "high-modernist" ideology of centralized state planning.

Although globalization should not be construed solely as a reaction against modernity, the latter term nevertheless requires some explication in order to see more clearly the reasons for the social and psychological dislocations that globalization produces. Globalization may be good news to those who reap its political or economic benefits, but it's bad news not only to those who don't but also and in a deeper sense to those whose self-definition and worldviews were originally shaped and continue to be dominated by modernist beliefs, institutions, and technologies. The ideology of modernity, like that of any other age, both constitutes and mirrors not only prevailing institutions and social practices but also and perhaps more fundamentally what it means to be a citizen or even human. This observation bears directly on the pragmatist argument of this book inasmuch as the modern supremacy of the nation-state crucially depended, and in large degree still depends, upon the conceptual dualisms of modernity's "rationality project" (Stone 2002). Martin Albrow makes this connection explicit in claiming that the power of "the Modern Project . . . derived from the way individual lives were bonded into the overall scheme of the nation-state, with rationality as the bonding substance" (1997, 189). That the transition from modernity to globalization is so often agonizing owes to the power of these dualisms (which Albrow calls dichotomies) to constitute modern individuals, who to their peril resist the implications of globalization by interpreting its strange new demands in terms of the dualisms to which they can imagine no alternative.

Public administration's standard narrative is the "governance chapter" of modernity's metanarrative. The governance chapter chiefly restates several of the broader themes of the modern metanarrative in the specialized, though often inconsistent, languages of management, economics, and normative political theory. The modernist belief in positive, universal knowledge, for example, grounds the standard narrative's faith in technical expertise, which ostensibly provides the instrument for achieving progress administratively by manipulatively controlling citizens and organization members. By the logic of market economics, modern society is conceived as an aggregation of self-interested, utility-maximizing individuals, suggesting to one branch of the standard narrative that citizens are essentially customers whose preferences it is government's chief obligation to satisfy. And the modern era's commitment to justice, predicated upon the principle of distributional equity, is then implemented impersonally according to bureaucratic standards of uniformity.

That this brief list of the standard narrative's recurring themes contains internal tensions should come as no surprise, because neither modernist ideology nor the standard narrative makes any pretense to be orthodoxy free of contradictions. Like a dysfunctional family, modernity's mutually opposing principles of free-market anarchy and bureaucratic control "enable" one another by producing pathologies that only incompletely and temporarily cancel out one another, if indeed they do so at all. Adherents to both principles share a common stake, however, in the bonding substance (their perverse "family value") of instrumental rationality—the radical separation of thinking from doing—which renders their theoretical differences as little more than a petty but interminable family squabble over the details about how most efficiently to adjust means to ends. Extending the metaphor a final step, the modern nation-state acts like an ineffectual social worker, who, instead of healing the family's internal wounds, tries, though with meager success, merely to shield its members from abuse by their similarly dysfunctional neighbors.

The modern metanarrative's tale of progress ends unhappily with the twentieth century's unremitting succession of cataclysms and disasters: wars provoking still other wars, famine, pandemic disease, holocausts of ethnic cleansing, and, only slightly less horrific, an ever-widening chasm between rich and poor, the erosion of civil society's institutions, and the disintegration, either already complete or imminent, of many nation-states (Kaplan 1997). Rather than serving as the century's engine of inexorable progress, rationality collapsed between its own irreconcilable polarities. Although the successor narrative of globalization has still to be written, drafts of its preface now appear in at least two competing versions: one of despair about an emergent "new world disorder"[2] still possibly reversible by reasserting modernity's promise of progress through rational control, and another hopefully anticipating an interdependent "*brave* new world" about which, this time, Huxley's phrase betrays no hint of doleful irony.

"Practical Maturity"

If reverting to modernity's assumptions and solutions is no longer possible, the realistic alternative appears to lie in inventing strategies and encouraging social practices for making the best of those social, political, and economic conditions now classified under the heading of globalization. An admittedly selective sampling of the now abundant commentaries on what globalization portends provides grounds for cautious optimism. In Mulgan's new world of connexity—of interdependence to replace the old "polarity of independence and dependence" (1997, 174)—the principle of reciprocity befits a new culture "more attuned to difference, more at ease with discussion, more open" (16). In a similar vein, Albrow writes that "globality . . . releases free-floating sociality" (1997, 111) and "promotes the endless renewability and diversification of cultural expression rather than homogenization or hybridization" (144). And Rosenau, commenting on the aftermath of cold-war-era superpower domination, describes "a new form of anarchy [that] has evolved in the current period—one that involves not only the absence of a highest authority, but also encompasses such an extensive disaggregation of authority as to intensify the pace at which transnational relations and cross-border spill-overs are permeating the Frontier, even as it also allows for such greater flexibility, innovation, and experimentation in the development and application of new control mechanisms" (1997, 151–52). Whether a global ethos so depicted—of interdependence, experimentation, difference, and reciprocity—can effectively shield against the ravages of international terrorism, mitigate the market's hegemony as the world's cardinal organizing principle, withstand the counterforces of religious and nationalistic orthodoxy, and guide recovery from inherited calamities is, of course, an open question, to which providing an answer constitutes the new era's signature challenge. Globalization makes archaic the conventional polarities—most especially, in the United States, between "liberals" and "conservatives"—in terms of which public discourse still misleadingly divides the principal opposing political camps. As the struggle between the worldviews of modernity and globality makes increasingly clear, the more relevant distinction is between the former's paradoxical mixture of rationalism and moralism and the latter's rejection of the modernist dualisms that prevent both individuals and societies from forging the social bonds needed for prospering in, and indeed surviving, an uncertain future.

My prologue defined the painful stage of adolescence as the irresolvable tension between the adolescent's dependence on parental authority and his or her impulse to escape from it in order to achieve independence. Just as John Dewey's opening epigraph urges that we "get over" philosophical questions rather than "solve" them, maturity requires the individual to get over the adolescent paradox by dissolving rather than trying to reconcile its polar requirements. Because, in adolescence, dependence and independence are arranged hierarchically, *reconciliation* reduces to a euphemism for subordinating the latter to the former. Thus, if maturation requires dissolving the adolescent paradox, it can be neither attained nor even contemplated so long as the opposing poles of the paradox are retained.

In a world no longer dominated by modernity's dualisms, however, what *could* maturity mean in more specific terms? And, would "mature" citizens and public officials stand a realistic chance of effectively collaborating on projects of common concern while at the same time accepting their differences? Addressing the first question, Zygmunt Bauman has described morally mature people of the global age as those who grow "to need the unknown, to feel incomplete without a certain anarchy in their lives," as those "who learn to love the 'otherness' among them" (1998, 46–47). "Anarchy" in the sense that Bauman intends, however, does not connote the absence of social relationships; rather, it implies the presence of forms of relating governed by practical requirements for collaborative action. Moral maturity in this sense would thus appear to complement Mulgan's depiction of societies now emerging in modernity's aftermath: "Traditional agrarian societies have some of the properties of childhood, in that they place people in dependence on authorities, both temporal and spiritual. Modern societies are the equivalent of adolescence, since they value above everything the freedom to make yourself, to escape and to satisfy your desires. The emerging societies that take stock of connexity, by contrast, are becoming adult through accepting that they live in a web of mutual interdependence" (1997, 17). If maturity in the global age can roughly be taken to mean the simultaneous embrace of *inter*dependence and difference, then the second question—of how (and whether) mature yet diverse people might actually collaborate with one another—takes on special urgency. Is maturity, in a word, practical?

This question is hardly new to public administration, but it is typically raised reluctantly by the field's standard narrative. Although "participative management" and "citizen participation" have long received ritualistic endorsement as examples of democratic administrative and political practices, both are often construed in procedural terms, as providing formal "mechanisms" by which administrators or citizens can gain "access" to decision-making arenas. More importantly, however, each fits uncomfortably alongside the standard narrative's core beliefs about administration's proper relation to democracy. When democratic governance, for example, is construed conventionally as public officials' representing citizens' preexisting interests, and when administration is conceived as applying professional expertise in order to satisfy those interests efficiently, then how to promote collaborative interaction between and among citizens and administrators must remain a peripheral concern. Both chapter 5's critique of administrative expertise and chapter 6's critique of democratic representation, however, suggest that the question of how to promote a form of democracy *re*conceived as collaborative interaction should be acknowledged as the field's central challenge. A public administration no longer obliged to defend collaboration's legitimacy as a philosophical proposition is therefore free to confront that challenge on practical terms.

To state the question more concretely: What social and institutional conditions are required for effective collaboration? Because this is a practical rather than a "legitimacy" question, readers should not be surprised that its most promising answers issue from the management literature rather than from public administration's normative discourse. Perhaps the best (not to mention the most widely read) recent synthesis of management and social science research on how collaboration within diverse groups can actually work is James Surowiecki's best-seller, *The Wisdom of Crowds* (2004). Subtitled *Why the Many Are Smarter Than the Few and How Collective Wisdom Shapes Business, Economies, Societies, and Nations,* Surowiecki's book combines extensively documented reasons for experts' chronic failures with a description of "wise crowds": groups of "naïve, unsophisticated agents" (107) who under the right circumstances make better decisions than either their smartest individual members or the experts in whom they sometimes *un*wisely vest decision-making power. Although Surowiecki does not address globalization directly, the four conditions he cites as characterizing wise crowds closely parallel some of the chief features of the global era described earlier: "diversity of opinion (each person should have some private information, even if it's just an eccentric interpretation of known facts), independence (people's opinions are not determined by the opinions of those around them), decentralization (people are able to specialize and draw on local knowledge), and aggregation (some mechanism exists for turning private judgments into a collective decision)" (2004, 10). These four conditions, Surowiecki says, pertain to groups dealing with any of three kinds of problems: *cognition* problems (those having right answers or solutions), *coordination* problems (in which all members simultaneously try to adjust their own behavior to that of other group members), and *cooperation* problems ("getting self-interested, distrustful people to work together, even when narrow self-interest would seem to dictate that no individual should take part" [xviii]).

Because cognition problems admit definitive solutions, the often remarkable superiority of groups over individual decision makers is easier to document for these problems than for the other two kinds.[3] But public administrators and citizens more typically confront problems requiring coordination and cooperation, whose solutions can seldom be judged from an "objective" standard of correctness. For these latter kinds of problems success depends on whether participants can jointly agree on *what* they ought to do (not on *why* they ought to do it) *or* on the emergence of mutually beneficial outcomes from their interaction even in the absence of explicit agreement. Effective groups ("wise crowds") evince, it would appear, several of the characteristics of globalized societies described earlier. First, their membership tends to be highly diverse rather than homogeneous, which has the advantage that individual errors won't "systematically point . . . in the same direction" (41), tending instead to cancel out (or "intelligently veto," recalling a prominent phrase from chapter 4) one another. Tolerating, even encouraging, dissent is thus preferable to consensus, especially in early stages of group decision making. Second, unlike the use of rational analysis, which requires prior agreement about (or the authoritative imposition of) values and ends, diverse groups "can coordinate themselves to achieve complex, mutually beneficial ends even if they're not really sure, at the start, what those ends are or what it will take to accomplish them" (107). In pragmatic fashion, ends and means are "fused," or mutually constituted, in courses of action, making abstract discussion of values superfluous. And third, cooperation crucially depends, not on agreement about values and ends, or even on mutual trust among the group's members, but on what Robert Axelrod (1984) describes as "the durability of the relationship" (qtd. in Surowiecki 2004, 117).[4] "People who repeatedly deal with each other over time," Surowiecki says, "recognize the benefits of cooperation, and they do not try to take advantage of each other, because they know if they do, the other person will be able to punish them" (117). If mutual trust emerges as a by-product of these durable relationships, so much the better; but "All you really [need to] trust is that the other person will recognize his self-interest" (124), coupled with safeguards against cheating. Thus when imperfect individual judgments are properly aggregated, group intelligence is usually superior to individual intelligence. Or, as Malcolm Gladwell (Surowiecki's colleague at the *New Yorker*) puts essentially the same point, the myth of individual talent "assumes that people make organizations smart. More often than not, it's the other way around" (2002, 32).

Democracy, Practical Maturity, and the Problem of Moralism (Revisited)

In his final chapter, Surowiecki proposes that democracy may be best understood as a practical way for dealing with problems of coordination and cooperation in order to make intelligent decisions. Other accounts of what democracy is chiefly for—that it "gives people a sense of involvement and control over their lives [and that] . . . individuals have the right to rule themselves" (2004, 262)—are still valid and important, but they are secondary to democracy's more basic function of enabling intelligent collaborative action. Echoing the unitary conception of democratic governance (summarized at the beginning of this epilogue), Surowiecki concludes that democracy's enduring question is "How do we live together?" (271). (Except for one insignificant word difference, his question, coincidentally though not surprisingly, is identical to my rewritten version of public administration's final exam question posed at the end of chapter 6: How *shall* we live together?)[5]

Democracy and practical maturity share the pragmatist attribute of dissolving the dualisms inherited from the modern era by collapsing the distinction between their heretofore polarized elements. Democracy, reconceived as a unitary, or process, idea, dissolves the dualisms between thinking and doing and between ends and means by revealing collaborative action as its essential property; while practical maturity, by dissolving the adolescent dilemma between dependence and independence, reveals interdependence as *its* essential property. Collaboration can only work when people perceive, acknowledge, and act in full recognition of their interdependence, therefore suggesting that *democracy is simply practical maturity writ large.* If this conclusion is accurate, then Albrow's contention that the global age requires "an overall change in the basis of action and social organization for individuals and groups" (1997, 4) puts in concrete terms the challenges posed by the question of how we might best live together.

Practical maturity offers an antidote, not only to the rationalist mindset that has fueled the modern era's failed ambitions, but also to rationalism's companion malady, moralism. I argued in chapter 2 that pragmatism, including the notion of practical maturity that it implies, dissolves the distinction between the practical and the moral. Practical maturity and moral maturity are one and the same thing owing to their (and thus *its*) common focus on creating contexts that foster collaborative action rather than on trying to settle ostensibly prior questions about values with the help of philosophers and "normative" theorists. Moralism—which I earlier defined as a posture toward discourse and action in which moral, or value, questions precede, and are radically distinct from, practical questions—presupposes a logically impossible form of moral justification (Fish 1999; Harmon 2003, 2005); but, more significantly, the mistaken belief in the possibility of moral justification erects the chief ideological barrier to living together in the global age, or indeed in any other. Moralism is dangerously beside the point by virtue of its obsession with the pseudoproblem of relativism, which only disguises what is truly at stake, namely, learning how to live together amid heretofore unimagined diversity and uncertainty.

At least since the tragic events of September 11, 2001, two rhetorical symbols—patriotism and values—have come to dominate moralist public utterances. Moralists have now joined with a vengeance the ranks of Samuel Johnson's "scoundrels"[6] by waging a "war on terrorism" that seeks odious statutory refuge behind a hastily enacted Patriot Act (Beresford 2004), whose even most circumspect detractors moralists reflexively label as *un*patriotic. Never mind that the moralistic framing of that "war" only compounds rather than honestly confronts the longer-term practical and immensely difficult problem identified in chapter 2, namely, fostering the conditions under which people who now see their interests as served by committing terrorist acts would in the future be less likely to do so. If patriotism is the nation-state's most conspicuous moralist symbol of international divisiveness, then the moralistic rhetoric about "values" surely qualifies as its domestic counterpart in America's current political dialogue. *Values* is an empty word that people use to make their opinions appear morally respectable while at the same time concealing both their substantive meaning and the consequences they imply. Abstract talk about values is simultaneously an avoidance and a deception (and very often a *self*-deception), an irony that Michael Kinsley (2004) captured neatly in concluding a recent op-ed column. "A country whose political dialogue is all about values," he wrote, "is either a country with no serious problems or a country hiding from its serious problems."

Academic discourse about public administration's legitimacy question, though (happily) free of the seamier qualities that currently infect public debate over patriotism and values, nevertheless merits the label of moralism for much the same reason. Even when its arguments are skillfully crafted and guided by the purest of motives, public administration's standard narrative, like all moralist discourse, asks an unanswerable question, the consequence of which is to hide from the serious problems that it ought to face. If public administration had no serious problems, such discourse might be indulged as a harmless diversion to occupy professors' spare time. Such a presumption would of course be untrue, and would also imply a grossly unfair aspersion on the undeniably serious and sincere efforts of so many scholars to grapple with questions about public administration's proper relationship to democracy. This acknowledgment, however, makes all the more poignant the standard narrative's central irony: that its moralistic stance toward public administration's role in democratic governance prevents it from addressing the most compelling democratic challenge of the global age: the simultaneously moral and practical challenge of living together.

A Postscript on the Personal/Political Nature of Epistemological Choice

While I was talking with colleagues about an early draft of chapter 3, one of them asked me why dissolving the dualism between thinking and doing was necessarily better than affirming it. Why should a social science epistemology that construes human action holistically be preferred over an epistemology depicting action in terms of discrete "moments" of stimulus and response (and thus of cause and effect), which a "primal" dualism between thinking and doing would seem to dictate? The question was certainly reasonable, but the answer seemed so intuitively obvious to me that I was unprepared to reply concisely. So, on a conciliatory note (and also buying time) I began by conceding that no "knockdown" arguments favoring one epistemological stance over another were really possible, but then I attempted to provide just such an argument by reminding my questioner that, unlike Dewey's unitary conception of action, the thinking/doing dualism committed the "empiricist's fallacy" of hypostatizing variables by falsely attributing causal power to abstract concepts. Because the others present had regarded, or so I sensed, my earlier discussion of this argument as among the more opaque portions of my presentation, the conversation pretty much stopped at that point. My "gotcha" response had fallen flat.

Later that evening a more sensible answer came to mind, one that is more fully consistent with my initial admission of the impossibility of conclusive, knockdown arguments. In view of that impossibility, social science researchers need to acknowledge that their choices of epistemologies, theories, and methodologies necessarily entail personal, moral, and political choices. That is, they should avoid recourse either to the spurious safety of purely logical (and therefore impersonal) justification or to protection by the illusion of value-free (and therefore morally and politically neutral) empirical evidence.

Such choices are personal at least partly in the prosaic sense that researchers inevitably differ from one another in what they find interesting. At least to a degree, there can be no more accounting for taste in epistemological and theoretical preferences than in movies or cuisine. To reduce the personal to a matter of mere preference (as mainstream economists and rational choice theorists might have it), however, risks losing sight of a deeper sense of the personal as it bears upon choices among scholarly orientations. Morgan describes "[t]he pursuit of scientific truth [as] . . . a particular way of making and remaking ourselves, or in Heidegger's terms, just one 'project' among others, and is of as much significance because of its implications for the development and well-being of all those humans involved with or influenced by this activity as it is for the 'knowledge' it generates" (1983, 373). Making and remaking ourselves through our choices of scholarly pursuits, however, cannot be accurately understood as actions taken by isolated individuals. The unfortunate conflating of the "personal" with the "individual" obscures the truth that the personal is in fact the *social*—and therefore the moral—not just in terms of the consequences that a researcher's choice of a scholarly orientation might have on other researchers and eventually even citizens, but also, conversely, in terms of *their* influence on the personal making and remaking of the individual researcher. Refusing to face responsibility, both *for* the products of one's research and *to* others who might profit or suffer from its consequences, is inadmissible once the personal is appreciated in social and therefore moral terms.

Just as the personal cannot be divorced from the social and the moral, neither can the latter be sensibly divorced from the political. Morgan does acknowledge the political nature and consequences of scholarly choices; but, owing to his own epistemological stance denying the possibility of secure foundations from which to adjudicate competing knowledge claims, he urges a catholic attitude endorsing, though not uncritically, a diversity of theoretical social science viewpoints. He is sympathetic, for example, to Feyerabend's (1975) maxim "Anything goes!" so long as it is augmented by a dialectical approach in which insights from diverse viewpoints are deliberately, even sharply, counterposed. The more compelling Morgan's argument for theoretical diversity in general seems to be (and it is indeed compelling on its own terms), the more paradoxical and perhaps even self-defeating the task appears of mounting an argument supporting a particular theoretical viewpoint, especially one that takes seriously its political commitments. The dialectic Morgan proposes, after all, requires advocates for opposing viewpoints who believe that they have good and sound reasons for preferring *their* theoretical approaches over others. Might not successful argument—which is to say, cogent comparison of one's preferred theory with rival approaches—have the paradoxical consequence of reducing the very diversity that sustains the dialectic?

Which brings me back to the question I began with: Can I plausibly argue for a pragmatist epistemology that dissolves the dualisms of public administration's standard narrative, do so without resorting to bogus knockdown arguments, *and* respect a healthy diversity of theoretical approaches (including some that I may not like)—all at the same time? Clearly, I would not have written chapter 3 (and indeed the entire book) unless I believed it possible to do all three. The answer to my questioner, necessarily couched in the form of a personal/moral/political declaration of sorts, builds upon an early sentence in that chapter in which I proposed that the dualism between thinking and doing serves as a micro-level analogue to all of the other dualisms of public administration's standard narrative. That is, the "epistemological errors" of the reflex arc concept (remember the empiricist's fallacy) are recapitulated at the macro level in institutional roles that demarcate thinkers (and thus deciders) from doers (implementers). That demarcation qualifies as political insofar as it implies relations of power. Recall that, beginning with the thinking/doing dualism, all of the standard narrative's dualisms connote not only an analytical separation of two elements (or "moments") but also a temporal, normative, and by implication authoritative priority between them as well. The first element not only precedes but also drives or determines the second element. Thus, thinkers have, or are "legitimately" granted, power, while doers either don't have it or can only acquire it "illegitimately" by means of stealth or deception—for example, under the guise of neutral competence. Similarly, the institutional subordination of doing to thinking qualifies as organizational by implicitly prescribing a particular form of institutional authority, namely, hierarchy. Superior/subordinate relationships naturally, even inevitably, follow from an epistemology that depicts doing as, quite literally, the servant of thought.

Despite the order in which I have discussed the various dualisms, however, it would be misleading to conclude that a subject as intellectually rarefied as social science epistemology can fairly be blamed for, or credited with, producing either radical disparities of political power or the predominantly bureaucratic form of organization of which hierarchy is the cardinal defining feature. At most, but still importantly, empiricist social science might plausibly be cited for its complicity, even if unwitting, in perpetuating those institutions of which it is nevertheless far more a product than a cause. (My "reductionist" strategy of first discussing the micro-level thinking/doing dualism before considering the other dualisms was therefore mainly chosen for convenience—for providing, as Edward O. Wilson [1998, 58] earlier suggested, "good points of entry into otherwise impenetrably complex systems"—not because I assumed any micro-to-macro causal direction.)

Still, the link between the epistemological on the one hand and the political and the organizational on the other requires elaboration, including some comment on the likely causal relation between them. When I enclosed the phrase "epistemological errors" in quotation marks, I did so in order to cast doubt on the assumption that epistemological battles could be fought in an arena wholly separate from that of more visible and consequential political and bureaucratic wars. Epistemological "errors," that is, mirror problematic political judgments. Frederick Thayer (1980) has argued quite directly that "epistemology *is* organization theory." He defines epistemology as a structure of authoritative relations specifying both *who* decides upon the rules of valid knowledge and *what* those rules are. The "who" and the "what" are inseparable. "Objective knowledge," in Thayer's view, can only be sustained when some people are empowered, or (more likely) somehow manage to accumulate the power, to define what counts as objective knowledge. To put his point another way, hierarchy is the organizational equivalent of, and is functionally a precondition for, "objectivity," a word advisedly enclosed by scare quotes in order to signify its organizationally contingent character. *Hierarchy is thus just another name for the authoritative separation of thinkers from doers.* His preferred epistemology of intersubjectivity (whose meaning empiricism limits to a methodological technique for guarding against observer error or bias) is, or could be, sustained by structured relationships governed by norms of, indeed requirements for, consensual agreement. Rather than being restricted to the gated community of social science theory and research, the notion of intersubjectivity connotes to Thayer more broadly, as it were, a preferred epistemology of everyday life in all its varied social, cultural, political, and organizational forms.

Having reflected upon my colleague's original question, I am in a position to provide a more honest answer, including an explanation of why my initial stab at a knockdown argument was not only disingenuous in the light of my earlier disclaimer but could not have succeeded in any event. The empiricist's fallacy of hypostatizing variables can be regarded *as* a fallacy only if as one has already chosen to honor—to grant a kind of a priori legitimacy to—people's own accounts of their experience. These accounts seldom speak of causes (save those of people's own subjective creation) and effects, nor are explanations that are cast in terms of stimulus and response or of independent and dependent variables always and self-evidently suitable for explicating their richness and ambiguity. Rather than coming so neatly packaged, first-person accounts blur the boundaries of, invert the priority of, or contradict the "moments" of the empiricist dualism between thinking and doing.

This should not be construed, however, as a blanket indictment of theories and methodologies predicated on that dualism, or as a claim that first-person accounts, especially if accepted uncritically, can tell the whole story—as if there were a "whole" story to tell. Although my earlier training as an interpretivist theorist in part explains my instinctive respect for and deference to people's "disorderly" accounts of their actions (this, then, is the personal part of my declaration), I am also mindful of their limitations. To begin with, sometimes people just don't tell—or don't *like* telling a researcher—the truth. And, people's (including my own) capacity for self-deception and artful rationalization sometimes seems limitless. More to the point, however, such accounts typically exclude, or at most hint at only indirectly and unreflectively, alternative structural, psychoanalytic, and (yes) empiricist explanations that might reveal them as incomplete, naive, or impractical for dealing sensibly with public problems. Problems, however, do not come predefined, which raises the question of whose problem definitions should count. Judgments about this question are themselves personal, moral, and political; and my interpretivist proclivities make me wary of problem definitions that suit the methodological tastes of the researcher at the expense of the problem definitions of those outside the academy. In view of this declaration, then, I am not only content with, but also eagerly invite, a diverse array of theoretical and methodological approaches, but with the attached condition that they show due respect for—that they not ignore—the often muddled, contradictory, ambiguous, and paradoxical accounts of their research subjects' lived experience.

My second reason for preferring Dewey's unitary conception of action over the thinking/doing dualism is more straightforwardly political, namely, that the institutional subordination of doers to thinkers—for which that dualism provides epistemological plausibility—constitutes the most elemental precondition for power disparities. If others might be sanguine about those disparities rather than troubled by them, I can think of no knockdown arguments showing why they ought to feel otherwise. There is really not much more to say to such people. For those scholars, however, who *are* troubled by them—whose normative image of democratic governance is one of mutual collaboration between and among citizens and public officials in both defining and contending sensibly with problems of shared concern—then a chief part of their task seems clear: namely, by means of critique to assist in revealing how taken-for-granted and historically contingent beliefs about the subordination of doing to thinking prevent people from realizing that normative image. Urging a critical scholarly role is, of course, hardly novel as a general proposition; but the thinking/doing dualism, along with the other dualisms of public administration's standard narrative, have yet to receive the sustained critical attention that they clearly warrant.

Notes

Prologue

1. Other scholars might cite one or another of Gulick's contemporaries as preceding him in first announcing the demise of public administration's notorious dichotomy, and I would pose no serious objection to such claims. In view of Gulick's richly deserved stature, however, as an original and important contributor to the field's literature for more than half a century, I was inclined to search no further than his 1933 article "Politics, Administration, and the New Deal," in which he describes public administrators as deeply enmeshed in policy concerns, within, as he puts it, "a seamless web of discretion and action" (61). The theme of administrative discretion and involvement in the policy process recurred in his later writings, including a 1955 article titled "Next Steps in Public Administration." For an excellent summary of Gulick's life and published works, see Brian Fry's *Mastering Public Administration.*

Chapter 1

1. Van Riper (1984) has concluded that Wilson's essay had virtually no influence (although some of his later books *did*) on public administration thinking from the time of its publication until the conclusion of World War II. Van Riper notes that he could "find absolutely no citation in footnote or index to 'The Study of Administration'" (207) in the principal public administration and political science texts published in the first quarter of the twentieth century.

2. Wilson never used the word *dichotomy;* nor, for that matter, did Waldo in *The Administrative State.*

3. Despite the importance and originality of Waldo's critique in *The Administrative State* of what later came to be known as the politics/administration

dichotomy, he nevertheless left unchallenged the logical positivist epistemological foundations on which, according to Simon (1947), the analytical distinction between the two spheres rested. (Although, in his 1948 edition, Waldo makes no mention of *logical* positivism, he does discuss briefly an older variant of positivism.) In the introduction to the 1984 edition he indirectly concedes that this omission made his own position against the dichotomy vulnerable to the kinds of epistemological arguments that Simon (1952) made in support of it.

4. The importance of this conflation will be revisited in chapter 6 when I consider Thomas Catlaw's (2003) critique of the notion of representation.

5. During the past twenty years, the so-called New Public Management (NPM) has represented an effort to combine, in the context of my own terminology, splitting and reconciling strategies. One of its chief advocates, Laurence Lynn (1997), describes public management as "the executive function in government," whose generic question may be stated as: "Under what circumstances, and how, do executives and the executive function make a difference to the success of public policy and public agencies?" (7). The domain of the NPM is thus the intersection between public administration (in particular those scholars who traditionally have sought to reconcile the often competing requirements of administrative efficiency and the "rule of law") and rational policy analysis (whose characteristically "scientific and disinterested" [87] analytic approaches work best when political, normative, and statutory considerations may be effectively bracketed out). Like virtually all contributors to public administration's standard narrative, the NPM rejects both the factual accuracy and even the normative desirability of a dichotomy between policy and administration but still retains the functional distinction between those two domains. By doing so the NPM, in effect, regards public administration's final exam question as an important one to ask. In various endnotes to chapters 2, 5, and 6, I will comment on why, from a pragmatist vantage, its answers are unsatisfactory.

6. For an excellent intellectual history of pragmatism from its origins to the close of the twentieth century, see Diggins's *The Promise of Pragmatism* (1994). Menand's story ends with Dewey's death at midcentury, while Diggins provides a comprehensive and critical history of pragmatist thought extending almost fifty years beyond Dewey's death. Especially engaging are his critique of the neopragmatist revival initiated chiefly by Rorty, its alliance with poststructuralism and postmodernism, and the internal debates currently raging among pragmatist scholars.

7. In *Pragmatism: A Reader,* Menand includes, in addition to excerpts from the works of the four founding luminaries, selections by important contemporary contributors to pragmatist thought, including Richard Rorty, Hilary Putnam, Richard J. Bernstein, Cornel West, and Richard A. Posner.

Chapter 2

1. Although contributors to what I term the normativist literature (in particular the literature of administrative ethics) and the rationalist literature in American public administration only infrequently cite or explicitly challenge each other's ideas, Catron and Denhardt (1994) correctly note that, since the 1940s, the periodic resurgences of the administrative ethics literature have been energized in part by a dissatisfaction with the near hegemony of rationalist thinking in both management science and policy analysis. The normativists' dissatisfaction, however, has been expressed mainly as a critique of these fields' failure to pay adequate attention to democratic "values" (Nigro and Richardson 1990). As I will argue in this and later chapters, the purported neglect of the "value dimension" misconstrues what is at issue by leaving intact the conceptual distinction between values and facts.

2. As the principal genre of the standard narrative's normativist wing, the contemporary administrative ethics literature includes contributions that extend the core ideas of virtually all the major perspectives in philosophical ethics. For a representative sampling of public administration discussions of deontological ethics, inspired initially by Kant and later extended by Rawls (1971), see Pops (1991), Frederickson and Hart (1985), Chandler (1994), and Geuras and Garofalo (1996); for virtue ethics, see Lilla (1981), Hart (1994), and Cooper (1990); for moral/cognitive development, especially regarding the controversy between Kohlberg (1971) and Gilligan (1982), see Stewart and Sprinthall (1994); for public citizenship and ethics, see Cooper (1991), Frederickson (1982), and Gawthrop (1984); for democratic (including "regime") values and ethics, see Burke (1986) and Rohr (1989); and for communitarian ethics, inspired by C. Taylor (1985), MacIntyre (1984), and Walzer (1983), see Cooper (1987, 1991) and Hart and Wright (1998). Utilitarian ethics is less prominently represented in the administrative ethics literature, an interesting exception being Gormley's (2001) discussion of murder mysteries as fodder for analysis from the standpoint of both "act" and "rule" utilitarianism. Utilitarianism has exerted far greater influence on the rationalist wing of public administration's standard narrative than on its normativist wing, in particular, on public choice theory (Buchanan and Tullock 1962; V. Ostrom 1974) and "incrementalist" policy analysis (Braybrooke and Lindblom 1963).

3. The likelihood of such conflict, however, has been wisely acknowledged by New Public Management scholars such as Robert Behn (1999). Behn notes that, given their passion for "results" rather than the formalities of bureaucratic procedures, NPM advocates "must not only demonstrate that their strategy [i.e., of empowering public managers to play an active role in the policy process and to respond aggressively to citizens' needs] is more effective or more efficient.

They must also demonstrate that it is politically responsible. Those who seek to create a new paradigm of public management have the burden of providing a correlative concept of democratic accountability" (132). "Is it possible," in other words, "to permit empowered, responsive civil servants to make decisions and be innovative and still have democratic accountability?" (159). Behn, in effect, initially appears to accept (by briefly restating) my original formulation of public administration's final exam question from chapter 1, and seems to promise an eventual "theoretical" answer to it. He ultimately sidesteps the question, however, by concluding, somewhat enigmatically, that "we will not answer the accountability question for performance by engaging in deep, theoretical thinking. . . . [Instead], the answer to the accountability question can only emerge from practice—evolving from a variety of efforts by the class of new public managers who do not obscure their accountability but define and clarify it" (159–60). The tensions, and possibly even the irresolvable conflicts, between and among the principles of efficiency, responsiveness, and accountability to the rule of law that so trouble public administration traditionalists such as Moe and Gilmour (1995) remain unresolved by Behn's answer.

I will argue in chapter 4 that the standard narrative's (including the NPM's) preoccupation with efficiency and effectiveness, by presupposing the dualism between ends and means, cannot come to terms with the normative/political problem of how social processes and institutions constitute and reshape people's conceptions of their wants, needs, and interests. If, as I argue there, normative judgments about ends are properly made "internally"—that is, from the standpoint of the social and political processes (or "means") by which those ends are produced—then the NPM's commitment to "results" and "performance" is revealed as just one more version of old-fashioned (ends/means) instrumental logic.

4. More precisely, Easton defined *policy* as the "authoritative allocation of values" but regarded *politics* and *policy making* as virtually equivalent terms. He later characterized *values* as "ultimately [reducible] . . . to emotional responses conditioned by the individual's total life-experiences" (1953, 221), which give rise to people's preferences for particular things or benefits. The "authoritative" aspect of policy lies in the power of government to allocate—"make accessible" (130)—certain things to some people while denying them to others.

5. Whether Rorty's "new" pragmatism, based as it is on a radical critique of the purportedly representational role of language, is better than Dewey's original version is hotly contested among public administration pragmatists. For a lively exchange see Shields (2003, 2004) (who takes Dewey's side) and Miller (2004) (Rorty's) in two recent issues of *Administration and Society*.

6. Sometimes pejoratively labeled the "new managerialism," the NPM movement appears to qualify as an exception to this rule. Inspired in part by

Osborne and Gaebler's *Reinventing Government* (1992), the NPM might, though perhaps controversially, be described as extending many key rationalist assumptions and beliefs of market economics and management theory. For a sampling of key contributions to the current NPM literature see Lynn (1997, 1998) and Behn (2001).

7. Moralism, as I have defined it here, typically presupposes what Fox terms a "foundational" conception of public administration ethics, namely, "any ethical argument which takes the form of deducing the appropriate judgment or behavior located in the flux and flow of actual life (physis) from putatively higher, more general or abstract laws, principles, or standards seen as located above and outside that flow regardless of how those rules are derived" (1994, 86).

8. In a July 2, 2002, e-mail announcement to the Communitarian Network, Amitai Etzioni, editor of *The Responsive Community,* advertised the title of the symposium as "Can Relativists Condemn Terrorism?" This is slightly different from the title that actually appears in the journal: "Can Postmodernists Condemn Terrorism?" I list the published version in the Works Cited, but I have used the e-mail version of the symposium's title in the text for obvious reasons. The symposium's lead article, contributed by Stanley Fish, is titled "Don't Blame Relativism" and is followed by nearly a dozen brief replies.

9. In *Philosophy and the Mirror of Nature,* Rorty offers the following comment on why those who construe objectivity as "correspondence" or "representation" in empirical descriptions of the physical world commit essentially the same sort of error as those who argue for an "objective" (universalist) theory of values:

> [E]ven philosophers who take the intuitive impossibility of finding conditions for "the one right thing to do" as a reason for repudiating "objective values" are loath to take the impossibility of finding individuating conditions for the one true theory of the world as a reason for denying "objective physical reality." Yet they should, for formally the two notions are on a par. The reasons for and against adopting a "correspondence" approach to moral truth are the same as those regarding truth about the physical world. . . . [T]he usual excuse for invidious treatment is that we are shoved around by physical reality but not by values. Yet what does being shoved around have to do with objectivity, accurate representation, or correspondence? Nothing, I think, unless we confuse *contact* with reality (a causal, non-intentional, non-description-relative relation) with *dealing with* reality (describing, explaining, predicting, and modifying it—all of which are things we do under descriptions). (1979, 374–75, emphasis in source)

Chapter 3

1. In the discipline of sociology, reconciling micro and macro levels chiefly involves explaining the mutually constitutive relation between human agency and social structure. This has been the project, to cite perhaps the most noteworthy example, of sociologist Anthony Giddens's (1976, 1977, 1984) "structuration theory." As two of Giddens's interpreters summarize the core of his approach:

> Structuration theory [attempts to show] . . . how "social structures are both constituted by human agency, and yet at the same time are the very *medium* of this constitution" (Giddens 1977, 121, italics original). This is what is meant by "duality of structure," the central concept in Giddens' structuration theory, and the means by which he seeks to avoid a dualism of agency and structure. Giddens stresses that "to enquire into the structuration of social practices is to seek to explain how it comes about that structures are constituted through action, and reciprocally how action is constituted structurally" (Giddens 1976, 161). (Bryant and Jary 1991, 7)

2. In 1976, Vickers made this observation in conversation with Bayard L. Catron, who then related it to me.

3. As any beginning methodologist knows, deciding which variables are "dependent" and which are "independent" cannot be determined by or inferred from statistical tests, but only from commonsense experience with and intuitions about the subject matter. The specification of some variables as dependent and others as independent is a technical way of attributing causality. In the absence of these attributions, statistical correlations in and of themselves cannot tell us anything about causality, which is to say that they cannot "explain," because explanation, in order to be nontrivial, connotes causal direction.

4. That the distinction between "empirical," or "positive," theory and "normative" theory in political science and economics emerged at about the time *Administrative Behavior* appeared, and when behavioralism began to dominate American social science, is probably not coincidental. For a discussion of the problematic nature of this distinction, see White 1978.

5. For an extended discussion of the inseparability of the normative and the empirical in the field of cognitive developmental psychology, see Kohlberg 1971.

6. Commenting on Simon's claim that pragmatism influenced his writing of *Administrative Behavior,* Snider has commented:

> [B]y the time of Simon's doctoral work, pragmatism had been captured by logical positivism, and the two philosophies, to many observers, had

> become one. Thus, in *Administrative Behavior,* Simon was able to claim the authority of pragmatism as well as that of logical positivism. . . . Simon embraced pragmatism, but only as logical positivism-pragmatism. . . .
>
> [Owing to his endorsement of the value/fact dichotomy], it is ironic that Simon, in a work in which he claimed the sanction of James and Dewey, may actually have moved public administration even further from their pragmatism. (2000, 346)

7. I have borrowed the term "problem-driven" from Flyvbjerg (2001), who uses it to describe a key feature of *phronetic* social science, which I discuss briefly below.

8. For an analysis of the debate between Habermas and Foucault, see chapter 6 in Flyvbjerg (2001), "The Significance of Conflict and Power to Social Science," pp. 88–109.

9. Action research should by no means be construed as "anti-statistics," although its characteristic approach to statistical analysis, deriving from the so-called Bayesian Theorem, makes very different assumptions about the relation between researcher and research subjects than does the better-known "classical" statistical approach that empiricists typically use. White and Gates (1974) have written perhaps the only (and, unfortunately, much-neglected) treatise on Bayesian statistics from a public administration perspective, arguing for its unique suitability for analyzing problems of social service delivery and for facilitating collaborative problem solving in organizational situations where problem-relevant knowledge is inherently fluid.

Chapter 4

1. The problematic nature of the ends/means dualism has been a recurring theme in the influential writings of Charles E. Lindblom ever since the publication of his classic "The Science of Muddling Through" (1959). He has revisited that theme in several of his later works, including *A Strategy of Decision* (Braybrooke and Lindblom 1963) and *Inquiry and Change: The Troubled Attempt to Understand and Shape Society* (1992).

2. Weick's question is actually a slight variation on E. M. Forster's (1927) earlier phrasing: "How can I *tell* what I *think* 'till I see what I say?" (97, emphasis added to indicate the differences from Weick's later version).

3. *Roget's Thesaurus* (Luzzatto and Morehead 1962, 292) lists five synonyms for *rational: sound, sane, logical, sensible,* and *reasonable.*

4. Tribe lists the three earlier "discontinuities"

> as the three ego-smashing divides that our species has already traversed in its intellectual history. The first crossing, signalled by the Copernican

> revolution if not earlier, dislodged man from his seat at the center of the universe by establishing a continuity in his perception between the earth he inhabited and the physical bodies he observed in the heavens. The second, heralded by Darwin, dethroned mankind from its secure place at the pinnacle of life by bridging the gap that had separated it from the rest of the animal kingdom. And the third crossing, due largely to the work of Freud, challenged the supremacy and autonomy of the human ego by linking the primitive and archaic in man with the civilized and the evolved. (1973, 617)

5. In *Responsibility as Paradox* (1995, 187–91) I discussed MacIntyre's concept of practice as it bears on the mutually opposing meanings of administrative responsibility.

6. O. C. McSwite is the pseudonym under which Orion F. White and Cynthia J. McSwain have written during since 1990. This accounts for my use of the plural form of personal pronouns in referring to their recent work.

7. For a recent exchange of opinions on the subject, see the 2001 *Public Administration Review* symposium (though not actually labeled as such) that begins with Lynn's "The Myth of the Bureaucratic Paradigm." Earlier important works representing the New Public Management side include Osborne and Gaebler (1992), Behn (2001), and Lynn (1997, 1998). Traditionalist skeptics of the NPM include Carroll (1995), Frederickson (1996), Moe (1994), and Moe and Gilmour (1995).

Chapter 5

1. In *Consequences of Pragmatism,* Rorty notes that "When the pragmatist attacks the notion of truth as accuracy of representation he is thus attacking the traditional distinctions between reason and desire, reason and appetite, reason and will. For none of these distinctions make sense unless reason is thought of on the model of vision, unless we persist in what Dewey called 'the spectator theory of knowledge'" (1982, 164). (Rorty's colleague Richard Bernstein [1971, 174], incidentally, credits the "'spectator' theory of the knower" to C. S. Peirce rather than to Dewey.)

2. Lending support to both a Rortian and an interpretivist view, Gareth Morgan's (1997, 1998) recent writings in effect define organizations as the products of the metaphors by which managers manage.

3. Hubert and Stuart Dreyfus argue in *Mind over Machine* (1986) that true expertise, in contrast to the rationalist stereotype of it, consists of behavior that is intuitive and holistic rather than linear, sequential, and divisible into separate phases of planning, deciding, and acting. True experts, unlike merely "profi-

cient performers," base their judgments chiefly on long experience in discerning relevant contextual factors bearing on effective performance.

4. Commenting on Dewey's view, Evans concludes: "For making the difficult, value-laden choices among alternatives, there is no expertise as such; decisions that will affect lives and livelihoods belong to the democratic and cooperative process of social inquiry involving all who might be affected" (2000, 314). The fuller implications of this statement will become clearer in chapter 6's discussion of Catlaw's conception of administration as "a politics of the subject."

5. Equally problematic, therefore, is Hill and Lynn's (2004) formulation of the public manager's central question: "Does my program work?" (3). To what extent, that is, does this or that program achieve public goals or contribute to governmental outcomes? Because the question is essentially instrumental, it is vulnerable to the same kinds of objections against the managerialist bias, discussed in chapter 4, found elsewhere in the literature of public administration's standard narrative. That chapter's critique of ends/means logic challenged managerialism's underlying normative/ideological belief that "results" and "performance" can be judged in reference to pre-given ends, purposes, or goals, independent of any normative assessment of the social processes through which they are formulated.

In the context of the present chapter, however, the question "Does my program work?" seems virtually identical to, and is thus objectionable for the same reasons as, the question "Does this theory work?" For example, Hill and Lynn note that determining why government programs do or don't work requires "an understanding of complex relationships in human, social, and organizational affairs. The use of theory in identifying these relationships is critical, but theories must be carefully tested rather than assumed or asserted to be true" (3). They later stress the importance of determining "whether the results of these dispersed efforts are cumulating to more general insights of practical value" (5). My quarrel with Hill and Lynn is not with their general proposition that, in effect, "more research is needed," but with some of the assumptions they seem to make about the relationship between theory and practice. The first is the assumption that a particular theory's "practical value" to public managers is necessarily, or even likely to be, a function of the theory's generality. In this chapter's section on "Theories and Clocks," for example, I argued that the generality criterion is often incompatible with the combination of two other criteria—accuracy and simplicity—that managers are likely to regard as more relevant to their own *practical* tests of a particular theory's value. As MacIntyre (1984) has noted in this regard, the best (i.e., most practical) "theoretical generalizations" can be little more than proverbs. Second, generality is typically valued by researchers because of its promise of predictive power, thus ignoring the relevance of the managers' idiosyncratic, contextual, and "local knowledge" in determining the degree of their programs' success. From a pragmatist vantage, "predictions" of program success or failure are as often as not self-fulfilling prophecies owing to the interactive relation between knowledge and action. Third, the instrumental relation between theory and practice assumed in Hill and Lynn's statement takes for granted the highly dubious epistemological dualism between thinking and doing (criticized in chapter 3). The acceptance of that dualism virtually guarantees the practical irrelevance of the empiricists' research program, to which the New Public Management is a prominent contributor, by ignoring the role of managers' normative commitments to *make* (or not make) particular theories—and thus their programs—work.

6. For a controversial and highly readable assessment of theory's status in the contemporary "culture wars," see Terry Eagleton's *After Theory* (2003).

7. Richard Bernstein's *Praxis and Action* (1971) remains one of the most comprehensive treatments of the history of and controversies surrounding the notion of praxis.

8. For an early, perhaps still the best, discussion of the term, see Manfred Stanley's "Technicism, Liberalism, and Development" (1972).

Chapter 6

1. The twenty-two dualisms, including the principal five dualisms to which the preceding five chapters are chiefly devoted as well as seventeen others also considered, are listed here in order of their appearance in the book:

politics (policy)/administration
value/fact
thinking/doing
holism/reductionism
cause/effect
independent variables/dependent variables
fact/theory
normative theory/empirical theory
expertise/experimenting
politics/organizing
ends/means
problems/solutions
substance/process
subject/object (subjective/objective)
what/who (how)
reason/desire (thought/feeling)
democracy/efficiency-effectiveness

principal/agent
individual/community
experience/belief
giving reasons/rationalizing
theory/practice

2. In *Postmodern Public Policy,* Hugh T. Miller (2002) explains how the criterion of universality ("generality" squared) underwrites modernist conceptions of public policy. In an argument that complements Catlaw's proposal for a "politics of the subject," Miller claims that modernist policies require for their implementation the impersonal, standardizing procedures implicit in the ends/means logic of Weber's ideal-typical bureaucracy. The policy/bureaucracy linkage, Miller says, inevitably privileges "order, pattern, and system" (6) at the expense of individual differences. The plurality of interests in a diverse citizenry are thus homogenized in modernism's "administered society" through policies appealing to "higher" (which is to say, universal) values or standards.

3. Catlaw's critique of the doctrine of popular sovereignty illuminates why the New Public Management, despite its avowed rejection of the dichotomy between politics and administration, is nevertheless a deeply conservative movement by virtue of its retaining a clear functional distinction between those two domains. The NPM's often-repeated claim of having formulated a radically new "paradigm" located at the intersection between public administration and public policy analysis would appear to be considerably weakened by his analysis. Any theoretical perspective making that functional distinction thereby advances what Catlaw calls "a theory of dual sovereignty":

> This means that justification for the separation between politics and administration is based on the sovereignty of each over distinctive domains of knowledge—political knowledge and factual knowledge. Concomitant with their realms of sovereignty, the theory of dual sovereignty draws a clear relationship between the *formal structure* of scientific and political rationalities. Politics possesses a legal or legalistic rationality that expresses the will of the People; administration exercises a scientific rationality over a body of facts. (2003, 16, emphasis in source)

Catlaw cites several historical and contemporary proponents of the theory of dual sovereignty, including Frank Goodnow (1900), Luther Gulick (1937), Herbert Simon (1947), Vincent Ostrom (1974), and, finally, Laurence Lynn (1997), perhaps the NPM's leading contemporary spokesman. Catlaw regards Lynn, as well as the rest of the NPM movement, as merely modestly extending the work of those earlier, and distinctly conservative, theorists. Lynn (who affirms that "American government is accountable to the freely expressed will of the people;

popular sovereignty is more than myth" [1997, 9]) remains a conventional dualist "because, most basically, he is concerned with public management as [a conceptually distinct] domain of knowledge. Public management proves its worth by virtue of what it *knows*" (Catlaw 2003, 30, emphasis in source). Its knowledge is essentially factual, *scientific* knowledge, in obvious contrast to the *political* knowledge that represents the People's will. Catlaw allows, however, that the NPM "does . . . profess to know more than technical facts" (30), citing Lynn's view that public management necessarily contains elements of both "art" and "science" in order to deal with the ambiguities of inherently unstable governance practices.

4. Originally published in 1962, Bernard Crick's classic *In Defence of Politics* (4th ed., 1992) anticipated by forty years certain aspects of Catlaw's critique. Crick held politics, which he defined as an ongoing process for conciliating diverse interests, to be a far superior—and in practice, a freer and more democratic—kind of governance to the "unsatisfactory and unpolitical" (59–60) conceptions of democracy based on the principle of majority consent and sustained by the "sadly empty doctrine" (60) of the popular sovereignty. "It should be the test," he continued, "of whether a man values liberty effectively, of whether he is in earnest about free politics to see if he is willing to recognize the meaninglessness of this rhetorical phrase" (60).

5. "A politics of the subject," based as it is on an a priori acceptance of individual differences, echoes Crick's (essentially Aristotelian) belief that *politics,* by connoting the presence of those differences, also implies in a normative sense their toleration as a precondition for the process—politics—by which they might be reconciled. The prior existence of anything like the popular sovereignty or even a widely shared consensus about the substantive content of the common good are not only unnecessary but also distinctly *un*political. Any truly "common good," Crick writes, "is itself the process of practical reconciliation of the interests of the various 'sciences,' aggregates, or groups which compose a state; it is not some external and intangible spiritual adhesive, or some allegedly objective 'general will' or 'public interest.' These are misleading and pretentious explanations of how a community holds together. . . . The moral consensus of a free state is not something mysteriously prior to or above politics: it is the activity (the civilizing activity) of politics itself" (1992, 23). Some key differences, however, between the positions of Crick and Catlaw should be noted. Unlike Crick, Catlaw focuses on the importance of social, including political, processes in *constituting* individual "interests," not simply in dealing with preexisting ones. And where Crick stresses politics' role as a conciliator of those interests, Catlaw emphasizes their collaborative creation.

6. I developed the notion of policy as a regrettable necessity in *Action Theory for Public Administration* (1981). Starting with the face-to-face encounter as the most elemental unit of social interaction, I identified standardized administra-

tive procedures and policy outcomes as normatively second-best expedients to be resorted to when "disaggregated" decisions produced through face-to-face interaction were either practically unfeasible or unnecessary. Examples of appropriately "aggregated" decisions of the sort that are assumed by bureaucratic rules and policies "include, first, pure public goods, whose benefits and costs are not meaningfully divisible; second, cases in which the consequences of a decision made by one person or group may negatively affect so vast a number of others that face-to-face negotiation among all concerned is not feasible; and third, situations in which the population affected by a given problem or issue is highly homogeneous. . . . In these situations potential outcomes of face-to-face deliberations may be so predictable that [face-to-face] . . . deliberations would be regarded as superfluous" (85). As we have already seen from Catlaw's analysis, however, homogeneity should not be automatically presupposed; at the very least, it requires empirical validation on a case-by-case basis.

7. I do not mean to suggest by this that public administrators therefore lack particular skills, knowledge, and experience (e.g., about public finance and budgeting, public personnel, and public law) that are more or less distinctive and have no clear counterparts in private-sector organizations. Rather, my critique has been directed against the idea of administrative expertise as ideally consisting of positive, value-neutral knowledge to be used, in manipulative fashion, in achieving predefined policy and managerial objectives.

8. The question, to be sure, can be and has been asked by nonpragmatists, too. To mention only one prominent example, "How ought we to live?" is the central question explored in Robert Bellah et al.'s 1985 best-seller *Habits of the Heart: Individualism and Commitment in American Life.*

9. Like many other proverbs, this one is more often spread orally than in writing. I first heard it in conversation with my colleague Peter Vaill, who credits one of his mentors at UCLA, Robert Tannenbaum, with, if not actually coining the proverb, at least passing it on to him.

10. Farmer borrows this term from Marcuse's *One-Dimensional Man* (1964).

Epilogue

1. One important change in academic public administration curricula implied by this commitment would be to replace current introductory research methods and statistics courses with courses in action research.

2. I have borrowed this phrase, somewhat out of context, from the title of Ken Jowitt's 1993 book (subtitled *The Leninist Extinction*) analyzing the decline of the Soviet system from the standpoint of Western liberal imperatives.

3. Surowiecki begins *The Wisdom of Crowds* with a case, first reported a century ago by the British scientist Francis Galton, of a weight-judging contest held at a livestock exhibition in rural England. Visitors to the exhibition were invited

to guess the weight of a recently "slaughtered and dressed" ox. Galton tabulated 787 entries, most submitted by people having little if any expertise about livestock, and performed a series of statistical tests on the results. Anticipating a "dumb answer" owing to the preponderance of non-experts participating, Galton was astounded by the accuracy of their collective guess. "The crowd had guessed that the ox, after it had been slaughtered and dressed, would weigh 1,197 pounds. After it had been slaughtered and dressed, the ox weighed 1,198 pounds. In other words, the crowd's judgment was essentially perfect" (2004, xiii).

Inspired by this story, I conducted a similar (albeit spur-of-the-moment) experiment in a section of my introductory MPA course by asking the eighteen students to guess the year in which Charles Darwin had published *The Origin of Species.* None of the students knew that the publication year was 1859, and none accurately *guessed* it during the experiment; in fact, no individual guess was closer than three years of the correct year. The experiment was flawed by my having asked the students to state their guesses orally, violating Surowiecki's condition of "independence" in wise groups. The students' collective (average) guess turned out to be 1856—pretty good, but not as impressive as the result Galton had reported about the ox. However, a few minutes after I had tabulated and averaged the eighteen guesses and announced the result, two of the students confessed that they had actually stated guesses of twenty years *earlier* than they had originally intended. To avoid embarrassment, they had changed their guesses at the last moment upon hearing the guesses reported by other students whom they believed were better informed. The class's *adjusted* collective guess, therefore, was 1858. (The following year I conducted the experiment again, this time with a class of twenty-four students. Their average guess was 1860, one year after *Origin's* publication.)

4. For a complementary argument in public choice theory, see Elinor Ostrom's *Governing the Commons: The Evolution of Institutions* (1990).

5. I first heard about and then read *The Wisdom of Crowds* after I had finished writing chapter 6.

6. In *The Life of Samuel Johnson,* James Boswell quotes his subject's famous declaration that "Patriotism is the last refuge of a scoundrel" (1791, 182).

Works Cited

Adams, Guy B., and Danny L. Balfour. 2004. *Unmasking administrative evil.* Rev. ed. Armonk, NY: M. E. Sharpe.

Albrow, Martin. 1997. *The global age: State and society beyond modernity.* Stanford, CA: Stanford Univ. Press.

Allison, Graham T., Jr. 1971. *Essence of decision: Explaining the Cuban Missile Crisis.* Boston: Little, Brown.

Argyris, Chris, and Donald A. Schön. 1974. *Theory in practice: Increasing professional effectiveness.* San Francisco: Jossey-Bass.

Axelrod, Robert. 1984. *The evolution of cooperation.* New York: Basic Books.

Barrett, William. 1978. *The illusion of technique: A search for meaning in a technological civilization.* New York: Anchor Books.

Bateson, Gregory. 1972. *Steps to an ecology of mind.* New York: Ballantine.

Bauman, Zygmunt. 1998. *Globalization: The human consequences.* New York: Columbia Univ. Press.

Behn, Robert D. 1999. The new public-management paradigm and the search for democratic accountability. *International Public Management Journal* 1 (2): 131–65.

———. 2001. *Rethinking democratic accountability.* Washington, DC: Brookings Institution Press.

Bellah, Robert N., Richard Madsen, William M. Sullivan, Ann Swidler, and Steven M. Tipton. 1985. *Habits of the heart: Individualism and commitment in American life.* New York: Harper and Row.

Beresford, Annette D. 2004. Homeland security as an American ideology: Implications for U.S. policy and action. *Journal of Homeland Security and Emergency Management* 1 (3), Article 301. Available at http://bepress.com/jhsem/vol1/iss3/301.

Berger, Peter L., and Thomas Luckmann. 1967. *The social construction of reality.* Garden City, NY: Doubleday.

Bernstein, Richard J. 1971. *Praxis and action.* Philadelphia: Univ. of Pennsylvania Press.

——. 1991. *The new constellation: The ethical-political horizons of modernity/postmodernity.* Cambridge: MIT Press.

Bhaskar, Roy. 1978. *A realist theory of science.* Hassocks, England: Harvester.

Boswell, James. 1791. *The life of Samuel Johnson.* London: Penguin, 1979.

Braybrooke, David, and Charles E. Lindblom. 1963. *A strategy of decision: Policy evaluation as a social process.* Glencoe, IL: The Free Press of Glencoe.

Bryant, Christopher G. A., and David Jary. 1991. Introduction: Coming to terms with Anthony Giddens. In *Giddens' theory of structuration: A critical appreciation,* ed. Christopher G. A. Bryant and David Jary, 1–31. London: Routledge.

Buchanan, James M., and Gordon Tullock. 1962. *The calculus of consent: Logical foundations of constitutional democracy.* Ann Arbor: Univ. of Michigan Press.

Burke, John P. 1986. *Bureaucratic responsibility.* Baltimore: Johns Hopkins Univ. Press.

Carroll, James D. 1995. The rhetoric of reform and political reality in the National Performance Review. *Public Administration Review* 55 (3): 302–12.

Catlaw, Thomas J. 2003. The biopolitical state: Public administration and the fabrication of "the people." PhD diss., George Washington Univ.

Catron, Bayard L., and Kathryn G. Denhardt. 1994. Ethics education in public administration. In *Handbook of administrative ethics,* ed. Terry L. Cooper, 49–61. New York: Marcel Dekker.

Chandler, Ralph Clark. 1994. Deontological dimensions of administrative ethics. In *Handbook of administrative ethics,* ed. Terry L. Cooper, 147–56. New York: Marcel Dekker.

Cohen, Michael D., James G. March, and Johan Olsen. 1972. The garbage can model of organizational choice. *Administrative Science Quarterly* 17 (1): 1–25.

Cooper, Terry L. 1987. Hierarchy, virtue, and the practice of public administration: A perspective for normative ethics. *Public Administration Review* 47: 320–28.

——. 1990. *The responsible administrator.* 3rd ed. San Francisco: Jossey-Bass.

——. 1991. *An ethic of citizenship for public administration.* Englewood Cliffs, NJ: Prentice Hall.

Crick, Bernard. 1992. *In defence of politics.* 4th ed. Chicago: Univ. of Chicago Press.

Croly, Herbert. 1963. *The promise of American life.* New York: E. P. Dutton.

Dahl, Robert A. 2002. *How democratic is the American Constitution?* New Haven, CT: Yale Univ. Press.

Denhardt, Kathryn G. 1988. *The ethics of public service.* Westport, CN: Greenwood Press.

Derrida, Jacques. 1982. *Margins of philosophy.* Chicago: Univ. of Chicago Press.

Dewey, John. 1896. The reflex arc concept in psychology. In *John Dewey: The early works, 1882–1898,* vol. 5, ed. J. A. Boydston, 96–109. Carbondale: Southern Illinois Univ. Press, 1972.

———. 1976–83. *John Dewey: The middle works, 1899–1924,* ed. J. A. Boydston. 5 vols. Carbondale: Southern Illinois Univ. Press.

Diggins, John Patrick. 1994. *The promise of pragmatism: Modernism and the crisis of knowledge and authority.* Chicago: Univ. of Chicago Press.

Donaldson, Lex. 1985. *In defence of organization theory: A reply to critics.* Cambridge, UK: Cambridge Univ. Press.

Dray, W. H. 1967. Holism and individualism in history and social science. In *The encyclopedia of philosophy,* vol. 4, ed. Paul Edwards, 53–58. New York: Macmillan.

Dreyfus, Hubert, and Stuart Dreyfus. 1986. *Mind over machine: The power of human intuition and expertise in the era of the computer.* New York: Free Press.

Eagleton, Terry. 2003. *After theory.* New York: Basic Books.

Easton, David. 1953. *The political system.* New York: Knopf.

Eaton, Dorman B. 1879. *Civil service in Great Britain.* 46th Cong., 2nd sess., House, Ex. Doc. 1, Part 7. Washington, DC: Government Printing Office.

Etzioni, Amitai, ed. 2002. Symposium: Can postmodernists condemn terrorism? *The Responsive Community* 12 (3): 27–61.

Evans, Karen G. 2000. Reclaiming John Dewey. *Administration and Society* 23 (3): 308–28.

Farmer, David John. 2003. Power of refusal: Introduction to the symposium. *Administrative Theory and Praxis* 25 (2): 173–82.

Festinger, L., H. W. Riecken Jr., and S. Schachter. 1956. *When prophecy fails.* Minneapolis: Univ. of Minnesota Press.

Feyerabend, Paul K. 1975. *Against method.* London: New Left Books.

Fish, Stanley. 1999. *The trouble with principle.* Cambridge: Harvard Univ. Press.

———. 2002. Don't blame relativism. *The Responsive Community* 12 (3): 27–31.

Flyvbjerg, Bent. 2001. *Making social science matter: Why social inquiry fails and how it can succeed again.* Trans. Steven Sampson. Cambridge, UK: Cambridge Univ. Press.

Follett, Mary Parker. 1918. *The new state: Group organization, the solution of popular government.* New York: Longmans, Green.

———. 1924. *Creative experience.* New York: Longmans, Green.

———. 1940. *Dynamic administration.* Ed. Henry C. Metcalf and L. Urwick. New York: Harper and Brothers.

Forster, E. M. 1927. *Aspects of the novel.* London: Edward Arnold, 1961.

Foucault, Michel. 1997. *Ethics: Subjectivity and truth.* Vol. 1. Ed. Paul Rabinow. New York: The New Press.

———. 2000. So is it important to think? In *The essential works of Michel Foucault, 1954–1984,* vol. 3: *Power,* ed. J. D. Faubion, 454–58. New York: Free Press.

Fox, Charles J. 1994. The use of philosophy in administrative ethics. In *Handbook of administrative ethics,* ed. Terry L. Cooper, 83–105. New York: Marcel Dekker.

Fox, Charles J., and Hugh T. Miller. 1995. *Postmodern public administration.* Thousand Oaks, CA: Sage.

Frederickson, H. George. 1982. The recovery of civism in public administration. *Public Administration Review* 45:501–8.

——. 1996. Comparing the reinventing government movement with the new public administration. *Public Administration Review* 56 (3): 263–70.

——. 1997. *The spirit of public administration.* San Francisco: Jossey-Bass.

Frederickson, H. George, and David K. Hart. 1985. The public service and the patriotism of benevolence. *Public Administration Review* 45:547–53.

Friedman, Milton. 1953. The methodology of positive economics. In *Essays in Positive Economics,* 3–43. Chicago: Univ. of Chicago Press.

Friedrich, Carl J. 1940. Public policy and the nature of administrative responsibility. In *Public policy,* ed. Carl J. Friedrich and Edward S. Mason, 3–24. Cambridge: Harvard Univ. Press.

Fry, Brian. 1989. *Mastering public administration: From Max Weber to Dwight Waldo.* Chatham, NJ: Chatham House.

Gadamer, Hans-Georg. 1975. *Truth and method.* London: Sheed and Ward.

Garfinkel, Harold. 1967. *Studies in ethnomethodology.* Englewood Cliffs, NJ: Prentice-Hall.

Gawthrop, Louis C. 1984. Civis, civitas, and civilitas: A new focus for the year 2000. *Public Administration Review* 45:547–53.

Geertz, Clifford. 1973. *The interpretation of cultures.* New York: Basic Books.

Geuras, Dean, and Charles Garofalo. 1996. The normative paradox in contemporary public administration theory. *Administrative Theory and Praxis* 18 (2): 2–13.

Giddens, Anthony. 1976. *New rules of sociological method: A positive critique of interpretive sociologies.* New York: Basic Books.

——. 1977. *Studies in social and political theory.* New York: Basic Books.

——. 1984. *The constitution of society.* Berkeley: Univ. of California Press.

Gilligan, Carol. 1982. *In a different voice.* Cambridge: Harvard Univ. Press.

Gladwell, Malcolm. 2002. The talent myth: Are smart people overrated? *New Yorker,* July 22, 28–33.

Goodnow, Frank. 1900. *Politics and administration.* New York: Macmillan.

Gormley, William T., Jr. 2001. Moralists, pragmatists, and rogues: Bureaucrats in modern mysteries. *Public Administration Review* 61 (2): 184–93.

Gould, Stephen Jay. 1989. *Wonderful life: The Burgess Shale and the nature of history.* New York: Norton.

——. 2003. *The hedgehog, the fox, and the magister's pox.* New York: Harmony Books.

Gulick, Luther. 1933. Politics, administration, and the New Deal. *Annals of the Academy of Political and Social Science* 169 (September): 55–66.

———. 1937. Notes on the theory of organization. In *Papers on the science of administration,* ed. Luther Gulick and Lyndall Urwick, 3–45. New York: Institute of Public Administration.

———. 1955. Next steps in public administration. *Public Administration Review* 15 (2): 73–76.

Gunnell, John G. 1993. Relativism: The return of the repressed. *Political Theory* 21 (4): 563–84.

Habermas, Jürgen. 1970. *Toward a rational society.* Trans. Jeremy R. Shapiro. Boston: Beacon Press.

———. 1971. *Knowledge and human interests.* Trans. Jeremy R. Shapiro. Boston: Beacon Press.

Harmon, Michael M. 1981. *Action theory for public administration.* New York: Longman.

———. 1989a. "Decision" and "action" as contrasting perspectives in organization theory. *Public Administration Review* 49 (2): 144–50.

———. 1989b. The Simon/Waldo debate: A review and update. *Public Administration Quarterly* 12:437–51.

———. 1995. *Responsibility as paradox: A critique of rational discourse on government.* Thousand Oaks, CA: Sage.

———. 2003. Why principles can't justify: A pragmatist commentary on the affirmative action debate. *Administrative Theory and Praxis* 25 (1): 91–103.

———. 2005. Five good reasons not to act on principle (Or, why you probably can't act on principle, anyway). *Administrative Theory and Praxis* 27 (2): 238–76.

Hart, David K. 1994. Administration and the ethics of virtue: In all things, choose first for good character and then for technical expertise. In *Handbook of administrative ethics,* ed. Terry L. Cooper, 107–23. New York: Marcel Dekker.

Hart, David K., and N. Dale Wright. 1998. "The civic good": "The public interest" of civic humanism. *Administrative Theory and Praxis* 20 (4): 406–21.

Hill, Carolyn J., and Laurence E. Lynn Jr. 2004. Governance and public management: An introduction. *Journal of Policy Analysis and Management* 23 (1): 3–11.

Himmelfarb, Gertrude. 1995. Preface. In *This will hurt: The restoration of virtue and civic order,* ed. Digby Anderson, vii–xi. London: Social Affairs Unit.

Hirschman, Albert O. 1971. *Exit, voice, and loyalty.* Cambridge: Harvard Univ. Press.

Holmes, Oliver Wendell. 1870. Codes, and the arrangement of the law. In *The collected works of Justice Holmes: Complete public writing and selected judicial opinions of Oliver Wendell Holmes,* ed. Sheldon M. Novick, 1:212–22. Chicago: Univ. of Chicago Press, 1995.

———. 1920. The path of the law. In *Collected legal papers,* 167–202. New York: Harcourt, Brace and Howe.

Hummel, Ralph P. 1982. *The bureaucratic experience,* 2nd ed. New York: St. Martin's Press.

James, William. 1898. Philosophical conceptions and practical results. In *Pragmatism,* ed. F. H. Burkhardt, 255–70. Cambridge: Harvard Univ. Press, 1975.

———. 1907. A defense of pragmatism II: What pragmatism means. *Popular Science Monthly,* April, 351–64.

Jowitt, Ken. 1993. *New world disorder: The Leninist extinction.* Berkeley: Univ. of California Press.

Kaku, Michio. 1994. *Hyperspace: A scientific odyssey through parallel universes, time warps, and the tenth dimension.* New York: Anchor Books.

Kaplan, Robert. 1997. Was democracy just a moment? *Atlantic Monthly,* December, 55–80.

Katz, Daniel, and Robert L. Kahn. 1966. *The social psychology of organizations.* New York: Wiley.

Kinsley, Michael. 2004. When ideology is a value. *Washington Post,* Nov. 28, B7.

Knapp, Steven, and Walter Benn Michaels. 1997. From "Against theory." In *Pragmatism: A reader,* ed. Louis Menand, 364–80. New York: Vintage Books.

Kochis, Bruce. 2005. On lenses and filters: The role of metaphor in policy theory. *Administrative Theory and Praxis* 27 (1): 24–50.

Kohlberg, Lawrence J. 1971. From is to ought: How to commit the naturalistic fallacy and get away with it in the study of moral development. In *Cognitive development and epistemology,* ed. T. Mischel, 151–235. New York: Academic Press.

Kull, Steven. 2004. *The separate reality of Bush and Kerry supporters.* PIPA/Knowledge Networks. Oct. 21.

Lilla, Mark T. 1981. Ethos, "ethics," and public service. *The Public Interest* 63:3–17.

Lindblom, Charles E. 1959. The science of muddling through. *Public Administration Review* 19 (1): 79–88.

———. 1992. *Inquiry and change: The troubled attempt to understand and shape society.* New Haven, CT: Yale Univ. Press.

Louch, A. R. 1969. *Explanation and social action.* Berkeley: Univ. of California Press.

Lowi, Theodore. 1969. *The end of liberalism.* New York: Norton.

Luzzatto, Jack, and Loy Morehead, eds. 1962. *The new American Roget's college thesaurus.* New York: Signet Books.

Lynn, Laurence E., Jr. 1997. *Public management as art, science, and profession.* Chatham, NJ: Chatham House.

———. 1998. The new public management: How to transform a theme into a legacy. *Public Administration Review* 58 (3): 231–37.

———. 2001. The myth of the bureaucratic paradigm: What traditional public administration really stood for. *Public Administration Review* 61 (2): 144–57.

MacIntyre, Alasdair. 1984. *After virtue: A study in moral theory.* 2nd ed. Notre Dame, IN: Notre Dame Univ. Press.

Mangham, Iain L. 1995. MacIntyre and the manager. *Organization* 2 (2): 181–204.

March, James G. 1976. The technology of foolishness. In *Ambiguity and choice in organizations,* ed. James G. March and Johan Olsen, 69–81. Bergen, Norway: Universitetsforlaget.

Marcuse, Herbert. 1964. *One-dimensional man: Studies in the ideology of advanced industrial society.* Boston: Beacon Press, 1991.

McSwite, O. C. 1995. Humanism and pseudo-critique: The danger of missing the postmodern moment. *Organization* 2 (2): 233–40.

———. 1997. *Legitimacy in public administration: A discourse analysis.* Thousand Oaks, CA: Sage.

———. 2001. Theory competency for MPA-educated practitioners. *Public Administration Review* 61:111–14.

Menand, Louis. 1997. An introduction to pragmatism. In *Pragmatism: A reader,* ed. Louis Menand, xi–xxxiv. New York: Vintage Books.

———. 2001. *The metaphysical club: A story of ideas in America.* New York: Farrar, Straus and Giroux.

Miller, Hugh T. 2002. *Postmodern public policy.* Albany: State Univ. of New York Press.

———. 2004. Why old pragmatism needs an upgrade. *Administration and Society* 36:243–49.

Miller, Hugh T., and Cheryl S. King. 1998. Practical theory. *American Review of Public Administration* 28 (1): 43–60.

Moe, Ronald C. 1994. The "reinventing government" exercise: Misinterpreting the problem, misjudging the consequences. *Public Administration Review* 54 (2): 11–22.

Moe, Ronald C., and Robert S. Gilmour. 1995. Rediscovering principles of public administration: The neglected foundation of public law. *Public Administration Review* 55 (2): 135–46.

Moore, G. E. 1903. *Principia ethica.* London: Cambridge Univ. Press.

Morgan, Gareth, ed. 1983. *Beyond method: Strategies for social research.* Beverly Hills, CA: Sage.

———. 1997. *Images of organization.* 2nd ed. Thousand Oaks, CA: Sage.

———. 1998. *Imaginization: New ways of seeing, organizing, managing.* Thousand Oaks, CA: Sage.

Mosher, Frederick C. 1968. *Democracy and the public service.* New York: Oxford Univ. Press.

Mulgan, Geoff. 1997. *Connexity: How to live in a connected world.* Boston: Harvard Business School Press.

Nigro, Lloyd G., and William D. Richardson. 1990. Between citizen and administrator: Administrative ethics and PAR. *Public Administration Review* 50: 623–35.

Nørretranders, Tor. 1998. *The user illusion: Cutting consciousness down to size.* Trans. Jonathan Sydenham. New York: Penguin.

Oakeshott, Michael. 1991. *Rationalism in politics and other essays.* Indianapolis: Liberty Fund.

Osborne, David, and Ted Gaebler. 1992. *Reinventing government: How the entrepreneurial spirit is transforming the public sector.* Reading, MA: Addison-Wesley.

Ostrom, Elinor. 1990. *Governing the commons: The evolution of institutions.* New York: Cambridge Univ. Press.

Ostrom, Vincent. 1974. *The intellectual crisis in American public administration.* Rev. ed. University: Univ. of Alabama Press.

Outhwaite, William. 1983. Toward a realist perspective. In *Beyond method: Strategies for social research,* ed. Gareth Morgan, 321–30. Beverly Hills, CA: Sage.

Parsons, Talcott. 1951. *The social system.* New York: Free Press.

Peirce, Charles Sanders. 1878. How to make our ideas clear. *Popular Science Monthly,* January, 286–302.

——. 1991. A definition of pragmatism. In *Peirce on signs: Writings on semiotic by Charles Sanders Peirce,* ed. James Hoopes, 246–48. Chapel Hill: Univ. of North Carolina Press.

Pops, G. M. 1991. Improving ethical decision making using the concept of justice. In *Ethical frontiers in public management,* ed. James S. Bowman, 261–85. San Francisco: Jossey-Bass.

Posner, Richard A. 1997. A pragmatist manifesto. In *Pragmatism: A reader,* ed. Louis Menand, 418–35. New York: Vintage Books.

Putnam, Hilary. 1981. *Reason, truth, and history.* Cambridge: Cambridge Univ. Press.

Rabinow, Paul, ed. 1984. *The Foucault reader.* New York: Pantheon Books.

Raskin, Marcus G. 1987. Conclusion: A manifesto of reconstructive knowledge. In *New ways of knowing: The sciences, society, and reconstructive knowledge,* ed. Marcus G. Raskin and Herbert J. Bernstein, 268–86. Totowa, NJ: Rowman and Littlefield.

Ravetz, J. R. 1971. *Scientific knowledge and its social problems.* New York: Oxford Univ. Press.

Rawls, John. 1971. *A theory of justice.* Cambridge: Harvard Univ. Press.

Redford, Emmett S. 1969. *Democracy in the administrative state.* Oxford: Oxford Univ. Press.

Rittel, Horst W. J., and Melvin Webber. 1973. Dilemmas in a general theory of planning. *Policy Sciences* 4 (2): 155–69.

Rohr, John A. 1984. The constitutional world of Woodrow Wilson. In *Politics and administration: Woodrow Wilson and American public administration,* ed. Jack Rabin and James S. Bowman, 31–50. New York: Marcel Dekker.

———. 1986. *To run a constitution: The legitimacy of the administrative state.* Lawrence: Univ. of Kansas Press.

———. 1989. *Ethics for bureaucrats.* 2nd ed. New York: Marcel Dekker.

Rorty, Richard. 1979. *Philosophy and the mirror of nature.* Princeton, NJ: Princeton Univ. Press.

———. 1982. *Consequences of pragmatism.* Minneapolis: Univ. of Minnesota Press.

———. 1989. *Contingency, irony, and solidarity.* New York: Cambridge Univ. Press.

———. 1991. *Objectivity, relativism, and truth: Philosophical papers.* Vol. 1. New York: Cambridge Univ. Press.

Rosenau, James N. 1997. *Along the domestic-foreign frontier: Exploring governance in a turbulent world.* Cambridge, UK: Cambridge Univ. Press.

Rosenbloom, David H. 1983. Public administrative theory and the separation of powers. *Public Administration Review* 43 (3): 219–27.

———. 1984. Reconsidering the politics-administration dichotomy: The Supreme Court and public personal management. In *Politics and administration: Woodrow Wilson and American public administration,* ed. Jack Rabin and James S. Bowman, 103–18. New York: Marcel Dekker.

Runciman, W. G., ed. 1978. *Max Weber: Selections in translation.* Cambridge, UK: Cambridge Univ. Press.

Sabatier, Paul, ed. 1999. *Theories of the policy process.* Boulder, CO: Westview Press.

Sartre, Jean Paul. 1956. *Being and nothingness: An essay on phenomenological ontology.* Trans. H. E. Barnes. New York: Philosophical Library.

———. 1989. Dirty hands. In *No exit and three other plays.* New York: Vintage International.

Schmidt, Mary R. 1993. Government: Alternative kinds of knowledge and why they are ignored. *Public Administration Review* 53:525–30.

Schön, Donald A. 1983. *The reflective practitioner: How professionals think in action.* New York: Basic Books.

Schutz, Alfred. 1967. *The phenomenology of the social world.* Evanston, IL: Northwestern Univ. Press.

Scott, James C. 1998. *Seeing like a state: How certain schemes to improve the human condition have failed.* New Haven, CT: Yale Univ. Press.

Searle, John. 1984. *Minds, brains, and science.* Cambridge: Harvard Univ. Press.

———. 1985. *Speech acts: An essay in the philosophy of language.* Cambridge, UK: Cambridge Univ. Press.

Shafritz, Jay M., and E. W. Russell. 2003. *Introducing public administration.* 3rd ed. New York: Longman.

Shields, Patricia M. 2003. The community of inquiry: Classical pragmatism and public administration. *Administration and Society* 35:510–38.

———. 2004. Classical pragmatism: Engaging practitioner experience. *Administration and Society* 36:351–61.

Silverman, David. 1971. *The theory of organisations.* London: Heinemann.

Simon, Herbert A. 1947. *Administrative behavior: A study of decision-making processes in administrative organizations.* 3rd ed. New York: Free Press, 1976.

———. 1952. Development of theory of democratic administration: Replies and comments. *American Political Science Review* 46:494–96.

Snider, Keith F. 2000. Expertise or experimenting. *Administration and Society* 23 (3): 329–54.

Stanley, Manfred. 1972. Technicism, liberalism, and development. In *Social development,* ed. Manfred Stanley, 274–325. New York: Basic Books.

Stewart, Debra W., and Norman A. Sprinthall. 1994. Moral development in public administration. In *Handbook of administrative ethics,* ed. Terry L. Cooper, 325–48. New York: Marcel Dekker.

Stone, Deborah. 2002. *Policy paradox: The art of political decision making.* Rev. ed. New York: Norton.

Surowiecki, James. 2004. *The wisdom of crowds: Why the many are smarter than the few and how collective wisdom shapes business, economies, societies, and nations.* New York: Doubleday.

Svara, James H. 2001. The myth of the dichotomy: Complementarity of politics and administration in the past and future of public administration. *Public Administration Review* 61 (2): 176–83.

Taylor, Charles. 1985. *Philosophical papers.* Cambridge, UK: Cambridge Univ. Press.

Taylor, Frederick W. 1947. *Scientific management.* New York: Harper and Brothers.

Thayer, Frederick C. 1972. General system(s) theory: The promise that could not be kept. *Academy of Management Journal* 15 (4): 481–94.

———. 1980. Organization theory as epistemology: Transcending hierarchy and objectivity. In *Organization theory and the new public administration,* ed. Carl Bellone, 113–39. Boston: Allyn and Bacon.

———. 1981. *An end to hierarchy and competition: Administration in the post-affluent world.* 2nd ed. New York: Franklin Watts.

Thorngate, W. 1976. "In general" vs. "It depends": Some comments on the Gergen-Schlenker debate. *Personality and Social Psychology Bulletin* 2:404–10.

Tribe, Laurence H. 1973. Technology assessment and the fourth discontinuity: The limits of instrumental rationality. *Southern California Law Review* 46: 617–59.

Van Riper, Paul P. 1984. The politics-administration dichotomy: Concept or reality? In *Politics and administration: Woodrow Wilson and American public administration,* ed. Jack Rabin and James S. Bowman, 203–18. New York: Marcel Dekker.

Vickers, Geoffrey. 1995. *The art of judgment: A study of policy making.* Thousand Oaks, CA: Sage.

Waldo, Dwight W. 1948. *The administrative state: A study of the political theory of American public administration.* 2nd ed. New York: Holmes and Meier, 1984.

———. 1952. Development of theory of democratic administration. *American Political Science Review* 46:81–103.

———. 1968. Scope of the theory of public administration. In *Theory and practice of public administration: Scope, objectives, and methods,* ed. James C. Charlesworth, 1–26. Philadelphia: American Academy of Political and Social Science.

Walzer, Michael. 1983. *Spheres of justice.* New York: Basic Books.

Wamsley, Gary L., Charles T. Goodsell, John A. Rohr, Camilla M. Stivers, Orion F. White, and James F. Wolf. 1990. Public administration and the governance process: Shifting the political dialogue. In *Refounding public administration,* ed. Gary L. Wamsley, 31–51. Newbury Park, CA: Sage.

Weber, Max. 1954. *Max Weber on law in economy and society.* Vol. 1. Ed. M. Reinstein. Cambridge: Harvard Univ. Press.

———. 1968. *Economy and society.* Ed. Guenther Roth and Claus Wittich. Berkeley: Univ. of California Press.

Weick, Karl E. 1979. *The social psychology of organizing.* 2nd ed. Reading, MA: Addison-Wesley.

White, Orion F. 1973. The concept of administrative praxis. *Journal of Comparative Administration* 5 (2): 55–86.

———. 1978. Beyond the "empirical theory versus normative theory" double bind. Paper prepared for the National Conference on Programmatic Uses of Experiential Learning in Professional Education, May 24–26, Dallas, TX.

White, Orion F., and Bruce L. Gates. 1974. Statistical theory and equity in the delivery of social services. *Public Administration Review* 34 (1): 43–51.

White, Orion F., and Cynthia J. McSwain. 1983. Transformational theory and organizational analysis. In *Beyond method: Strategies for social research,* ed. Gareth Morgan, 292–305. Beverly Hills, CA: Sage.

———. 1990. The Phoenix project: Raising a new image of public administration from the ashes of the past. In *Images and identities in public administration,* ed. Henry D. Kass and Bayard L. Catron, 23–59. Newbury Park, CA: Sage.

Whitehead, Colson. 2000. *The intuitionist.* New York: Anchor Books.

Wilson, D. J. 1995. Fertile ground: Pragmatism, positivism, and the linguistic turn. In *Pragmatism: From progressivism to postmodernism,* ed. R. Hollinger and D. Depew, 122–41. Westport, CT: Praeger.

Wilson, Edward O. 1998. *Consilience.* New York: Knopf.

Wilson, Woodrow. 1887. The study of administration. In *Classics of public administration,* ed. Jay M. Shafritz and Albert Hyde, 3–17. Oak Park, IL: Moore, 1978.

Index